BASIC TEXAS BIRDS

TEXAS NATURAL HISTORY GUIDES™

BASIC
TEXAS BIRDS

A FIELD GUIDE

MARK W. LOCKWOOD

Photographs by Greg W. Lasley, Tim Cooper,
and Mark W. Lockwood

UNIVERSITY OF TEXAS PRESS

Austin

Publication of this book was aided by the generous support of the RGK Foundation, Mildred Wyatt-Wold, and the Corrie Herring Hooks Endowment.

LIBRARY OF CONGRESS CATALOGING-IN-PUBLICATION DATA

Lockwood, Mark.
  Basic Texas birds : a field guide / Mark W. Lockwood ; photographs by Greg W. Lasley, Tim Cooper, and Mark W. Lockwood. — 1st ed.
    p. cm. — (Texas natural history guides)
  Includes bibliographical references and index.
  ISBN-13: 978-0-292-71349-9 (pbk. : alk. paper)
  ISBN-10: 0-292-71349-5 (alk. paper)
1. Birds—Texas—Identification. I. Title.
QL684.T4L626 2007
598.09764—dc22

                               2006035914

To my parents,
Robert and Sharon Lockwood,
for those nights at the kitchen table
and everything else.

CONTENTS

Contents

ACKNOWLEDGMENTS

I thank Lorraine Atherton, Eric Carpenter, Richard Conner, Rob Fergus, and Cindy Lockwood for comments made on previous drafts. I would also like to thank Greg Lasley, Tim Cooper, and John Ingram for allowing the use of their many fantastic photos that illustrate this work. The maps found with each species are adaptations of those used in the *TOS Handbook of Texas Birds* (Lockwood and Freeman, 2004).

BASIC TEXAS BIRDS

INTRODUCTION

Texas has a large and varied birdlife, as diverse as the landscapes of the great state itself. Ecological diversity plays a major role in defining Texas birdlife, but other factors are also important. The state's location in the southern latitudes and central longitude of the United States is one of the primary factors responsible for the wide range of species found here. These factors make Texas an excellent place to study birds, and almost anywhere in the state allows for a rewarding birdwatching experience. That is why Texas is now a destination for birders from all over the United States and even the world. This book is an introduction to some of the more common birds that might be encountered across the state.

The diversity of Texas can accommodate the full range of birding experience, from casual neighborhood observations to remote expeditions. Many people first become interested in birds simply by looking at the species that are attracted to their backyard. This often leads to exploring the parks or natural areas close to where they live. For some, their interest develops into a lifelong obsession. Birders in Texas can start a long spring vacation by watching migrants along the Coastal Prairies, then move on to the Lower Rio Grande Valley to have a peek at a more tropical birdlife before finishing up in the Hill Country or the Trans-Pecos. As the seasons change, so does the diversity of the birdlife. These changes offer new opportunities to study a different group of birds, even in the backyard or at a local park. Varying factors, such as weather and the available food crop, have a strong influence on bird distribution, which makes every year different. When looking at the entire state, this can have a profound influence on which species are present. For example, poor food crops in the Rocky Mountains can bring jays and finches into the western part of the state where they would be very rare or absent under normal circumstances. Severe freezes that extend well into northern Mexico have been known to cause that area's birds to disperse when the tender tropical habitats they occupy are damaged by the cold weather. Some of the birds end up in the Lower Rio Grande Valley. All of these factors add to the allure of Texas to birders. Truly dedicated birders who travel from region to region generally expect to observe more than 400 species within the state in a single year.

If this book, or the exploration of the birds of your yard or a nearby park, sparks the need for more information about the birdlife of Texas, many other books can be helpful. In particular, identification guides to the birds of the United States are quite useful. Two popular guides are the National Geographic Society's *Field Guide to the Birds of North America* (National Geographic Society, 2003) and *The Sibley Guide to Birds* (Sibley, 2000) or Sibley's supplementary guides that cover the eastern and western portions of North America (Sibley, 2003). In addition, the Texas Ornithological Society's *TOS Handbook of Texas Birds* (Lockwood and Freeman, 2004) takes a closer look at the status and distribution of birds of the state as a whole. Similar books examine specific regions, such as *Birds of the Texas Hill Country* (Lockwood, 2001), *Birds of the Trans-Pecos* (Peterson and Zimmer, 1998), *Birds of the Texas Panhandle* (Seyffert, 2001), and *Birds of Northeast Texas* (White, 2001), to name a few. These are not illustrated field guides but rather additional tools to help observers better understand what is known about the distribution and abundance of the birds of a particular region. The Texas Parks and Wildlife Department also produces regional checklists for most of the major ecological regions of the state. All of these resources are a great help in sorting out the diversity of Texas birds.

THE TEXAS LIST AND ITS NOMENCLATURE

Within the Lone Star state, 629 species of birds have been documented. The Texas Ornithological Society, through the Texas Bird Records Committee (TBRC), maintains the list of accepted species found in the state. This list increases by one to a few species most years. Most of these gains are the result of new discoveries that have been well documented; however, others are the result of taxonomic decisions by the American Ornithologists' Union (AOU) through its Committee on Classification and Nomenclature. This group maintains the checklist of birds for North America and reviews scientific papers that provide data supporting reclassifications, either separating one species into more species or lumping two or more species into one. The taxonomic treatment and species sequence in this book follow the *Check-list of North American Birds, Seventh Edition* (AOU, 1998). Annual supplements to the check-list are published each July in *The Auk,* the quarterly journal of the AOU. The entire list of birds that have been accepted by the TBRC can be found in this book in the Appendix at the end of the species accounts.

For a species to be considered for inclusion on the Texas Ornithological Society's list, there must be a known specimen, a recognizable and confirmed photograph or video, or a recognizable and confirmed audio recording of that species from the state. When a species that is not on the Texas state list is discovered, documentation that meets one of those criteria must be obtained and reviewed to be accepted by the TBRC. More information about the TBRC and a list of species for which documentation is requested are available at http://texasbirds.org/tbrc/.

HOW TO USE THIS BOOK

The purpose of this book is to introduce the reader to the birds of Texas by looking at a cross section of commonly occurring species, some of which are likely to be encountered anywhere in the state. The book is an introductory tool that includes a broader spectrum of natural history information about each species than would be found in a typical field guide. When observing birds, however, a more inclusive field guide is needed to make comparisons of similar species and to have a wide range of illustrations of even common birds.

This book takes a close look at 161 species that are considered commonly occurring birds in Texas. Considering that the book discusses only about 30 percent of the species found in Texas, the selection of which species to include was a difficult task. The primary consideration was to choose a variety of birds that occur commonly across the state and are likely to be encountered by most Texas birders anywhere in the state. Several exotic species are established and abundant throughout Texas, such as the Rock Pigeon (*Columba livia*), the Eurasian Collared-Dove (*Streptopelia decaocto*), the European Starling (*Sturnus vulgaris*), and the House Sparrow (*Passer domesticus*), but they were purposefully excluded from this book in order to focus on native species. It was also important to make sure all regions of the state are well represented by selecting common birds within each region, even if they are not common statewide. For example, the Laughing Gull is abundant along the coast but fairly rare inland. The third concern was to represent the full range of Texas birdlife. The TOS list divides the birds of Texas among more than 40 broad taxonomic groups, from large waterfowl like swans and geese to tiny hummingbirds to more than 40 kinds of sparrows. To give the reader a representative cross section of Texas birdlife, an effort was made to include a sprinkling of species from a wide variety of those groups, but even then, all the families of birds that occur in Texas are not represented here.

Besides the 161 common species, this book describes 23 other species often referred to as Texas specialties; their species accounts are marked with an asterisk (*). Generally speaking, Texas specialties are not found regularly anywhere else in the United States. Most are more tropical species that reach the northernmost point of their distribution in the Lower Rio Grande Valley. A few are more specialized birds that are for one reason or another restricted to specific habitats within the state.

Each species account includes information about the bird's natural history, identification (a description of its physical appearance), habitat, and status in Texas (where and when it is likely to be found). There is also a section that discusses similar species that might cause confusion when trying to identify a bird in the field. The abundance and geographic distribution for each species are described and augmented by a map for each account. For those species that are migratory, a typical migration window is included under the Status and Distribution heading.

Maps

The maps included within each species account reflect the typical expected range for that species. Some of the species that don't have a statewide distribution might be expected to occur outside the mapped range from time to time. In addition, many of these species may be very rare in areas outside the mapped range. These maps are adapted from those produced for the *TOS Handbook of Texas Birds* (Lockwood and Freeman, 2004).

Map Key

Year-round occurrence

Winter occurrence

Summer occurrence

Migration route

Irregular occurrence

STATUS AND ABUNDANCE DEFINITIONS
The definitions of status and abundance in this book follow those listed in the *TOS Handbook of Texas Birds* (Lockwood and Freeman, 2004).

Status

Permanent Resident: Occurs regularly within the defined range throughout the year; implies a stable breeding population

Summer Resident: Implies a breeding population, although in some cases this population may be small

Summer Visitor: Implies a nonbreeding population or lingering migrants or winter residents

Winter Resident: Occurs regularly within the described range generally between December and February

Winter Visitor: Does not occur with enough regularity or in large enough numbers to be considered a winter resident

Migrant: Occurs as a transient passing through the state in spring or fall (certain species may be migrants in some regions and residents in others)

Local: May be found only in a specific habitat or geographical area within any region, possibly in small numbers (e.g., Red-cockaded Woodpecker and Colima Warbler)

Vagrant: Has wandered outside its normal range, either as a migrant or through irregular wandering

Abundance

Abundant: Always present in such numbers and with such a general distribution that in its proper habitat, many may be found in a given day

Common: Always present in such numbers that one may expect to find several in a day

Uncommon: Normally present in proper habitat, but one cannot be sure of finding one in a day

Rare: On the average, occurs only a few times a year in a given area or not at all. It is always a surprise to see one.

Very Rare: Not expected, occurs with some regularity, although not on an annual basis

Casual: Between 6 and 15 records accepted for the state by the TBRC; only one or a few records for any given area, but reasonably expected to occur again

Accidental: Average of one or two records every 10 years

Irregular: May occur in large numbers, but not expected every year

Natural Areas of Texas

For those species that have a regional distribution in the state, their status and distribution is often defined by the ecological region of the state in which they occur. In order to make those designations more meaningful, it is important to have an understanding of the ecological diversity of the state. Texas is often divided into natural or ecological regions that are defined by geology and vegetation. I prefer to follow the natural area boundaries developed by the Lyndon B. Johnson School of Public Affairs of the University of Texas at Austin (1978). The Lyndon B. Johnson School divided the state into 11 regions with some additional subregions. For ease of use, however, I have combined a few of the regions so that only 8 natural areas are used in this book (map 1).

Texas becomes more arid from east to west, and that defines the vegetation present in a particular area. Between the mesic

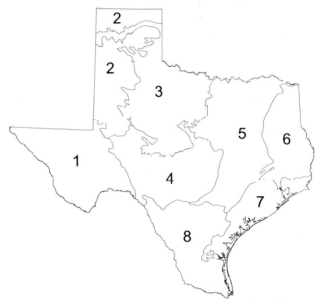

Map 1. Physiographic regions of Texas as defined by the LBJ School of Public Affairs of the University of Texas. (1) Trans-Pecos, (2) High Plains, (3) Rolling Plains, (4) Edwards Plateau, (5) Post Oak Savannah and Blackland Prairies, (6) Pineywoods, (7) Coastal Prairies, and (8) South Texas Brush Country.

Pineywoods region in the east, which receives more than 50 inches of precipitation annually, and the deserts of far west Texas, where as little as 8 inches of precipitation occurs each year, there are many habitats and niches that support the diverse birdlife of the state.

The **Pineywoods** area is the easternmost ecological region in the state. In general, the Pineywoods are nearly level, with elevations ranging from 200 to 500 feet above sea level. As the name implies, forests with a mix of pines and hardwoods dominate the vegetation communities within the Pineywoods. Native pines common to the region are loblolly (*Pinus taeda*), shortleaf (*P. echinata*), and longleaf (*P. palustris*). Throughout the uplands, hardwoods are found in mixed stands with pines. Common hardwoods in the region include sweetgum (*Liquidambar styraciflua*), various oaks (*Quercus* spp.), elms (*Ulmus* spp.), cottonwoods (*Populus* spp.), and hickories (*Carya* spp.), as well as water tupelo (*Nyssa aquatica*), blackgum (*N. sylvatica*), and bald cypress (*Taxodium distichum*). The open pine forests characteristic of this ecological region are maintained by frequent fires during the growing season. In the absence of wild fires, intensive management is required to prevent a dense understory of woody vegetation from developing and ultimately stopping the regeneration of the pines.

The **Coastal Prairies** include prairies, marshes, estuaries, and dunes on a nearly level plain, which extends along the Gulf Coast from Mexico to Louisiana and includes the barrier islands. The Coastal Prairies reach up to 80 miles inland from the Gulf, with elevations that range from sea level to 150 feet. The transition from the Coastal Prairies to the Pineywoods and Post Oak Savannah is abruptly delineated except along drainages where riparian corridors extend into the prairies. The region grades more evenly into the South Texas Brush Country, narrowing to include the barrier islands and a thin corridor along the Laguna Madre south of Baffin Bay. The natural vegetation of the Coastal Prairies is tallgrass prairie and oak savannah. Many of these grasslands, however, have been invaded by trees and shrubs, such as the exotic Chinese tallow (*Sapium seb-*

iferum), native honey mesquite (*Prosopis glandulosa*), and various acacias. One of the primary reasons these woody plants have been so successful in invading the Coastal Prairies is the long-term suppression of fire in this habitat. Prairies are maintained by the regular occurrence of fire, which recycles nutrients and controls invasive woody species. Gulf cordgrass (*Spartina spartinae*), big bluestem (*Andropogon gerardii*), little bluestem (*Schizachyrium scoparium*), indiangrass (*Sorghastrum nutans*), and gulf muhly (*Muhlenbergia capillaris*) are common native grasses in these prairies.

West of the Pineywoods, a large area with belts of forest, savannah, and grassland makes up the **Post Oak Savannah** and **Blackland Prairies**. The Post Oak Savannah region is found just to the west of the Pineywoods and grades into the Blackland Prairies to the south and west. This area is a gently rolling wooded plain with a distinctive pattern of post oak (*Quercus stellata*) and blackjack oak (*Q. marilandica*) in association with tall grasses. This basic vegetation type also characterizes the Cross Timbers subregion, which is included in this region in this book. The southwestern boundary with the South Texas Brush Country is indistinct. The Blackland Prairies intermingle with the Post Oak Savannah in the southeast and have divisions known as the Grand, San Antonio, and Fayette prairies. This region was once an expansive tallgrass prairie dominated by little bluestem, big bluestem, indiangrass, tall dropseed (*Sporobolus asper*), and Silveus dropseed (*S. silveanus*). About 98 percent of the Blackland Prairies has been under cultivation for the past century. Many other areas of remaining prairie have been invaded by woody plants.

The **South Texas Brush Country** is an area of brushlands primarily found south of the Balcones Escarpment. The vegetation of this region is dominated by brushy species including mesquite, live oak, acacias, lotebush (*Zizyphus obovata*), spiny hackberry (*Celtis pallida*), whitebrush (*Aloysia gratissima*), and Texas persimmon (*Diospyros texana*). The Lower Rio Grande Valley is found at the southern tip of this region. This distinctive subregion lies in the subtropical zone and is located within the delta of the Rio Grande and its alluvial terraces. Many species of plants reach their northern distribution in the Lower Valley. Historically, the floodplain of the Rio Grande supported a more diverse hardwood woodland that included sugarberry (*Celtis laevigata*), cedar elm (*Ulmus crassifolia*), ebony (*Pithecellobium flexicaule*), and anacua (*Ehretia anacua*). The Texas sabal (*Sabal texana*) was a locally common component of that woodland. With the construction of numerous dams along the Rio Grande, the seasonal flooding that maintained the natural vegetation along the floodplain has ceased, and brush species from the north are invading this area. Another important subregion is the **Coastal Sand Plain,** an area of deep sands found south of Baffin Bay that borders the narrow extension of the Coastal Prairies inland to eastern Jim Hogg County. The sand plain is stabilized by vegetation for the most part and is largely dominated by live oak mottes.

The **Edwards Plateau** is also commonly referred to as the Hill Country. This region includes the Llano Uplift or Central Mineral Region. The Balcones Escarpment bounds the Edwards Plateau on the east and south. This region is deeply dissected with numerous streams and rivers. The Balcones Canyonlands form the true Hill Country along the escarpment and are dominated primarily by woodlands and forests, with grasslands restricted to broad divides between drainages. Protected canyons and slopes support forests of Ashe juniper (*Juniperus ashei*) and oak. The dominant oak species differ depending on the location but include Lacey oak (*Quercus laceyi*), Texas red oak (*Q. buckleyi*), and plateau live oak (*Q. fusiformis*). Much of the northern and western plateau is characterized by semiopen grasslands and shrublands on the uplands with riparian corridors along the drainages.

The **Rolling Plains** are situated between the High Plains and the Cross Timbers and Prairies in the north-central part of the state. These plains are nearly level or rolling and were originally covered by prairie. The Rolling Plains are divided from the High Plains by the steep Caprock Escarpment. The vegetation of this region was described as tall- and midgrass prairie with a wide variety of grasses present, including little bluestem, big bluestem, sand bluestem (*Andropogon gerardi*), sideoats grama (*Bouteloua curtipendula*), indiangrass, and buffalograss (*Buchloe dactyloides*). Overgrazing and reduction of fires have transformed much of the Rolling Plains from a mid- and tall-grass prairie to an open shrubland dominated by mesquite and juniper. Many rivers and streams have eroded away the Caprock Escarpment to form canyons. The largest and best known is **Palo Duro Canyon**. The canyons or breaks of the Canadian River are also included in this region. The Rolling Plains and the Edwards Plateau are ecologically similar, but a distinct geological change defines the boundary. The Concho Valley lies along this boundary.

The **High Plains** are bounded by the Caprock Escarpment and dissected by the Canadian River. These plains are nearly level, with many shallow playa lakes. The original vegetation of the High Plains consisted generally of mixed and shortgrass prairie and was free from brush. The species of grasses present varied based on soil types. In areas with clay soils, blue grama (*Bouteloua gracilis*) and buffalograss were common. On sandy soils, grasses such as little bluestem, sideoats grama, and sand dropseed (*Sporobolus cryptandrus*) dominated. Today, about 60 percent of the High Plains is in agricultural production, much of which is used to produce row crops. The southern extension of the High Plains, south of the Canadian River, is known as the Llano Estacado. The area around Lubbock, including the surrounding counties, is known as the **South Plains**.

The **Trans-Pecos** of far west Texas includes the northern extension of the Chihuahuan Desert. There are many small mountain ranges within the region, with the Davis, Chisos, and Guadalupe mountains being the best known. Guadalupe Peak, at an elevation of 8,751 feet, is the highest point in Texas. Desert grasslands and desert scrub are found at lower elevations, although very little desert grassland persists today. The vegetation found at the mid-elevations in the mountain ranges is dominated by pinyon pines (*Pinus cembroides, P. edulis,* and

P. remota) and junipers; the upper elevations support pines (*P. ponderosa* and *P. arizonica*). Creosote bush (*Larrea tridentata*), tarbush (*Flourensia cernua*), and various acacias are found in the lowland basins. The **Stockton Plateau** is the subregion found west of the Pecos River, including most of Terrell and southern Pecos counties, occupying a transitional zone between the Edwards Plateau and the Chihuahuan Desert. The dominant vegetation type is mesquite and redberry juniper (*Juniperus pinchotii*) savannah. The Stockton Plateau is sometimes included as a subregion of the Edwards Plateau.

SPECIES ACCOUNTS

**BLACK-BELLIED
WHISTLING-DUCK***
Dendrocygna autumnalis

BACKGROUND

One of the most strik-
ing ducks found in
Texas, with long legs and a long neck.
Very gregarious, they can sometimes be
found in flocks of more than 1000 birds.
This duck is nocturnal in nature and can
often be seen flying between feeding and roosting
sites at dawn and dusk. During the day, they are often encountered loafing in parks or around bodies of water. As the name
suggests, they have a very nasal, whistling call that is given frequently when in flight. Whistling-ducks were formerly known
as tree-ducks because a few of the species in the genus nest in
cavities, including the Black-bellied. There are eight species of
whistling-ducks, and they can be found on all continents except
Antarctica.

IDENTIFICATION The adults are unmistakable, with their brown
body color combined with a black belly and white wing patches,
which are revealed as broad stripes in flight. The bright red bill
and gray face are also key characteristics of the species. In flight
they have a hump-backed look, with the long neck dipped
slightly. The long legs extend well beyond the short tail. The
black of the belly extends throughout the underside of the
wings, contrasting sharply with the distinctively patterned
upper surface. Ducklings are tan overall with two broad black
stripes on the face, reminiscent of a female Masked Duck. As
the young mature they molt into a plumage that is similar to
the adult but is primarily composed of varying shades of brown,

14

rather than the more distinctive colors they will acquire within a few weeks.

SIMILAR SPECIES There are really no birds in Texas that can be confused with the Black-bellied Whistling-Duck. There is, however, another species in the genus present in the state, the Fulvous Whistling-Duck (*Dendrocygna bicolor*). This species has a rich tawny plumage, but it shares the same body shape with the Black-bellied and is similar in size.

HABITAT This species is found in a variety of habitats ranging from wooded swamps to city parks. The primary requirements are large trees where potential nesting cavities can be found. They will readily use nesting boxes if the opening is of sufficient size. Large concentrations can be found in rice fields on the upper and central coasts in the late summer and fall.

STATUS AND DISTRIBUTION Uncommon to common resident, although generally less common in winter, from the central Edwards Plateau southward and along the Coastal Prairies. Continues to expand its range northward and eastward. Now a regular visitor to the northern Edwards Plateau and can be found as far north as Tarrant and Dallas counties. Isolated breeding populations have become established in the southern Rolling Plains as well. Irregular visitor to the remainder of the state, primarily between March and November.

Black-bellied Whistling Duck, adult. Photo by Tim Cooper.

SNOW GOOSE
Chen caerulescens

BACKGROUND The worldwide population of the Snow Goose has increased dramatically in recent decades, and as a result the number of these geese that winter in Texas has proportionally increased. The increase has damaged both the breeding and winter habitats, although the change has been more dramatic on the breeding grounds in the Arctic. With the increase in overall population, there has also been an expansion of the wintering range in Texas. This species was formerly a rare winter visitor to many areas of the state away from the Coastal Prairies, but now substantial numbers can be found on the High Plains and locally elsewhere in the state. The dark morph, which is much less common, was formerly considered a separate species called the Blue Goose.

IDENTIFICATION White-morph birds have entirely white plumage with the exception of the primaries, which are black. The bills and legs are pink in adults. Immature white-morph birds have a grayish tint to their plumage, particularly the upperparts. Dark-morph birds have white heads and necks but slate blue-gray body plumage. The wings are considerably lighter gray, contrasting sharply with the darker body when seen in flight. Immature dark-morph birds are gray-brown overall.

SIMILAR SPECIES The only species that is likely to cause confusion is the diminutive Ross's Goose (*Chen rossii*). Although Ross's Goose is considerably smaller than the Snow Goose, close examination is often required to separate the two species. This is partially because the Snow Geese that winter in Texas are of a smaller subspecies and are often referred to as Lesser Snow Geese. Adult Snow Geese can be distinguished by their large, rather long pink bills, with a prominent black area where the mandibles come together, called the grin patch. Ross's Goose also has a dark morph that is very rare and can be distinguished from a blue-morph Snow Goose in that the dark coloration of the upperparts extends to include the crown.

Snow Goose, white morph. Photo by Tim Couper.

HABITAT These geese rely heavily on agricultural areas in all of the regions of the state where they occur. On the Coastal Prairies between Houston and Corpus Christi they favor rice and grain fields in particular. On the High Plains, winter wheat fields are often used.

STATUS AND DISTRIBUTION Common to abundant migrant through the state, particularly in the eastern half. Abundant winter resident along the Coastal Prairies, and common to locally abundant in the Panhandle southward through the South Plains. Also an uncommon and local winter resident in the western Trans-Pecos and in agricultural areas in the South Texas Brush Country. Can occur as a winter visitor almost anywhere in the state. Fall migrants arrive in early October; wintering birds generally remain until mid-March, although a few linger as late as early April.

CACKLING GOOSE
Branta hutchinsii
and
CANADA GOOSE
Branta canadensis

BACKGROUND Until recently the Cackling Goose was considered a subspecies of the Canada Goose, distinguished mainly by its small size. Its classification as a separate species has raised a host of questions about identification and led to more scrutiny of white-cheeked geese. The size variation in these two species can be quite striking. The largest subspecies of the Canada Goose may be as much as seven times larger than the typical Cackling Goose. The subspecies that occurs in Texas is called Richardson's Cackling Goose (*B. h. hutchinsii*).

IDENTIFICATION These geese are easily identifiable, with their black heads and necks contrasting sharply with the prominent white cheeks. The body plumage is generally light gray for most individuals found in Texas, but some can be dark gray. The real challenge is separating the two sister species from one another. Most of the Canada Geese found in the northwestern part of Texas belong to a small subspecies, *B. c. parvipes,* which is more difficult to distinguish from Cackling Geese as the large size differential may not be apparent. A key feature of Canada Geese is the longer bill, which is close to three-quarters the width of the head. Cackling Geese have much stubbier bills, rarely half the width of the head. The two species have very different calls, and this can be a good field characteristic if a small number of birds are present so that their

Richardson's Cackling Goose. Photo by Mark W. Lockwood.

Lesser Canada Goose (*B. c. parvipes*). Photo by Mark W. Lockwood.

calls can be easily discerned. Cackling Geese have a higher, more nasal call compared to the familiar honking call of the Canada.

SIMILAR SPECIES No other species are likely to be confused with either of these species. The Brant (*B. bernicla*) is similar in size and also has a black neck and head, but it lacks the distinctive white cheek patches.

HABITAT Both species frequent man-made impoundments for roosting and scatter into nearby agricultural areas for feeding. They also frequent smaller ponds and city parks.

STATUS AND DISTRIBUTION Both species are uncommon to common migrants throughout the state. Canada Geese winter throughout the state, sometimes in large numbers, but are generally abundant only on the High Plains and common only along the upper and central coasts. The Cackling Goose is much more common on the High Plains than on the Coastal Prairies and is casual in the Trans-Pecos. Canada Geese are rare along the lower coast but can be locally uncommon during some years. Fall migrants of both species begin to appear in late September, with the majority of the wintering population arriving in late October. Most have departed by March. The Canada Goose is a summer resident in north-central Texas and, in small numbers, the Panhandle and South Plains. The status and distribution of the Cackling Goose in Texas is generally poorly understood.

WOOD DUCK
Aix sponsa

BACKGROUND

Wood Ducks are often shy and retiring in habit, keeping to secluded wooded swamps and protected wetlands. They are, however, also encountered in city parks and other areas more conducive to easy observation, where the spectacular plumage of the male can be fully appreciated. These ducks are cavity nesters, which is one reason they prefer heavily wooded wetlands. The availability of natural cavities is often a limiting factor on the number of pairs in specific areas, but these birds will readily use nest boxes.

IDENTIFICATION Adult males are unmistakable with their brightly colored plumage. In breeding plumage the male has an elongated crest, and the head is iridescent green and purple. The chin and throat are white with two extensions onto the face and neck. A thin white line extends from the bill back through the crest. The bill is primarily red and white with a black tip. The underparts are multicolored, with a reddish breast and yellowish sides that are separated by single black and white bars. The upperparts are dark with greenish iridescence. In the nonbreeding, or eclipse, plumage, the male retains this basic pattern, but it is overlaid with browns and is considerably muted. Adult females are grayish brown overall. They share the bushy crest of the male, although it is much reduced. Females have a broad white eye-ring that tapers into a postocular stripe. The underparts are gray-brown and streaked with tan and white. The speculum is green in both sexes.

SIMILAR SPECIES The male Wood Duck is truly unmistakable. Although the male Green-winged Teal (*Anas crecca*) shares a few similarities, the white throat and multicolored underparts of the Wood Duck set it apart from the primarily gray teal. The female Hooded Merganser (*Lophodytes cucullatus*) is similar in shape and overall coloration to a female Wood Duck and is found in similar habitats, but Hooded Mergansers have a somewhat differently shaped head and lack the white around the eye and heavy streaking on the underparts.

HABITAT Primarily forested wetlands, but found in more open habitats as well, particularly in winter.

STATUS AND DISTRIBUTION Locally uncommon to common resident in the eastern three-quarters of the state, west to the eastern Panhandle and western Edwards Plateau. Uncommon resident along the Rio Grande in the western Trans-Pecos and in Starr and Webb counties in southern Texas. Except for in the Panhandle, this species is generally more common in winter as migrants from more northerly populations arrive.

Wood Duck, male. Photo by Tim Cooper.

AMERICAN WIGEON
Anas americana

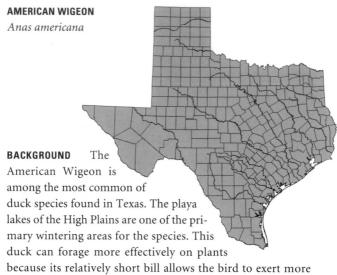

BACKGROUND   The American Wigeon is among the most common of duck species found in Texas. The playa lakes of the High Plains are one of the primary wintering areas for the species. This duck can forage more effectively on plants because its relatively short bill allows the bird to exert more force when tearing off small pieces of submergent plants and grasses. American Wigeons are the most likely of the dabbling ducks to be seen in wet pastures and meadows.

IDENTIFICATION The prominent white forehead and cap are distinguishing characters of adult males. The males also have a broad green stripe across the sides of the head starting just in front of the eye. Also look for the rose-colored breast and brownish red flanks. The female is patterned much like the male but lacks the white crown and green eye stripe. Both sexes share a distinctive wing pattern. The shoulder is bright white in the male and grayish white in the female, and the speculum (secondaries) is green in both species.

SIMILAR SPECIES The male is distinctive among Texas ducks. The female might be confused with females of several species, particularly when at rest, when the wing pattern is concealed. A characteristic shared by many species of ducks is a sharp line separating the head and neck from the contrasting breast plumage. The silvery blue bill and reddish brown breast distinguish the female American Wigeon from similarly patterned species, such as the Gadwall (*A. strepera*), Mallard (*A.*

platyrhynchos), and smaller teal. The Eurasian Wigeon (*A. penelope*), a very rare visitor to Texas, shares a similar overall pattern. The rufous head easily distinguishes the male, but identifying females can be tricky. Most female Eurasian Wigeons have a rufous head as well, but a few have a gray head and thus are difficult to distinguish from a female American Wigeon. The key feature is the white axillaries (the feathers connecting the under surface of the wing and the body) of the American Wigeon, which are gray in the Eurasian Wigeon.

HABITAT Found on freshwater ponds and lakes, saline and brackish marshes; will forage in wet meadows and pastures. American Wigeon is a common species inhabiting ponds in city parks.

American Wigeon, female on right and male on left. Photo by Mark W. Lockwood.

STATUS AND DISTRIBUTION Common to abundant migrant and winter resident. Migrants arrive in the fall during October; the last birds to leave in the spring remain until late May. Local summer visitor to the Panhandle and can occasionally be found in other areas of the state during that season. Evidence of nesting has never been uncovered in Texas.

MALLARD
Anas platyrhynchos

BACKGROUND

The male Mallard in breeding plumage is certainly one of the most recognizable ducks in Texas. These greenheads, as they are sometimes called, are both widespread and easily observable, making them a favorite of artists and waterfowl enthusiasts. Mallards are not only common in Texas but are also found across the entire northern hemisphere.

Populations of Mallards in Mexico and parts of Texas were previously considered a separate species, the Mexican Duck. The male Mexican Duck has plumage very similar to that of the female and lacks the characteristic green head familiar to the species. Mallards are also the ancestor of most domestic duck breeds.

IDENTIFICATION Adult males in breeding plumage have an iridescent green head with a bright yellow bill. These birds have a narrow white neck ring and a chestnut-brown breast. The remainder of the underparts and the upperparts are gray. The rump and undertail coverts are black. The tail is largely white with black central feathers that curl upward, unlike any other North

Mallard, male.
Photo by Mark
W. Lockwood.

American dabbling duck. Nonbreeding males are largely brown with hints of the breeding plumage underlaid, particularly the chestnut-brown breast and some green, usually on the crown. Adult females are brown

Mallard, female. Photo by Mark W. Lockwood.

overall and heavily mottled with buff, white, and darker brown. The head and neck are paler than the body. There is a dark line through the eye, and the crown is also darker than the rest of the head. The tail of the female Mallard is grayish white, and the female's bill is usually orange with some black mottling.

SIMILAR SPECIES The male in breeding plumage is unlikely to be confused with other ducks. Although the male Northern Shoveler (*A. clypeata*) also has a green head, its large spatulate bill easily distinguishes it from the Mallard. The male Red-breasted Merganser (*Mergus serrator*) has a similar plumage pattern, but it has a shaggy crest and a long, thin bill. The female Mallard can be more easily confused with other waterfowl, the Mottled Duck (*A. fulvigula*) in particular. Common residents along the Coastal Prairies, Mottled Ducks have a similar plumage pattern but are generally much darker on the body, with a dark brown tail.

HABITAT Virtually all wetland habitats.

STATUS AND DISTRIBUTION Common to abundant winter resident in the northern half of the state, becoming less common in the south. Fall migrants arrive in late October, and wintering birds are generally present until late April. Uncommon summer resident in the Panhandle, rare and local elsewhere in the state. Mexican Ducks are rare to locally common resident in the Trans-Pecos and along the Rio Grande south to the Lower Rio Grande Valley.

BLUE-WINGED TEAL
Anas discors

BACKGROUND
The Blue-winged
Teal is among the ear-
liest of the ducks to
return in fall from northern breeding
areas, and it is the last to depart in the
spring. Unusual among North American
ducks, they are long-distance migrants;
some birds winter as far south as central South
America. The main foods of this species include seeds and
aquatic plants, insects, and other invertebrates. It is reported to
be among the three most common ducks in North America,
along with the Mallard and Northern Pintail (*A. acuta*).

IDENTIFICATION The male is very distinctive, with a lead-gray
head and broad white crescent on its face. The underparts of
the male are buffy brown heavily speckled with black. The
female is fairly uniform brown with a paler head and neck. In
flight, both sexes show a pale blue shoulder and green speculum.

SIMILAR SPECIES The immature male Northern Shoveler (*A.
clypeata*) can have a white crescent on the face as well, but the
very large, spatulate bill and overall larger size easily distinguish
this species. It is often difficult to distinguish the female Blue-
winged from Cinnamon Teal (*A. cyanoptera*). In general,
female Cinnamon Teal are a warmer brown and have a plainer
face without a dark eye line. One of the best features in separating these species is the longer, more spatulate bill of the Cinnamon. The most obvious difference between female Green-
winged (*A. crecca*) and Blue-winged Teal is the wing pattern,

but the Green-winged is also smaller in overall size and has a smaller bill.

HABITAT Found in a variety of habitats, including freshwater and brackish marshes and other shallow wetlands.

STATUS AND DISTRIBUTION Common to abundant migrant throughout the state. Can be seen in migration during March and April and from late July through October. Uncommon summer resident throughout the Panhandle and South Plains as well as the upper Texas coast. Known to nest in various locations throughout most of the remainder of the state. In winter, uncommon to common along the Coastal Prairies and in the South Texas Brush Country. Wintering birds are uncommon to rare as far north as Travis, Burleson, and Montgomery counties.

Blue-winged Teal, male in foreground. Photo by Tim Cooper.

NORTHERN SHOVELER
Anas clypeata

BACKGROUND The large, spatulate bill of the Northern Shoveler easily separates it from all other waterfowl found in Texas. These ducks filter water through comblike projections along the edges of the bill in order to capture small swimming crustaceans. Shovelers can be locally abundant during the winter in Texas and form large flocks of several hundred individuals as they feed in shallow wetlands.

IDENTIFICATION Adult males in breeding plumage have an iridescent dark green head that contrasts sharply with a white breast. The belly and flanks are chestnut-brown, and the upperparts are largely black. The rump and undertail coverts are black, and the tail is primarily white. The upper wing is brightly colored, with a light blue shoulder and a green speculum separated by a white line. The bill is black, and the eyes are bright yellow. The male's nonbreeding plumage is much duller overall, with a wash of brown over the brighter pattern of the breeding season. Some individuals will also have an indistinct white crescent on the face behind the bill, reminiscent of a Blue-winged Teal (*A. discors*). Adult females are grayish brown overall and heavily mottled with buff,

Northern Shoveler, male. Photo by Greg W. Lasley.

Northern Shoveler, female. Photo by Greg W. Lasley.

white, and darker brown. The female has the same upper wing pattern as the male. The bill of the female is usually brownish olive with orange along the edges of the mandibles and at the base.

SIMILAR SPECIES The breeding plumage of the male Northern Shoveler is unique among Texas waterfowl. The male Mallard (*A. platyrhynchos*) also has a green head, but the body plumage is very different and less brightly colored. The male Red-breasted Merganser (*Mergus serrator*) has a similar plumage pattern, but it has a shaggy crest and a long, thin bill. Both Cinnamon (*A. cyanoptera*) and Blue-winged Teal have similar wing patterns, but both are much smaller species, and neither has a green head or white breast. The long, spatulate bill of the female Northern Shoveler separates it from all other waterfowl found in the state.

HABITAT Shallow wetlands, both fresh and saline. Particularly common on settling ponds at sewage treatment plants.

STATUS AND DISTRIBUTION Common to abundant migrant and winter resident throughout the state. Northern Shovelers arrive in Texas in early September and are present through mid-May. Uncommon summer visitor to the Panhandle, with a few nesting records. Elsewhere in the state, a rare and local summer visitor.

GREEN-WINGED TEAL
Anas crecca

BACKGROUND
The Green-winged
Teal is the smallest of
North America's dab-
bling ducks. It is also one of
the most common ducks found in
Texas. They migrate, mainly at night, in
large flocks, sometimes numbering a few
hundred individuals. The subspecies of Green-
winged Teal present in Texas is *A. c. carolinensis*, but there is a
single documented record of Eurasian Teal (*A. c. crecca*) from
the Village Creek Drying Beds, Tarrant County, on 30 January–
1 February 1994. The Eurasian Teal is distinguished by a hori-
zontal white stripe along the back, and it lacks the white stripe
on the side of the breast. Some authorities consider the Eurasian
Teal to be a separate species.

IDENTIFICATION A very attractive duck, the male has a chestnut
head with a dark green ear patch that extends back into a shaggy crest. The body plumage is mostly gray, becoming more
mottled on the flanks, with a prominent white vertical stripe
along the side of the breast. The central breast is buffy with
black spotting. The female is fairly uniform brown with a white
belly and a paler head and neck. This small duck has a proportionally small bill as well. Both sexes have a bright green speculum that has a buffy leading edge.

SIMILAR SPECIES The adult male is unlikely to be confused with
other ducks, although the Wood Duck (*Aix sponsa*) has a shaggy crest. Female Blue-winged Teal have a grayer brown plumage
with a brown belly and a longer bill. If seen in flight, the wing
pattern is strikingly different between these species. Female

Green-winged Teal, male. Photo by Greg W. Lasley.

Cinnamon Teal can usually be easily eliminated because of their much larger and longer bills.

HABITAT This duck prefers shallow freshwater and brackish wetlands with abundant emergent vegetation. They often loaf on larger bodies of water and forage along the shores.

STATUS AND DISTRIBUTION Common to abundant migrant, and uncommon to locally common winter resident throughout the state. Wintering birds are present from September through April. Fall migrants begin to appear in late August; spring migrants generally have departed by mid-May, but some have lingered as late as early June. Rare to occasional in the Panhandle and Trans-Pecos during the summer. There are, however, only two reports of nesting in Texas.

CANVASBACK
Aythya valisineria

BACKGROUND
The Canvas-back is one of several diving ducks that winter through-out Texas. These birds are generally more common on secluded bays and protected saltwater habitats than on inland reservoirs. They breed primarily in the prairie pothole region of central North America, and the overall population has fluctuated greatly over the past few decades. As a result, the Canvasback occasionally appears on lists of species of conservation concern. Wetland conservation on the breeding grounds is a primary concern for the long-term health of the Canvasback population. The species name comes from *Vallisneria americana,* the wild celery, which is a favored food.

IDENTIFICATION The shape of the head is an identifying feature of this duck. The forehead slopes into a long black bill, giving the head and bill an elongated profile. Males in breeding plumage have a chestnut head and neck. The breast is black, and the body is pale gray, often looking whitish. The rump, under-tail, and tail are black. In females and eclipse-plumage males, the head and neck are pale brown, contrasting slightly with a darker brown breast. The body plumage is brownish gray.

SIMILAR SPECIES The plumage of the Canvasback is similar to that of the Redhead (*A. americana*), particularly the male's breeding plumage, which in Redheads is grayer and less whitish on the body, with a brighter red head. Redheads differ in having a rounder head, thus lacking the sloping profile characteristic of a Canvasback. The bill is also shorter and blue with a black tip.

Female and nonbreeding male Redheads are browner overall.

HABITAT Found on lakes and reservoirs as well as saltwater habitats, primarily estuaries and protected bays.

STATUS AND DISTRIBUTION Uncommon to locally common migrant and winter resident throughout the state. Canvasbacks arrive in Texas in mid-October and remain through late March, but it is not unusual for a few to linger through the spring and occasionally into early summer. In a few instances birds have remained through the summer in the Panhandle, where there are only a few nesting records. There is also a single nesting record from the Trans-Pecos.

Canvasback, male. Photo by Tim Cooper.

REDHEAD
Aythya americana

BACKGROUND The Redhead is similar in color pattern to the Canvasback, and it also winters in large numbers in Texas. In fact, the lower Laguna Madre is one of the most important wintering areas in the world for this species. Hundreds of thousands of individuals converge on the Laguna Madre each winter; very large concentrations can easily be observed near Corpus Christi or Laguna Atascosa National Wildlife Refuge. The Laguna Madre is such an important wintering area because of the vast sea grass (*Halodule wrightii*) beds found in the shallow waters of the bay. Like the Canvasback, Redheads breed in the prairie pothole region of central North America, as well as other areas of the western United States. The overall population has remained fairly steady over the past half century, and it appears that the species is slowly expanding its breeding range eastward. Redheads are well known for laying eggs in other ducks' nests.

IDENTIFICATION The Redhead is a medium-sized diving duck, slightly smaller than a Canvasback (*A. valisineria*). Males in breeding plumage have a bright red head and neck. The breast is black, and the body is smoky gray. The rump, undertail, and tail are black. The bill is tricolored with a bluish base, a narrow white ring, and a black tip. Females and eclipse-plumage males are brown with a slightly darker crown than the remainder of the face. In flight Redheads have a long gray stripe along the trailing edge of the wing.

SIMILAR SPECIES The Redhead looks similar to a Canvasback, particularly males in breeding plumage. Redheads differ in hav-

Redhead, female on left and male on right. Photo by Greg W. Lasley.

ing a rounder head, thus lacking the sloping profile characteristic of a Canvasback. The male's breeding plumage is also grayer and less whitish on the body, and the head is a brighter red. The bill is shorter and blue with a black tip. Female and nonbreeding male Redheads are browner overall.

HABITAT Habitat specialist in winter, found primarily in shallow bays where sea grasses are abundant. Smaller numbers are found on inland reservoirs as well.

STATUS AND DISTRIBUTION Uncommon to common migrant throughout the state. Common to abundant winter resident along the central and lower coasts, primarily in the Laguna Madre. Also rare to locally common winter resident throughout the remainder of the state. Normally arrives in Texas in mid-October and remains through early April. Uncommon to locally common summer resident in the Panhandle, but there are relatively few nesting records. Also rare summer resident in El Paso and Hudspeth counties in the western Trans-Pecos.

RING-NECKED DUCK
Aythya collaris

BACKGROUND The Ring-necked Duck is a common wintering diving duck in Texas that favors shallower water than most of its relatives. The common name does not provide a good clue to identifying the species. Both the common name and the scientific name refer to an inconspicuous chestnut collar on the male. The feature is visible only in the field under excellent conditions and can most easily be seen when the bird is in the hand.

IDENTIFICATION This medium-sized diving duck is slightly smaller than a Redhead (*A. americana*). In all plumages, the peaked head separates it from other *Aythya* species. Males in breeding plumage have a purplish black head and neck. The breast and back are black, and the flanks are smoky gray. A bold white crescent separates the breast from the flanks. The rump, undertail, and tail are black. The bill has a broad white band with a black tip. Females are

Ring-necked Duck, male. Photo by Greg W. Lasley.

Ring-necked Duck, female. Photo by Greg W. Lasley.

brown with the same peaked head shape of the male. The face is paler than the remainder of the head. They also have a pale eye-ring and a thin postocular stripe.

SIMILAR SPECIES The waterfowl most likely to be confused with a male Ring-necked Duck are the Greater (*A. marila*) and Lesser (*A. affinis*) Scaup. Male Ring-necked Ducks have a much more angular profile with a peak on the back of the head. The body plumage is more bicolored, with dark upperparts contrasting with pale gray flanks. Female Ring-necked Ducks can be separated from female scaup by their distinctive head shape as well. They also have a white eye-ring and thin postocular stripe. The female Redhead is also similar but larger, with a rounded profile.

HABITAT Found in a variety of wetland habitats, although far more common on freshwater. Tends to favor relatively shallow water, less than five feet deep, for a diving duck. Most often found on reservoirs and other impoundments, including small ponds.

STATUS AND DISTRIBUTION Uncommon to locally common migrant and winter resident throughout the state. Ring-necked Ducks begin to arrive in Texas in mid-October and are generally present through mid-April. Rare summer visitor to the Panhandle, South Plains, and Trans-Pecos. Despite the almost annual occurrence of these ducks in summer, there are no nesting records for Texas.

LESSER SCAUP
Aythya affinis

BACKGROUND
Statewide, Lesser Scaup is the most common of the diving ducks to occur in Texas. Even so, the numbers for this species have been declining since the 1980s.

IDENTIFICATION Males have a glossy black head that has a purple sheen, although it can appear green in certain light and from different angles. The neck and breast are black, which contrasts sharply with the paler body. The flanks are white but are heavily marked with gray vermiculations. There is generally some contrast between the flanks and the darker gray back, which is also heavily marked with fine bars. The tail, uppertail coverts, and undertail coverts are black. A white speculum extends into a light brown stripe on the inner primaries. The bill is a light blue-gray with a small black nail, and the iris is yellow. The female has a brownish head, neck, and chest and an obvious white patch at the base of the bill. The remainder of the bird is also brown, but more mottled with white on the back and flanks.

SIMILAR SPECIES The Greater Scaup (*A. marila*) is extremely similar but slightly larger. Where Lesser Scaup usually show a peaked crown, Greaters have a more smoothly rounded head. Greater Scaup also exhibit a larger black nail on the bill tip and a white stripe extending beyond the speculum through most of the primaries. Male Greater Scaup usually have brighter white sides with little to no barring. The females are also quite similar, but Greaters have a noticeably heavier nail and usually have a pale patch on the sides of the head. Another similar duck is the

Ring-necked Duck (*A. collaris*), but it has a black back, and the bill has a prominent white ring above the nail. Female Ring-necked Ducks generally have a mottled face, an eye ring, and the same white ring on the bill as the male.

HABITAT Found on fresh and brackish wetlands along the coast and in open bays. Inland, they are found in large water impoundments most frequently, but they can be seen on small ponds and in city parks as well.

Lesser Scaup, male. Photo by Mark W. Lockwood.

STATUS AND DISTRIBUTION Common to abundant migrant and winter resident east of the Pecos River. In the Trans-Pecos, common migrant and uncommon to locally rare winter resident. The first migrants arrive in late September, but the bulk of the wintering population is not in place until late October. Spring migrants start heading north in late February, with most birds gone by late March, though a few linger into mid-May. Rare summer visitor to virtually any part of the state. There are only two reports of nesting for Texas: Muleshoe National Wildlife Refuge, Bailey County, in 1942, and a female with ducklings in southern Swisher County in early July 1977.

MASKED DUCK*
Nomonyx dominicus

BACKGROUND The Masked Duck is one of two stifftail ducks to occur in Texas, the other being the much more common Ruddy Duck (*Oxyura jamaicensis*). This Neotropical species is only an irregular visitor to the United States, with most records from Texas and Florida. A pattern of invasions into Texas has emerged, with large numbers of birds showing up every 20 to 30 years. The last such incursion lasted from 1992 through 1998.

IDENTIFICATION The male's breeding plumage is unmistakable: a bright blue bill contrasts sharply with the black face. The body is bright chestnut heavily marked with black. Adult females and winter plumaged males have brown to reddish brown plumage that is also heavily spotted with black. They have a dark cap with a tan head that shows two prominent dark lines. One of the

Masked Duck, male in breeding plumage. Photo by Mark W. Lockwood.

lines starts in the lores and
passes through the eye, while
the other cuts across the cheek.
Both sexes, in all plumages,
have a short tail that is occasionally held up out of the
water, although not as regularly
as seen in Ruddy Ducks.

SIMILAR SPECIES Female Ruddy
Ducks are occasionally confused with the Masked Duck.
The Ruddy Duck's plumage,
however, is grayer and the dark

Masked Duck, adult female. Photo by Mark W.
Lockwood.

cap extends down to the eye, leaving only one stripe through
the cheek. The pattern of Black-bellied Whistling-Duck ducklings is very similar to that of an adult female Masked Duck; the
ducklings, however, are structurally quite different. They more
closely resemble their parents and look rather long-necked and
large-headed, as well as having downy body plumage. They are
usually still dependent on the adults while in that plumage.

HABITAT Found on freshwater ponds or marshes with abundant
emergent vegetation.

STATUS AND DISTRIBUTION Rare and irregular visitor along the
coast and in the Lower Rio Grande Valley. Absent during most
years but can be locally uncommon during invasion periods.
They have been found in large concentrations during these
invasions, including a total of 37 individuals on a lake in San
Patricio County in February 1993. Only 2 of the 62 documented
records for the state are away from the Coastal Plains: one in El
Paso County on 11 July 1976 and another in Hays County on 20
September–early October 1980. There have been a number of
reports of nesting over the years, but the only well-documented
record was of a female with young at Anahuac National Wildlife
Refuge, Chambers County, in 1967. The Masked Duck is frequently claimed as a rare permanent resident in Texas, but there
is very little evidence to support this contention.

GREATER PRAIRIE-CHICKEN*
Tympanuchus cupido

BACKGROUND

Greater Prairie-Chickens were once a common sight in the grasslands of the eastern half of Texas and on the Coastal Prairies in the late 1800s. The conversion of these grasslands to agricultural uses took a heavy toll on these birds. Those formerly found in the Blackland Prairies have been completely gone from Texas since the early 1900s, and those on the Coastal Prairies are on the brink of extinction. The sub-species of Greater Prairie-Chicken that is still found in Texas is popularly known as Attwater's Prairie-Chicken, *T. c. attwateri.* An aggressive conservation effort is under way to save this endangered subspecies, including a captive breeding program and close monitoring of the birds in the wild. The remaining populations are found at the Attwater Prairie Chicken National Wildlife Refuge and the Texas Nature Conservancy's Texas City Preserve. Many of the birds found at these locations were raised in captivity. The Greater Prairie-Chickens formerly found on the Blackland Prairies and elsewhere in the eastern portion of the state belonged to a separate subspecies, *T. c. pinnatus.* They were common in these tallgrass prairies from north-central and northeastern Texas southward to Travis County. By 1920, they were largely gone. The last of these birds was reported in 1956 from Smith County.

IDENTIFICATION This medium-sized grouse is generally brown

Attwater's Greater Prairie-Chicken, male. Photo by Greg W. Lasley.

and heavily barred with black. It has a short, blackish tail. Males have long "ear" tufts on the neck, which point forward during courtship displays. Males also have a yellow comb above the eyes and a large yellow-orange area of skin on the side of the neck that is inflated during the courtship display.

SIMILAR SPECIES Within its very limited range there are no species that could potentially be mistaken for a prairie chicken. The Lesser Prairie-Chicken is similar in size to Attwater's subspecies, but it is paler and less heavily barred. These two species do not occur in the same region; Lesser Prairie-Chickens are found in the northwestern part of the state.

HABITAT Tallgrass coastal prairie. The type of habitat used varies throughout the year. Areas of shorter grass are used for courtship and feeding areas, and tall grasses are used for nesting and cover. It has been estimated that 97 percent of the habitat has been lost within the historic range.

STATUS AND DISTRIBUTION Extremely rare on prairies of the upper coast. This species is an extremely rare and local resident in Colorado and Galveston counties. Formerly found on the Coastal Prairies from the Louisiana border to Refugio County. The total population in the wild consists of fewer than 100 individuals.

LESSER PRAIRIE-CHICKEN*
Tympanuchus pallidicinctus

BACKGROUND Like the Greater Prairie-Chicken, the Lesser Prairie-Chicken has declined in overall abundance over the past few decades. Most of this decline involves the transition of grasslands to agricultural uses, but severe droughts on the southern Great Plains over the past century have also contributed to the deterioration of their habitat. Among North American grouse, only the Gunnison Sage-Grouse (*Centrocercus minimus*) has a smaller distribution and population than the Lesser Prairie-Chicken. Much of the remaining range of this prairie chicken is found in northwestern Texas. Like other species in the genus, Lesser Prairie-Chickens use leks, or booming grounds, for courtship displays. These elaborate courtship displays include confrontations between males. There are no true pair bonds, and the female alone cares for the young. This mating system allows the dominant males to produce most of the offspring.

IDENTIFICATION This medium-sized grouse is generally light brown overall but heavily barred with darker brown above and below. The tail is short and blackish. Males have long "ear" tufts on the neck, which point forward during courtship displays. Males also have a yellow comb above the eyes and a large reddish yellow area of skin on the side of the neck that is inflated during the courtship display.

SIMILAR SPECIES Within its range, only a female Ring-necked Pheasant (*Phasianus colchicus*) could potentially be mistaken for a prairie chicken. A female pheasant shares the overall light brown coloration of a Lesser Prairie-Chicken, but it is easily distinguished by its larger size and long pointed tail. Another key feature is the lack of heavy barring above and below on the female pheasant.

HABITAT Found in grasslands with scattered shrubs. In Texas, this habitat is primarily Havard or shinnery oak (*Quercus havardii*) in tall grass. Highest-quality habitat includes areas with a higher density of shrubs and taller grasses for nesting sites and somewhat more open areas for when the young leave the nest. Within these grasslands, there must be very open sites suitable for courtship displays. These booming grounds are now often located on areas of human disturbance, such as abandoned petroleum well sites and roadways.

STATUS AND DISTRIBUTION Rare to uncommon and local resident in the Panhandle and South Plains. There are currently two separate populations in Texas. One is found along the western South Plains from Bailey County south to Gaines County. The eastern population is found in the Panhandle from Lipscomb County south to Collingsworth County. The species formerly ranged south to Menard and Jeff Davis counties. In the past it moved to the south during the winter, but the last such incursion occurred during the winter of 1885–1886.

Lesser Prairie-Chicken, male. Photo by Mark W. Lockwood.

WILD TURKEY
Meleagris gallopavo

BACKGROUND The Wild Turkey is the largest North American game bird. Populations of turkeys were eliminated from much of its range by the early 1900s. The species has returned to much of the original range through reintroduction programs, most directed by state wildlife departments. Turkeys raised in captive breeding programs, however, have generally been unsuccessful in adapting to the wild. In contrast, wild birds captured and transported to new areas quickly became established and have flourished. As is well known, the male gobbles to attract females and struts with his tail fanned and body plumage raised. Turkeys are social and form flocks, sometimes very large ones, during the winter. They frequently choose winter roosting sites in large trees and are very faithful to these areas if left undisturbed. Three subspecies of Wild Turkey are found in Texas: the Eastern Wild Turkey (*M. g. silvestris*) the Rio Grande Wild Turkey (*M. g. intermedia*) and Merriam's Wild Turkey, (*M. g. merriami*). The Eastern Wild Turkey is found locally in the eastern third of the state, while Merriam's Wild Turkey is the bird seen in the mountains of the Trans-Pecos. The Rio Grande Wild Turkey is found in between, from the Panhandle south to the South Texas Brush Country.

IDENTIFICATION Males are dark brown overall with iridescent copper, bronze, and gold feathers. They also have brightly colored, nearly featherless heads. The tail of a male Wild Turkey is usually 12 to 15 inches long and has broad bands at the tip. Females have drabber plumage, usually brown and gray feathers.

SIMILAR SPECIES This turkey is distinctive among North American birds. Adult Turkey Vultures (*Cathartes aura*) also have featherless, bright red heads, but they lack the highly ornamented body plumage and tail. Another species of turkey, the Ocellated Turkey (*M. ocellata*), found in the Yucatan Peninsula southward into Belize and Guatemala, is smaller, with iridescent blues and greens replacing many of the coppery tones of the Wild Turkey.

Wild Turkey, displaying male. Photo by Tim Cooper.

HABITAT Found in open hardwood and mixed forests with scattered openings, including pastures or fields.

STATUS AND DISTRIBUTION Common to uncommon resident from the eastern Panhandle southward through the Rolling Plains to the Edwards Plateau. Common to uncommon in the South Texas Brush Country north of the Lower Rio Grande Valley and in the mountains of the central Trans-Pecos. Domesticated turkeys, however, are sometimes encountered in areas outside the known range.

SCALED QUAIL
Callipepla squamata

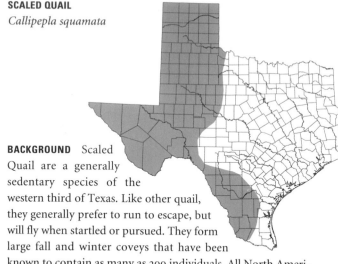

BACKGROUND Scaled Quail are a generally sedentary species of the western third of Texas. Like other quail, they generally prefer to run to escape, but will fly when startled or pursued. They form large fall and winter coveys that have been known to contain as many as 200 individuals. All North American quail, including the Scaled Quail, experience great fluctuations in abundance due to total rainfall during the breeding season. There can be very low numbers following dry years and very high numbers following years with above-average rainfall. Scaled Quail have declined dramatically since the 1940s, particularly on the South Plains and western Edwards Plateau. The reasons behind this decline are presently unclear but are probably related to habitat loss. Two subspecies of Scaled Quail are found in Texas. The subspecies found over most of the state is *C. s. pallida*, and *C. s. castanogastris* is present in the South Texas Brush Country. The latter has a chestnut patch on the belly and is darker in overall plumage, particularly on the upperparts.

IDENTIFICATION Rather plump looking, this quail has a short tail and gray plumage. The bluish gray body plumage is edged in black, giving the bird an overall scaled appearance. The sexes are similar, but the male has a more prominent white crest. Adult females have a smaller and buffer crest.

SIMILAR SPECIES It is unlikely that this distinctive bird would be confused with any of the other species of quail.

HABITAT This species is found most commonly in desert grasslands, mesquite savannah, and open brushy habitats. They are found less frequently in areas where there are pockets of native habitat surrounded by row crop agriculture or other heavily disturbed areas.

STATUS AND DISTRIBUTION Uncommon to locally common resident in the Trans-Pecos and from the Panhandle south through the western Rolling Plains and northwestern Edwards Plateau. Also locally common in the western South Texas Brush Country. Formerly ranged eastward to the eastern Rolling Plains and Edwards Plateau.

Scaled Quail. Photo by Mark W. Lockwood.

GAMBEL'S QUAIL
Callipepla gambelii

BACKGROUND

Gambel's Quail is more a symbol of the Sonoran Desert and Arizona than of Texas. This handsome quail reaches the eastern extreme of its range in the far western reaches of Texas. It has been found irregularly farther east than where it is generally thought to occur. Occasional sightings on the west side of Guadalupe Mountains National Park and in Big Bend Ranch State Park suggest that it is a low-density resident over a large area of west Texas. The reproductive success of Gambel's Quail, like many galliforms, depends on rainfall, which makes for great fluctuations in the size of the population in a given location. Those changes may explain why the species is found irregularly along the edges of its range in Texas. This quail was named after William Gambel, a naturalist from the Academy of Natural Sciences of Philadelphia, who first discovered the bird while working along the Santa Fe Trail in 1841.

IDENTIFICATION Gambel's Quail has the plump body shape and short tail typical of other quail. The overall plumage is gray, and both sexes have a teardrop-shaped plume. Adult males have a chestnut crown with a black face that extends down through the throat. Females lack this distinctive facial pattern. Both sexes have chestnut sides that are streaked with white; the rest of the underparts are whitish, except that the male has a black belly. The upperparts are gray. Occasional instances of hybrids between Gambel's and Scaled Quail (*C. squamata*) have been documented. These individuals most often look superficially

Gambel's Quail, male. Photo by Greg W. Lasley.

like Gambel's Quail, with a muted plumage pattern overlaid with heavy scaling similar to the typical plumage of a Scaled Quail.

SIMILAR SPECIES In Texas, Gambel's Quail is unlikely to be confused with any other species. The prominent teardrop-shaped plume, or double plume, is present in both sexes and not shared with any other quail in the state.

HABITAT In Texas, most commonly in the floodplain of the Rio Grande, where it is found in brushy drainages along the river. Also in mixed desert scrub in foothills of the Franklin Mountains and elsewhere.

STATUS AND DISTRIBUTION Common resident in the western Trans-Pecos from El Paso and Hudspeth counties southward along the Rio Grande to Presidio County.

NORTHERN BOBWHITE
Colinus virginianus

BACKGROUND
The advertising call of the male Northern Bobwhite is a familiar sound in much of Texas. The whistled *bob-WHITE* or *bob-bob-WHITE* is, of course, the source of the species' common name. Bobwhites are found in coveys except during the nesting season. These birds often roost in a circle with their heads pointing outward. This allows them not only to share body warmth but also to maintain a clear escape route. Northern Bobwhites (and other quail) are fully capable of flight, but they usually spend most of their time on the ground. When a covey or family group is flushed, they will burst into flight with individuals heading in all directions. Afterward, soft calls can be heard as they try to relocate one another. Northern Bobwhites exhibit the greatest range of geographical variation of any galliform, with many well-marked subspecies. There are 20 described subspecies, and some of the differences between these populations are striking, particularly in the plumage of the adult male.

IDENTIFICATION Northern Bobwhites are plump, short-tailed birds. They have an intricate body plumage with areas of chestnut, brown, and white. In males, the throat and eye stripe are white; these areas are buffy in the female. Females are also paler overall and browner, with less black and chestnut in the plumage. One very rare morph has a black face and very rufous body plumage, which masks other markings.

SIMILAR SPECIES There are no similar species within the range of

Northern Bobwhite, male. Photo by Tim Cooper.

this distinctive bird. The Montezuma Quail (*Cyrtonyx montezumae*) is superficially similar, and they do occur together on the southwestern Edwards Plateau. The Montezuma Quail has a very distinctive facial pattern with a rounded brown crest on the back of the head. Unlike the chestnut tones of the Northern Bobwhite, the Montezuma Quail has brown upperparts that are heavily marked with black and black underparts with white spots. The adult female is browner overall with a rounded crest as well.

HABITAT Bobwhites occupy a variety of habitats, including open woodlands, thickets, open brushy areas, grasslands with some woody cover, and cultivated areas with weedy or brushy edges.

STATUS AND DISTRIBUTION Locally uncommon to rare throughout the state east of the Pecos River. Rare and local resident in the Trans-Pecos west to southern Reeves County and eastern Terrell County. Also reported from Jeff Davis and Pecos counties. Northern Bobwhites have declined in recent years, particularly in the eastern half of the state, where they have become rare in many areas. They are still locally common in some of these areas and remain common in the Panhandle, South Plains, and western Rolling Plains.

MONTEZUMA QUAIL
Cyrtonyx montezumae

BACKGROUND
The Montezuma Quail has been known by a variety of common names over the decades: Harlequin Quail, Fool's Quail, and Mearn's Quail. Although the male has striking plumage, these birds rely on camouflage for protection. The brown crest and brown and black marked back of the male and the darker underparts allow them to blend in when they huddle down in tall grasses. They often go undetected until they burst straight up from the observer's feet. When the monsoon rains come to the mountains of the southwest, it is often easier to hear the males calling than it is to see one. Montezuma Quail have highly specialized long claws that are used for digging up bulbs and tubers.

IDENTIFICATION The adult male has a distinctive black-and-white facial pattern and a rounded brown crest on the back of the head. The upperparts are brown mottled with black, and the breast is dark chestnut. The sides and flanks are black and heavily spotted with white. Females are brown overall, with pinkish brown underparts. The upperparts are marked with black and tan streaks and spots. The females also have a rounded brown crest on the back of the head. In late summer, immature males can be seen with plumage that looks like a cross between male and female patterns. They develop the adult body plumage first but often have a pale gray face with just a hint of the coming pattern.

SIMILAR SPECIES The unique plumage pattern of the male Montezuma Quail is unlikely to be confused with any other quail. The Northern Bobwhite (*Colinus virginianus*) also has a patterned face, but its brown and chestnut coloration eliminates both sexes of that species.

HABITAT Open woodlands with abundant tall grasses. Also found in more open areas of tall grasses, with only scattered trees and shrubs. These birds are sensitive to changes in the quality of the grasslands and savannahs they inhabit. Research on the Edwards Plateau showed that when 40 to 50 percent of the tall grass cover is removed, the quail are extirpated.

STATUS AND DISTRIBUTION Uncommon and local resident in the Davis and Del Norte mountains of the Trans-Pecos. Elsewhere in the Trans-Pecos, they are rare to uncommon in the Chinati and Glass mountains and in the Sierra Vieja. Montezuma Quail were discovered in the Chisos Mountains in 2005, the first recorded there since reintroduction attempts in the 1970s. A remnant population remains on the southwestern Edwards Plateau, where the species is locally uncommon.

Montezuma Quail, male on left and female on right. Photo by Mark W. Lockwood.

COMMON LOON
Gavia immer

BACKGROUND The Common Loon is truly aquatic, spending most of its life in the water, coming onto land only to nest. Its legs are placed far back on its body to facilitate swimming, making the bird very awkward on land.

IDENTIFICATION This loon's nonbreeding plumage is gray overall. The upperparts are gray to gray-brown, with first-winter birds usually showing a more pronounced scalloped pattern. The underparts, including the throat, are white. The bird has a fairly prominent white collar and white crescents around the eye. The bill is silvery gray with a black upper edge. In late spring many individuals molt into breeding plumage just before leaving the state. These birds have a bold black-and-white plumage pattern. The head, neck, sides, and upperparts are black, and the back is heavily checkered with white. The chest is white, and an obvious white neck ring is marked with vertical black bars. The bill turns black as well.

SIMILAR SPECIES The Common Loon is the most likely species of loon to be encountered in Texas. The Red-throated Loon (*G. stellata*) and Pacific Loon (*G. pacifica*) are very rare winter visitors to the state and are both smaller than the Common. The Red-throated has a more slender bill that is usually held pointed slightly upward and is paler overall with a more rounded head. The Pacific Loon can be identified by an even division between gray and white down the side of the neck and the lack of a pale collar. The Yellow-billed Loon (*G. adamsii*) is accidental in the state; it is larger with a heavier pale bill, which is usually held pointed slightly upward. These birds also have a distinctive dark ear patch.

Common Loon, winter plumage. Photo by Mark W. Lockwood.

HABITAT In bays and estuaries as well as in the open Gulf close to shore. Also can be found on lakes and reservoirs that are deep enough to accommodate their feeding strategy of diving for fish.

STATUS AND DISTRIBUTION Uncommon to rare migrant throughout the state. Common winter resident in bays and estuaries along the coast, and uncommon to locally common on inland lakes and reservoirs. Less common and more local in the western half of the state, particularly on the High Plains and in the Trans-Pecos. On rare occasions, Common Loons will remain through the summer.

LEAST GREBE*
Tachybaptus dominicus

BACKGROUND   More
than 25 percent smaller
than a Pied-billed Grebe, the Least
Grebe is the smallest grebe in the United
States. The Least is more closely related to
the dabchicks of the Old World than any of
the New World species. Their small size and somewhat skulking behavior makes them easy to overlook. They
seem to be found most frequently on ponds with abundant vegetation both in the water and along the edges. They feed mostly
on aquatic insects, but they will also take very small fish. The
number of Least Grebes present at any particular location fluctuates greatly from year to year depending on rainfall. Research
has also shown that this species is sensitive to cold and tends to
decline temporarily following extended periods of unusually
cold weather.

IDENTIFICATION This grebe is very small, rather short-necked,
with bright golden yellow eyes. In the breeding season, they
have a blackish cap and throat contrasting somewhat with the
gray color of the face and neck. In the winter, they generally lose
the black color on the throat. The body is gray as well, noticeably darker on the upperparts. They have a white undertail that
can be very obvious on dry birds, giving them a fluffy look.
Actively feeding or skulking birds often look more streamlined,
and the undertail coverts are concealed. During the height of
breeding activity, the bill becomes almost black and is dark gray
through the remainder of the summer. For the rest of the year,

it is paler overall and can be almost pinkish on the lower mandible in some individuals.

SIMILAR SPECIES No other grebes combine a dark overall coloration with the bright yellow eye of the Least Grebe. The immature American Coot (*Fulica americana*) or Common Moorhen (*Gallinula chloropus*) may share a similar size and overall color, but they have the fluffy appearance of chicks and lack the brightly colored eyes.

HABITAT Most frequently found on small, shallow, secluded bodies of water protected by trees, brush, and other vegetation. Ponds with abundant emergent vegetation are thought to be the highest-quality habitat.

STATUS AND DISTRIBUTION Uncommon to locally common resident of the Lower Rio Grande Valley north along the Coastal Prairies to the central coast. Rare visitors at all seasons up the coast to the Louisiana border. Found inland with increasing regularity to Travis County. Most common on the lower coast and eastern Lower Rio Grande Valley. Some individuals retreat southward during the winter, particularly those from the northernmost portions of their range.

Least Grebe. Photo by Tim Cooper.

PIED-BILLED GREBE
Podilymbus podiceps

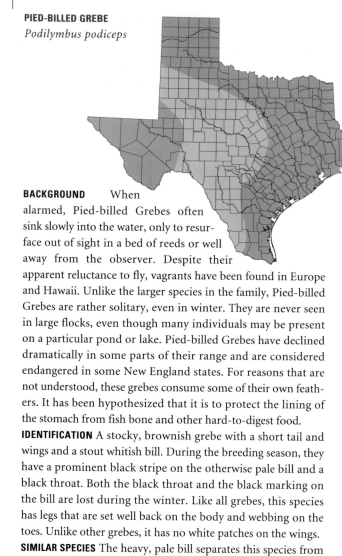

BACKGROUND   When alarmed, Pied-billed Grebes often sink slowly into the water, only to resurface out of sight in a bed of reeds or well away from the observer. Despite their apparent reluctance to fly, vagrants have been found in Europe and Hawaii. Unlike the larger species in the family, Pied-billed Grebes are rather solitary, even in winter. They are never seen in large flocks, even though many individuals may be present on a particular pond or lake. Pied-billed Grebes have declined dramatically in some parts of their range and are considered endangered in some New England states. For reasons that are not understood, these grebes consume some of their own feathers. It has been hypothesized that it is to protect the lining of the stomach from fish bone and other hard-to-digest food.

IDENTIFICATION A stocky, brownish grebe with a short tail and wings and a stout whitish bill. During the breeding season, they have a prominent black stripe on the otherwise pale bill and a black throat. Both the black throat and the black marking on the bill are lost during the winter. Like all grebes, this species has legs that are set well back on the body and webbing on the toes. Unlike other grebes, it has no white patches on the wings.

SIMILAR SPECIES The heavy, pale bill separates this species from other small grebes, which have thinner, black bills. Most of the other grebes that occur in Texas are more common in winter, and they exhibit gray (rather than brown) plumage.

HABITAT Found on almost any permanent body of water; less common on playas of the High Plains than on ponds elsewhere in the state. This species nests on ponds with abundant emergent vegetation. They do seem to tolerate slightly more open and less protected locations than do Least Grebes. Nonbreeding birds can also be found on salt water.

Pied-billed Grebe. Photo by Tim Cooper.

STATUS AND DISTRIBUTION Uncommon to common migrant and winter resident throughout the state. Rare to locally uncommon, but irregular, breeders in most areas of Texas. Along the Coastal Prairies and in south Texas, in particular, they can be locally common when high rainfall produces very favorable nesting conditions. Individuals found during the summer may not necessarily be nesting, and continued observations are required to confirm actual breeding.

AMERICAN WHITE PELICAN
Pelecanus erythrorhynchos

BACKGROUND
Unlike the Brown
Pelican (*P. occiden-
talis*), the American
White Pelican does not dive
for its food. Instead, it dips its head
underwater to scoop up fish. It is not
uncommon to see several individuals fishing
cooperatively. They move together, either in a
line or in a circle, to concentrate the fish, and then dip their
heads simultaneously to make the catch. With the exception of
a small population on the Texas coast, this species breeds
entirely on lakes on the Great Plains and intermountain West.

IDENTIFICATION The American White Pelican is large and mostly
white. The primaries and outer secondaries are black, contrasting strongly with the remainder of the wing. The bill is bright
orange and develops a fibrous plate on the upper mandible during the breeding season. During the nonbreeding season, the
bill normally fades to a yellowish orange. The feet and legs are
also orange. Immature birds often have some brown mottling,
particularly to the wings and back.

SIMILAR SPECIES Several species have the same basic plumage
pattern of the American White Pelican; none, however, shares
the unique bill of a pelican. The Snow Goose (*Chen
caerulescens*), Whooping Crane (*Grus americana*), and Wood
Stork (*Mycteria americana*) all have white body plumage with
some combination of black in the flight feathers. For the pelican, most of the flight feathers are black, but the innermost secondaries are actually white. Both the Snow Goose and Whooping Crane have only black primaries. The Wood Stork is the

American White Pelican. Photo by Mark W. Lockwood.

most similar to the pelican, but all of the flight feathers of the stork are black, and the stork's head is black.

HABITAT Shallow coastal bays, inlets, and estuaries that have exposed shoal and other loafing sites. These pelicans also use inland lakes and reservoirs in areas where the surface of the water does not freeze.

STATUS AND DISTRIBUTION Uncommon to common migrant over the eastern half of the state, becoming less common farther west. Common winter resident in the southern half of the state, particularly along the coast. There are only two nesting colonies in Texas, both along the central coast. Nonbreeding birds are frequently encountered around the state during the summer.

BROWN PELICAN
Pelecanus occidentalis

BACKGROUND
When feeding, Brown Pelicans dive into the water often from heights of up to 60 feet. The impact with the water is cushioned by small air sacs just beneath the skin. Devastated by the use of pesticides, the total number of Brown Pelicans in Texas in the early 1970s may have been as low as 12 to 15 individuals. Today the recovery of this species is one of the great success stories for endangered species. Through the reintroduction of additional birds, aggressive conservation efforts, and tighter controls on pesticide use, this species has begun to flourish, and there are now thousands of these birds along the coast. The biggest problem for the Brown Pelican was the use of DDT, which thinned the shells of its eggs. When the adult would start to brood the new eggs, they would break under the weight of the adult bird.

IDENTIFICATION This is a large bird, with a seven-foot wingspan. The body plumage is largely gray and brown. Adults in breeding plumage have a red-brown neck with a white forehead, crown, and throat. These areas are often tinged with yellow at the height of breeding condition, fading to white by the time the eggs hatch. In winter the entire head and neck become white with a yellow wash to the forehead and crown.

SIMILAR SPECIES There is nothing in Texas that can be mistaken for a Brown Pelican; however, another species of pelican is found in Texas, the American White Pelican (*P. erythrorhynchos*). As the name implies, it is white, with black wing tips and a yellow bill and pouch. American White Pelicans breed on the Great Plains and winter along the coast and on lakes throughout the interior of the state. Migrants can be seen almost anywhere in the state, often in large flocks.

HABITAT Found primarily on salt water, they use spoil and other islands in the bays for loafing and nesting. They feed in these bays as well as on the open Gulf.

STATUS AND DISTRIBUTION Common to uncommon resident along the coast. They routinely find their way inland along the Coastal Prairies, primarily in the late summer and fall. Casual to accidental farther inland, with records from all areas of the state. Most of the birds found far inland are immature or hatch-year individuals. Large nesting colonies are present on the upper and central coasts, and although none are known to breed along the lower coast, it seems only a matter of time before colonies become established there as well.

Brown Pelican, breeding plumage. Photo by Mark W. Lockwood.

DOUBLE-CRESTED CORMORANT
Phalacrocorax auritus

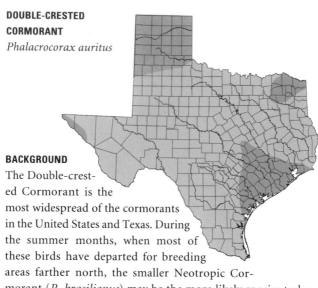

BACKGROUND

The Double-crested Cormorant is the most widespread of the cormorants in the United States and Texas. During the summer months, when most of these birds have departed for breeding areas farther north, the smaller Neotropic Cormorant (*P. brasilianus*) may be the more likely species to be seen. During the winter, flocks of cormorants can be seen throughout most of the state. These groups often fly in a V-formation and can be mistaken for geese. These birds seem to have a preference for perching on dead snags over water, and they are commonly seen sitting with their wings spread to dry. Cormorants feed largely on fish and are frequently wrongly blamed for low numbers of fish in reservoirs.

IDENTIFICATION

This large, somewhat gangly-looking cormorant has a large head and a long tail. Adults are black overall, with some iridescence in the plumage visible under certain conditions. They also have a distinct orange patch of bare skin on the throat. Immature birds are brown above with a whitish throat, foreneck, and breast, giving them a distinctly paler appearance. The white on the underparts of immature birds varies considerably and may include most of the underparts on some individuals. The unfeathered throat pouch is generally yellow to orangish yellow. In flight, Double-crested Cormorants have a distinctive crook in the neck, with the head up, just above the center line of the body.

Double-crested Cormorant. Photo by Tim Cooper

SIMILAR SPECIES The Neotropic Cormorant is similar in overall coloration, but it is smaller, with a different pattern on the head. Where the Double-crested has a large patch of orange skin on the throat, readily visible year-round, the Neotropic Cormorant has a much-reduced area that is duller in color. During the breeding season this smaller throat patch is edged in white in the Neotropic. In flight, the smaller size and smaller, less bulbous head are good field marks for distinguishing Neotropic Cormorants.

HABITAT Found primarily on large bodies of water where fish are abundant. Less frequently seen on large rivers and ponds. Also common along the coast in marine environments.

STATUS AND DISTRIBUTION Uncommon to abundant migrant and winter resident throughout much of the state. In the Panhandle and northern Rolling Plains, rare during the winter. In recent years, Double-crested Cormorants have become common in a few localities during summer in the Panhandle and the western Trans-Pecos. Also rare to uncommon in summer along the upper and central coast.

ANHINGA
Anhinga anhinga

BACKGROUND A common colloquial name for Anhinga is "snake bird," referring to its long neck and small head. It often swims with the body totally submerged, so that only the head and neck are above the surface of the water. Anhingas are well adapted to an aquatic life, with dense bones and feathers that become fully saturated with water. However, this requires that they seek out exposed perches where they can spread their wings and tail to allow them to dry and to soak up heat from the sun. They were also formerly known as Water Turkey, because their long, fan-shaped tail is somewhat reminiscent of the tail of a Wild Turkey. Anhingas are social and nest with other colonial waterbirds, such as herons, spoonbills, and ibises. They generally build their nests on branches that overhang the water so that the young birds can escape potential predators by jumping into the water.

IDENTIFICATION This slender-bodied waterbird has a small head on a long neck that is often held in a curved posture. The tail is long and fan-shaped, with a thin terminal band (white in males, tan in females). Males are black with silver and white markings on the scapulars and shoulders. The female's plumage is similar but duller, with a buffy head, neck, and breast. The bill is long and daggerlike.

SIMILAR SPECIES The two species most likely to be confused with an Anhinga are the Double-crested Cormorant (*Phalacrocorax auritus*) and the Neotropic Cormorant (*P. brasilianus*). In general, cormorants have a shorter tail and lack the large silvery wing patches, and their head is much larger and more bulbous. In addition, cormorants have a short, thick bill in comparison to the Anhinga's spearlike bill.

HABITAT Found most often in wooded swamps and other protected wetlands. They use areas with slow-moving or standing water and abundant perches available for drying and sunning.

STATUS AND DISTRIBUTION Uncommon summer resident along the Coastal Prairies and northward through the eastern half of the state. Rare to locally uncommon winter resident throughout the South Texas Brush Country and along the Coastal Prairies, becoming generally rare and local inland through the eastern third of the state.

Anhinga, female. Photo by Tim Cooper.

AMERICAN BITTERN
Botaurus lentiginosus

BACKGROUND

The American Bittern is a stocky and well-camouflaged heron that prefers to stay hidden in dense reed beds. A common behavior is to point its bill skyward so that the heavy streaking of the underparts blends in with the surrounding reeds. These birds (and many other herons) rely on stealth more than quickness to capture prey. They will often wait motionless for long periods to capture unsuspecting prey. They feed on a wide variety of organisms, including insects, amphibians, crayfish, small fish, and small mammals. Not surprisingly, they are much more active at dusk and dawn.

IDENTIFICATION This medium-sized heron is heavily streaked with brown below. The throat is white bordered with thick black malar stripes. In flight, the outer half of the wing is black, contrasting sharply with the brown inner half. The bill is greenish yellow with a blackish culmen. The legs are also greenish yellow.

SIMILAR SPECIES The Least Bittern (*Ixobrychus exilis*) is much smaller and very unlikely to be confused with an American Bittern. In addition, Least Bitterns have a dark green crown and back and prominent buffy wing coverts. Immature night-herons are more likely to cause an identification challenge. They have white spotting or streaking on the upperparts and lack the prominent black malar streaks of the American Bittern. The immature Yellow-crowned Night-Heron (*Nyctanassa violacea*) has a thicker bill that is black; the Black-crowned Night-Heron

(*Nycticorax nycticorax*) also has a thicker bill and a dark upper mandible. Both species lack the black primaries and outer secondaries of the American Bittern.

HABITAT Found primarily in freshwater marshes with tall, emergent vegetation. Impoundments where cattails are abundant are primary habitats, such as those at Brazos Bend State Park and Anahuac National Wildlife Refuge. More sparsely vegetated wetlands are also occasionally used, as are brackish and tidal marshes.

American Bittern. Photo by Tim Cooper.

STATUS AND DISTRIBUTION Rare to locally uncommon migrant in the eastern third of the state. Generally rare migrant in the western two-thirds of the state, becoming very rare to casual in the Trans-Pecos. Rare to uncommon winter resident on the Coastal Prairies and found at scattered localities farther inland as far as the Panhandle. There are summer records from almost all areas of the state and even a few nesting records.

LEAST BITTERN
Ixobrychus exilis

BACKGROUND Least Bitterns can be fairly common in areas of suitable habitat, but their small size and secretive habits can make them difficult to observe. They are very agile and are able to walk through dense reed beds, hunting insects and small aquatic organisms in areas of open water. They also prey on frogs and crayfish. Because they are able to straddle between reeds and move so freely, they can exploit hunting areas where the water is too deep for other species of birds that occur in these same reed beds, such as rails or other herons.

IDENTIFICATION The Least Bittern is the smallest heron found in Texas. These tiny herons are buffy in overall coloration, with a dark greenish black crown and back. The outer half of the wings is also blackish, contrasting strongly with the bright buff inner half of the wing. The face and sides of the neck down through the flanks are bright buff in color as well. The throat and belly are white and streaked with buff. The female is duller than the male in overall plumage and generally buffier overall.

SIMILAR SPECIES The diminutive size of the Least Bittern makes it very unlikely to be confused with most other herons that occur in North America. The species most likely to cause confusion is the Green Heron (*Butorides virescens*), which is fairly small but actually much larger than a Least Bittern. Green Herons lack the bright buff patches on the wings; in fact, their upperparts are entirely dark. Their underparts are also chestnut

Least Bittern. Photo by Mark W. Lockwood.

(in adults) or reddish brown (in immature birds), rather the distinctive buffy coloration of the Least Bittern.

HABITAT Found in both freshwater and brackish marshes where dense reeds and other emergent vegetation are present; most often in marshes where clumps of woody vegetation as well as open water are interspersed within the reed beds. Conservation lands such as Brazos Bend State Park and Anahuac National Wildlife Refuge offer excellent habitat.

STATUS AND DISTRIBUTION Rare to locally common summer resident throughout much of the eastern half of the state, becoming very rare and local farther west. Rare to uncommon migrant throughout the state, but difficult to detect, making the actual status difficult to determine. Also very rare winter resident along the Coastal Prairies.

GREAT BLUE HERON
Ardea herodias

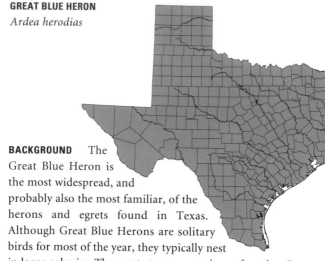

BACKGROUND The Great Blue Heron is the most widespread, and probably also the most familiar, of the herons and egrets found in Texas. Although Great Blue Herons are solitary birds for most of the year, they typically nest in loose colonies. The greatest concentrations of nesting Great Blues are on spoil and other islands on the central coast. In flight, Great Blues and other large herons fold their neck into an S-curve, bringing the head back to near the shoulders. Flying herons can be easily distinguished from cranes, which do not fold the neck at all in flight. A white subspecies, *A. h. occidentalis,* found primarily in southern Florida and the northern Caribbean, has strayed to Texas a few times. This subspecies was formerly known as the Great White Heron and was once considered a separate species.

IDENTIFICATION The largest heron found in the United States, the Great Blue Heron has a slaty blue-gray body plumage made up of long plumelike feathers. The head is white with a prominent black stripe starting behind the eye and ending in a thin black crest. The neck is long and gray with a black stripe, bordered in white, down the front. The thighs are rufous, and the long legs are dark.

SIMILAR SPECIES Sometimes confused with the Sandhill Crane (*Grus canadensis*) because they are both basically gray in color and are similar in size. Closer examination, however, reveals that the two species are not very similar in plumage. The Sandhill Crane is a uniform gray with a red cap of bare skin, and the Great Blue Heron actually has a much more ornate plumage.

HABITAT Almost all wetland habitats found in Texas. They can be found along the shores of large reservoirs or small ponds. They are also common in brackish and saltwater habitats as well.

STATUS AND DISTRIBUTION Uncommon to common summer resident throughout much of the state. Particularly common along the Coastal Prairies. During the fall and early winter, most birds move south out of the interior of the state to the Coastal Prairies. Large rookeries, or nesting colonies, are found at scattered locations across the state. They are especially common on coastal islands, where rookeries can contain many hundreds of nests. The white subspecies has been found on very rare occasions along the upper and central coasts.

Great Blue Heron. Photo by Tim Cooper.

GREAT EGRET
Ardea alba

BACKGROUND The Great Egret's distribution is almost worldwide; the species is found on all continents except Antarctica. The bird is also the symbol of the National Audubon Society, which was originally founded to help protect birds from being killed for their feathers.

IDENTIFICATION A large, all-white heron, this bird has long, all-black legs and feet, with a heavy, yellow bill. During the breeding season, the Great Egret develops a long plume on the back that extends beyond the tail. For a brief period at the height of breeding, the bill turns orange-yellow and the lores become lime-green.

SIMILAR SPECIES The Great Egret is one of several herons with primarily white plumage. The white-morph Reddish Egret (*Egretta rufescens*) is the most common of these in the same size range; it can be distinguished by its strongly bicolored bill with a pink base and black tip. The white-morph of the Great Blue Heron (*Ardea herodias*) is extremely rare in Texas; it has a

heavier bill, and the legs are yellowish green rather than black. There are also three small white egrets. The Snowy Egret (*E. thula*) has a black bill with yellow lores and yellow feet; in

Great Egret. Photo by Tim Cooper.

Great Egret, displaying. Photo by Mark W. Lockwood.

immature birds, the back of the legs is also greenish yellow. Immature Little Blue Herons (*E. caerulea*) have greenish legs and a bicolored bill that is primarily bluish gray in color. The breeding plumage of the Cattle Egret (*Bubulcus ibis*) has a golden wash over the head, back, and chest, but this stocky heron is all white during the remainder of the year, with a yellow bill and legs.

HABITAT Both freshwater and saltwater habitats. Can be found nesting with other colonial waterbirds on lakes, marshes, and estuaries. These birds will use almost any wetland habitat with the appropriate water depth when feeding, such as marshes, the edges of watercourses, ponds, lakes, tidal flats, and estuaries. They also use flooded agricultural areas, such as rice fields.

STATUS AND DISTRIBUTION Common resident along the Coastal Prairies. During the summer, locally common in the eastern and central portions of the state. Uncommon year-round visitor in the Trans-Pecos; has nested in a few locations. Rare to common postbreeding visitor to most of the state and can often be found in very large flocks, particularly along the coast, in late summer and early fall. Farther inland, uncommon to rare and irregular winter visitor to all areas of the state except the Panhandle.

SNOWY EGRET
Egretta thula

BACKGROUND

Snowy Egrets are a fairly common sight across Texas, but that was not always the case. Populations of this and many other egrets and herons were devastated in the nineteenth and early twentieth centuries, when plumes were greatly valued for adorning hats. Fortunately, through aggressive conservation actions, populations of Snowy Egret have flourished. They are fairly active when feeding and apparently use their brightly colored feet to attract prey items.

IDENTIFICATION This small white heron has a slender black bill contrasting sharply with yellow lores. The head and neck appear shaggy, as the feathers are long plumes. In adult plumage, the legs are entirely black and the feet are a bright golden yellow. In immature birds, the legs are mostly greenish yellow with varying amounts of black down the front of the leg. At the height of courtship activity, Snowy Egrets have long graceful plumes that curve upward on the back. During this time the facial skin and feet turn from yellow to orange.

SIMILAR SPECIES There are four white egrets that occur in the same habitats as the Snowy Egret. Two are easily distinguished by their much larger size: the Great Egret (*Ardea alba*) and the white morph of the Reddish Egret (*E. rufescens*). The Cattle Egret (*Bubulcus ibis*) is slightly smaller, but chunkier than a Snowy. The bill and legs of Cattle Egrets are yellow, and in breeding condition they have patches of golden yellow plumes. Immature Cattle Egrets have black bills and legs for a very short

Snowy Egret. Photo by Mark W. Lockwood.

period after they leave the nest, but these individuals lack the plumes of a Snowy Egret. The final similar species is the immature Little Blue Heron (*E. caerulea*). These birds normally have blue-gray bills and facial skin and greenish legs. They also have dusky tips to their flight feathers, but that is often easily overlooked.

HABITAT Found in almost all wetland habitats, including both freshwater and marine environs.

STATUS AND DISTRIBUTION Uncommon to common summer resident throughout much of the state west to the Rolling Plains and south along the Coastal Prairies to the Lower Rio Grande Valley. Rare to locally common summer resident in the Trans-Pecos; appears to be increasing as a summer visitor on the High Plains. During the winter, uncommon resident along the Coastal Prairies and rare to locally uncommon inland. Rare to uncommon migrant throughout the state.

LITTLE BLUE HERON
Egretta caerulea

BACKGROUND
Little Blue Herons are unique among Texas herons in that the adults and immature birds are dramatically different in coloration. Immature birds are white, like many other egrets, but the adults are slaty blue-gray. There are a number of hypotheses as to the advantages of this plumage change; perhaps the best is that immature birds can more easily integrate into flocks of other white egrets and thus gain a greater measure of protection from predators.

IDENTIFICATION The adult plumage of this medium-sized heron is slate-blue overall. In high breeding plumage, the head and neck become reddish purple. The bill is bicolored with a bluish gray base and a black tip. Immature birds are mostly white, with a bicolored bill similar to that of an adult. These birds also have gray tips to the outer primaries, but the characteristic is often difficult to observe in the field. They have dull greenish legs and feet. During the transitional period between immature and adult plumage, Little Blue Herons become mottled with patches of slate-blue.

SIMILAR SPECIES The species most similar to the Little Blue Heron is the Tricolored Heron (*E. tricolor*), which is slightly larger and has a white belly. It also has a distinctive white line down the throat and white head plumes. The dark-morph Reddish Egret (*E. rufescens*) is much larger and has gray and rufous plumage. Both color morphs of the Reddish Egret have a bicolored bill with a pink base and black tip. The immature Little

Blue Heron is similar to several small white egrets. The adult Snowy Egret (*E. thula*) has a uniform black bill with yellow lores and black legs. The breeding plumage of the Cattle Egret (*Bubulcus ibis*) has a golden wash over the head, back, and chest; this stocky heron is all white during the remainder of the year, with a yellow bill and legs.

HABITAT Freshwater swamps, ponds, and lakes as well as shallow bays and estuaries. These birds will use a variety of wetland habitats when feeding, including freshwater marshes, ponds, lakes, tidal flats, and estuaries.

STATUS AND DISTRIBUTION Common summer resident in the eastern third of the state and abundant along the Coastal Prairies. Rare to locally uncommon as postbreeding wanderers to the western two-thirds of the state. In winter, found primarily in the southern half of the state, but uncommon along the Coastal Prairies and rare inland in the eastern third of the state.

Little Blue Heron, adult. Photo by Tim Cooper.

REDDISH EGRET
Egretta rufescens

BACKGROUND Perhaps the most fascinating aspect of the behavior of the Reddish Egret is its feeding antics. The bird is an active feeder in shallow water, often running from one place to another capturing small fish and other aquatic organisms. It also engages in what is known as canopy feeding, foraging with its wings extended over the water. This produces areas of shadow where the bird can more easily spot prey items. No other species of heron found in North America uses this feeding technique. There are two color morphs of Reddish Egret; the dark morph makes up nearly 90 percent of the overall population. The reason for this polymorphism is poorly understood, and the

Reddish Egret, dark morph. Photo by Mark W. Lockwood.

advantages and disadvantages of the white morph have long been debated. A very small percentage of the population is calico, primarily dark-morph birds with scattered patches of white in the wings.

IDENTIFICATION Both color morphs have a shaggy look to the head and neck, black legs, and a pink bill with a black outer third. The dark morph, for which the species was named, has a rusty brown head and neck con-

Reddish Egret, white morph. Photo by Mark W. Lockwood.

trasting slightly with the slaty gray body plumage. The white morph has entirely white plumage.

SIMILAR SPECIES The dark morph is unlike any other species of heron, with its shaggy rufous head and neck. The Little Blue Heron (*E. caerulea*) and Tricolored Heron (*E. tricolor*) are much smaller and have blue-gray plumage. In both morphs, the Reddish Egret's strongly bicolored bill with a pink base separates this species from all other herons in Texas. Great, Cattle, and Snowy Egrets all have some passing resemblance to the white morph. The Great, however, is larger with a yellow bill, and the Snowy and Cattle Egrets are significantly smaller.

HABITAT Found primarily in shallow saltwater habitats, but occasionally in brackish wetlands as well. Postbreeding wanderers will use inland freshwater habitats; at other times of the year they are found infrequently in freshwater wetlands close to the immediate coast.

STATUS AND DISTRIBUTION Uncommon to locally common resident along the coast. More common on the central and lower coasts, with large numbers present in Matagorda Bay, Matagorda County, and the lower Laguna Madre. Very rare postbreeding visitor inland through the eastern third of the state. For reasons that are not readily apparent, the Reddish Egret is an almost annual visitor during all seasons to reservoirs in the Trans-Pecos, particularly Balmorhea Lake in Reeves County.

CATTLE EGRET
Bubulcus ibis

BACKGROUND

The origin of Cattle Egrets in the New World has been much debated. Some contend that they were introduced into Brazil; others believe they arrived on their own power. The species was unknown in Texas until late November 1955, when the first one was found on the central coast. The first nesting record was obtained a short three and one half years later. Now this species forms large rookeries across many areas of the state and has become a pest in some areas. Unlike many other herons, Cattle Egrets forage extensively in upland habitats.

IDENTIFICATION This medium-sized white heron looks somewhat chunkier than the other white egrets. Its posture is also more hunched, giving it a less graceful look. In breeding plumage, adults develop orange-buff patches on the crown, breast, and back. The bill and legs are yellow, although they become reddish in high breeding condition. Immature birds are white with a yellow bill and black legs. Nestlings have a black bill, which occasionally persists through the first summer and may cause some confusion with the Snowy Egret (*Egretta thula*). The Cattle Egrets, however, lack yellow lores.

SIMILAR SPECIES The Cattle Egret can be confused with other small, primarily white egrets found in Texas. The Snowy Egret has a uniformly black bill with yellow lores; its legs are either entirely black (in adults) or black in front and greenish yellow in back (in immature birds). Immature Little Blue Herons (*E.*

caerulea) have greenish legs and a bicolored bill, primarily bluish gray at the base with a black tip. These birds also have gray tips to the outer primaries, but the characteristic is often difficult to observe in the field. The Great Egret (*Ardea alba*) is much larger, with a long, slender neck. The white-morph Reddish Egret (*E. rufescens*) is also much larger; its distinctive bicolored bill has a pink base and black tip.

HABITAT A variety of wetland habitats including freshwater swamps, ponds, and lakes as well as shallow bays and estuaries. They also forage extensively in upland habitats, including pastures and fields.

STATUS AND DISTRIBUTION Common to abundant summer resident throughout most of the eastern half of the state, becoming more local in the west. Uncommon to rare winter resident along the Coastal Prairies and generally rare inland. Not present on the High Plains and northern Rolling Plains in winter.

Cattle Egret, breeding plumage. Photo by Mark W. Lockwood.

GREEN HERON
Butorides virescens

BACKGROUND
Green Herons are often overlooked because of their some-what cryptic habits. They prefer to forage in areas with more cover than many other herons in Texas, particularly along slow-moving creeks that have a well-developed riparian corridor. They generally choose these areas for nesting sites as well. The Green Heron belongs to a group of closely related birds that are sometimes considered one species. The larger species is called Green-backed Heron, and many North American field guides published in the 1980s have the Green Heron listed under this name. The relationship between the Green Heron and the widespread Striated Heron (*B. striatus*) is still not well understood; they could be considered one species again in the future.

IDENTIFICATION The Green Heron is rather small and compact. In adults, the head and underparts are deep chestnut with a glossy dark green cap. The upperparts are greenish black, including the wings. The bill has a dark upper mandible and yellow-green lower mandible. Leg color varies from orange to dull greenish yellow, depending on the time of year and breeding condition. Immature birds are heavily striped below with brownish red. The upperparts are brownish with buff spots, particularly on the wing coverts.

SIMILAR SPECIES The diminutive Least Bittern (*Ixobrychus exilis*) is much smaller and seems unlikely to be confused with a Green Heron. Least Bitterns have prominent buffy wing coverts that can be easily seen on both perched and flying birds. The American Bittern (*Botaurus lentiginosus*) is significantly larger and heavily streaked below, as is the immature Green Heron. The brown plumage, both above and below, also helps distinguish the American Bittern. Immature night-herons are larger and heavier bodied. They are also much browner in overall plumage, with white spotting or streaking on the upperparts.

HABITAT A wide variety of wetland habitats. Frequently seen in swamps, along wooded watercourses, ponds, and salt marshes. They tend to prefer areas with thick vegetation but will feed in open areas as well.

STATUS AND DISTRIBUTION Common summer resident throughout the eastern two-thirds of the state, becoming uncommon and more local west through the remainder of the state. Uncommon to common migrant statewide. During the winter, generally rare in the southern half of the state, but most common along the coast and in the Lower Rio Grande Valley, where they are locally uncommon.

Green Heron, adult. Photo by Tim Cooper.

BLACK-CROWNED NIGHT-HERON
Nycticorax nycticorax

BACKGROUND
Another wide-ranging species, this bird occurs on every continent except Australia and Antarctica. Although it is widespread in Texas, its nocturnal and crepuscular habits make it much less obvious than most of the other herons found in the state. These birds nest with other colonial waterbirds in large rookeries and even use the same feeding areas as other heron species, but they reduce the competition by feeding at night.

IDENTIFICATION This stocky, medium-sized heron has a short neck and legs. Adults have a distinctive black cap and back. The back contrasts strongly with the gray neck, wings, and rump. The underparts are white to pale gray. The bill is fairly heavy and black. The legs are yellow-green for most of the year. Immature birds are brown above with large pale spots on the back and wings. The underparts are paler and heavily striped with brown. This plumage gradually becomes more like the adult's, and older juveniles may appear to have adult plumage washed with brown.

SIMILAR SPECIES The adult Black-crowned Night-Heron is distinctive and unlikely to be confused with any other species. Immature birds, however, can be readily confused with immature Yellow-crowned Night-Herons (*Nyctanassa violacea*). The immature Black-crowned is browner than the immature Yellow-crowned, with bolder white spotting on the upperparts. Its bill is also longer and thinner, with a greenish yellow lower

Black-crowned Night-Heron, adult. Photo by Tim Cooper.

mandible. The entire bill is generally black in the Yellow-crowned. Finally, the legs are shorter, barely extending beyond the tail in flight. The American Bittern (*Botaurus lentiginosus*) is slightly larger and lacks the white spotting on the upperparts. Bitterns can also be distinguished by their prominent black malar stripes.

HABITAT A wide variety of wetland habitats, in both saltwater and freshwater environments. Due to their nocturnal habits, night-herons tend to be found in areas where roosting sites are close by, such as marshes, swamps, slow-moving watercourses with some riparian habitat, lakes, and even agricultural areas.

STATUS AND DISTRIBUTION Common resident along the Coastal Prairies. Farther inland, uncommon to rare summer resident in all areas of the state except the Pineywoods. From the South Plains north through the Panhandle, fairly common and can be a locally abundant summer resident. Rare to locally uncommon winter resident throughout the state, except in the Panhandle and Pineywoods, where it is only a casual visitor.

WHITE-FACED IBIS
Plegadis chihi

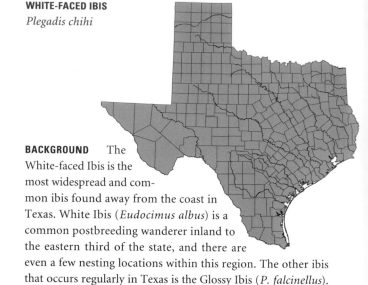

BACKGROUND The White-faced Ibis is the most widespread and common ibis found away from the coast in Texas. White Ibis (*Eudocimus albus*) is a common postbreeding wanderer inland to the eastern third of the state, and there are even a few nesting locations within this region. The other ibis that occurs regularly in Texas is the Glossy Ibis (*P. falcinellus*). A rare to locally uncommon resident on the upper and central coasts, the Glossy Ibis is difficult to distinguish from the White-faced except at close range.

IDENTIFICATION Adults in the spring and summer have a rich chestnut plumage with iridescent green and bronze in the wings and tail. The bright pink facial skin is ringed by white feathers. The bill and legs are gray, and the eyes are red. In the fall and winter, the facial skin often fades to gray, and most of the chestnut color on the body is lost. The body plumage becomes a dark greenish brown and the head and neck are finely streaked with white. Immature birds resemble winter adults but have brown eyes.

SIMILAR SPECIES The Glossy Ibis is very similar to the White-faced. Adults in breeding plumage can be fairly easily separated, but winter adults and immature birds are very difficult (often impossible) to identify with certainty. The adult White-faced Ibis in breeding plumage can be distinguished by the ring of white feathers around the face, pink facial skin, and red eyes. The breeding plumage of the adult Glossy Ibis features gray facial skin and a thin blue or white line bordering the feathers on the face. This line does not extend behind the eye. In winter the adult White-faced Ibis can be reliably identified only by eye color. The color and pattern of the facial skin can sometimes be used to identify first-winter birds. The dark body plumage of *Plegadis* ibises will separate them from other birds with long curved bills, such as curlews.

HABITAT The White-faced Ibis uses shallow freshwater habitats but will use brackish marshes as well. They are typically seen along the edges of ponds or lakes or in flooded fields. They nest on spoil and other coastal islands in bays but fly inland to feeding areas.

White-faced Ibis. Photo by Greg W. Lasley.

STATUS AND DISTRIBUTION Common to uncommon resident along the coast. As migrants from the Great Plains arrive in the fall, the number of birds present along the Coastal Prairies swells. Rare and localized breeder away from the coast as far north as the Panhandle. In most areas of the state, uncommon to common migrant. A few individuals will linger through the winter at inland locations, although this species is not expected in the Panhandle and South Plains at this season.

ROSEATE SPOONBILL
Platalea ajaja

BACKGROUND The Roseate Spoonbill is very distinctive, with its large spatulate bill and pink plumage. The bird uses the sensitive bill to capture tiny aquatic organisms, which are the spoonbill's primary food. It opens the bill and swings its head from side to side, grabbing prey items in shallow water. It flies with slow wing beats, often interspersed with glides. Spoonbills nest in colonies on coastal islands where trees and shrubs are established. They are often found in mixed rookeries with various species of herons and ibis.

IDENTIFICATION Adults are unmistakable with their bright pink plumage and large gray spoon-shaped bill. Adults have a naked head that is greenish gray. The plumage of the neck and upper back is white. The wings, lower back, and underparts are bright pink. The upper wing coverts are a vivid reddish pink, and the tail is bright orange. The head of immature birds is feathered and white. The neck and back are also white, and the remainder of the body is pale pink. The plumage color brightens gradually to the adult color during the first year after hatching.

SIMILAR SPECIES No other bright pink wading birds occur regularly in Texas. The large spatulate bill also readily identifies these birds. The Greater Flamingo (*Phoenicopterus ruber*) is a casual visitor along the Texas coast, but it has a very long neck and a short hooked bill with a black tip. Other species of flamingos have escaped captivity and have been seen on the Texas coast, including the Old World subspecies of Greater Flamingo.

Roseate Spoonbill. Photo by Tim Cooper.

HABITAT Found in tidal flats, shallow marshes, and swales in both freshwater and saltwater habitats. Birds that wander inland also use flooded fields and ponds.

STATUS AND DISTRIBUTION Locally common summer resident along the coast, becoming uncommon in the winter. Wanders inland annually after the breeding season and can become common in wetlands on the Coastal Prairies and as far inland as Travis County. Farther inland in the eastern third of the state, rare to very rare visitor during the summer and fall. Farther west, Roseate Spoonbills are accidental, with records west to the Trans-Pecos and north to the Panhandle.

BLACK VULTURE
Coragyps atratus

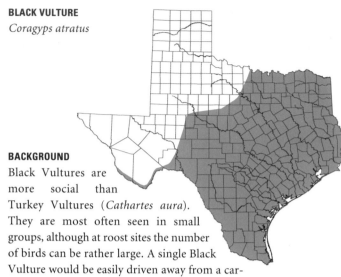

BACKGROUND

Black Vultures are more social than Turkey Vultures (*Cathartes aura*). They are most often seen in small groups, although at roost sites the number of birds can be rather large. A single Black Vulture would be easily driven away from a carcass by the larger Turkey Vulture, but when the Black Vultures arrive as a group, they can drive off a lone Turkey Vulture. Studies have shown that the Black Vulture lacks a highly developed sense of smell and has learned to follow Turkey Vultures to carcasses. Perhaps not surprising at all were the results of a study conducted in Pennsylvania and Maryland that radio-tagged a number of Black Vultures; the birds used primarily open habitats for foraging and particularly trolled along roads.

IDENTIFICATION Black Vultures are large soaring birds with blackish plumage. Adults have a small, naked, black or dark gray head. The wings are similar in color to the body plumage, with white linings to the outer primaries. Immature birds are similar to adults.

SIMILAR SPECIES The Turkey Vulture, the other vulture species found in Texas, has a quite different shape. Its wings are longer and narrower and lack the white patch on the outer primaries. The tail is longer and more rectangular, which gives the Turkey Vulture a very different shape in flight. The skin on the head of the immature Turkey Vulture is gray, but the plumage is much browner. The profile of the Common Black-Hawk (*Buteogallus* *anthracinus*) in flight is similar to a Black Vulture, but the hawk has a feathered head and a prominent white band on the tail.

HABITAT Generally in areas with lots of open space, but suitable roosting sites must be available in the general area. Roosting sites are most often undisturbed stands of large trees, but they will also use telephone poles and other man-made structures. Nesting sites such as abandoned buildings, rock outcrops, and hollow or fallen trees are also an important component.

STATUS AND DISTRIBUTION Common to locally abundant resident in the eastern two-thirds of the state. Locally uncommon resident along the Rio Grande from eastern Val Verde County to northern Presidio County in the Trans-Pecos. Some migrate out of Texas to spend the winter in more tropical areas, but the remaining birds are supplemented by migrants from more northern populations in the United States.

Black Vulture. Photo by Greg W. Lasley.

TURKEY VULTURE
Cathartes aura

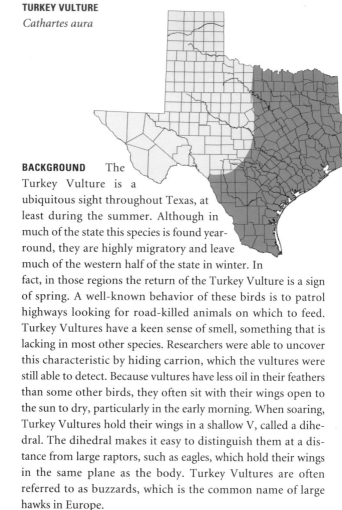

BACKGROUND The Turkey Vulture is a ubiquitous sight throughout Texas, at least during the summer. Although in much of the state this species is found year-round, they are highly migratory and leave much of the western half of the state in winter. In fact, in those regions the return of the Turkey Vulture is a sign of spring. A well-known behavior of these birds is to patrol highways looking for road-killed animals on which to feed. Turkey Vultures have a keen sense of smell, something that is lacking in most other species. Researchers were able to uncover this characteristic by hiding carrion, which the vultures were still able to detect. Because vultures have less oil in their feathers than some other birds, they often sit with their wings open to the sun to dry, particularly in the early morning. When soaring, Turkey Vultures hold their wings in a shallow V, called a dihedral. The dihedral makes it easy to distinguish them at a distance from large raptors, such as eagles, which hold their wings in the same plane as the body. Turkey Vultures are often referred to as buzzards, which is the common name of large hawks in Europe.

IDENTIFICATION Large soaring birds with a six-foot wingspan, adults have a small, naked, red head, white bill, and a blackish brown body, wings, and tail. Immature birds have a gray head and bill. In flight, the red head of the adult is often not readily visible. The flight feathers of these birds are gray, contrasting sharply with the dark coloration of the body. These feathers can appear almost white in certain lighting conditions.

SIMILAR SPECIES There is one other species of vulture found in Texas, the Black Vulture (*Coragyps atratus*). Black Vultures have a white patch in the outer primaries and have much shorter, broader wings. In addition, they have a short, square tail, the combination of which gives them a very different shape in flight. Black Vultures also have a naked head, but the skin is dark gray to black. The profile in flight of the Zone-tailed Hawk (*Buteo albonotatus*) is similar to a Turkey Vulture's, but the hawk has a feathered head and white bands in its tail.

Turkey Vulture. Photo by Tim Cooper.

HABITAT Found in open habitats, including everything from fields and pastures to urban environments. These gregarious birds are well known for roosting in groups on power-line towers. Vultures nest in small caves and other sheltered areas.

STATUS AND DISTRIBUTION Common to locally abundant summer resident throughout the state. Leaves most of the western half of the state during the winter. Common during winter in the eastern half of the state and in south Texas. In late fall, very large numbers migrate through southern Texas on their way to wintering areas farther south.

OSPREY
Pandion haliaetus

BACKGROUND The Osprey is sometimes referred to as the fish hawk because it feeds almost exclusively on fish. The structure of the Osprey, including its long wings, allows it to capture and carry large fish. Ospreys hunt for their prey by hovering over the water and then, when a suitable fish is located, diving with talons outspread. They have very long talons as well as barbed pads on their feet to help grasp fish. If successful, they fly to a perch, positioning the fish so that the head is pointed forward to cut down on wind resistance as much as possible. Although a very rare nester in Texas, Ospreys will readily build nests on man-made structures, particularly telephone poles. Ospreys (and many other birds of prey) were among the species hardest hit by DDT, but Osprey populations have rebounded since the ban on DDT in the early 1970s.

IDENTIFICATION This large, long-winged raptor is basically brown above and white below. Females can be identified by a heavily spotted brown band across the breast. On males, the banding is less distinct or may be entirely lacking. The head is white with a prominent dark line through the eye, continuing down the side of the head. Both the tail and flight feathers are heavily barred with brown and white. Immature Ospreys resemble adults, but the feathers on the upperparts are edged in buff, giving them a scaled appearance. In flight, Ospreys hold their wings bent back at the "wrist," giving them a distinctive shape.

SIMILAR SPECIES The species most likely to be confused with the

Osprey. Photo by Tim Cooper.

Osprey are the Red-tailed Hawk (*Buteo jamaicensis*) and White-tailed Hawk (*B. albicaudatus*). In all cases, the head pattern of the Osprey will eliminate other contenders.

HABITAT Lakes, rivers, and the immediate coast.

STATUS AND DISTRIBUTION Uncommon to rare migrant throughout most of the state. Spring migrants begin passing through the state in mid-March and can be seen through late May. The fall migration period is from early September to mid-November. Common to uncommon winter resident along the coast. Uncommon to rare in the eastern third of the state during winter and very rare to casual winter visitor to the High Plains and Trans-Pecos. Very rare and local breeder in the Pineywoods and along the upper coast. Nonbreeding individuals, however, are rare summer visitors elsewhere along the coast and in the eastern third of the state.

MISSISSIPPI KITE
Ictinia mississippiensis

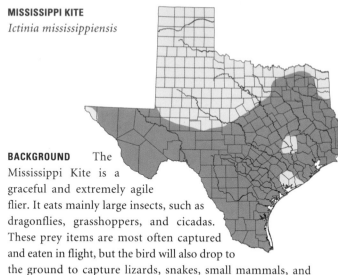

BACKGROUND   The Mississippi Kite is a graceful and extremely agile flier. It eats mainly large insects, such as dragonflies, grasshoppers, and cicadas. These prey items are most often captured and eaten in flight, but the bird will also drop to the ground to capture lizards, snakes, small mammals, and frogs. These birds are well-known for aggressively defending the nest, even attacking humans who wander too close. Golf courses with large, widely spaced trees provide excellent nesting areas for this species and also invite confrontations between the birds and golfers. Despite their aggressive behavior toward intruders, Mississippi Kites often nest in loose colonies and appear gregarious in many activities.

IDENTIFICATION These relatively small birds of prey have long, narrow, pointed wings. Adults are gray overall, slightly paler on the underparts and on the head. The upperparts are a dark slate gray with a panel of whitish secondaries, and the tail is black. Immature birds are streaked with rufous-brown below and have a prominently banded tail.

SIMILAR SPECIES The Peregrine Falcon (*Falco peregrinus*) is very similar in overall proportion. Both species share a similar wing shape and tail length in proportion to the body, but Peregrines are heavier bodied and as a result are more direct fliers. A feature that differentiates Mississippi Kites from falcons is the outermost primary: in the kite it is distinctly shorter than the next two feathers. White-tailed Kites (*Elanus leucurus*) are very similar in body shape and structure, but their plumage is mostly white in adults. Immature birds of this species have some rufous mottling on the underparts as well, but overall they are much lighter in color and have an obviously white tail. A male Northern Harrier (*Circus cyaneus*), although very different in overall body shape and size, shares a similar pattern of coloration.

HABITAT Found primarily in open habitats, including urban environments. They will also use woodland edges and riparian corridors.

STATUS AND DISTRIBUTION Common to uncommon migrant throughout the state. Common summer resident on the High Plains and Rolling Plains, also uncommon to rare summer resident in El Paso County and on the upper coast. Mississippi Kites have nested in many other areas of the state, including the Pineywoods, Blackland Prairies, and Post Oak Savannahs. The small overall population in these regions may be increasing locally. Migration occurs between early April and mid-May and late August to mid-October.

Mississippi Kite. Photo by Mark W. Lockwood.

BALD EAGLE
Haliaeetus leucocephalus

BACKGROUND
Congress selected the Bald Eagle as the national emblem of the United States in 1782. In spite of its prominence in American culture, the Bald Eagle was threatened with extinction in the lower 48 states because of DDT poisoning. Protection under the Endangered Species Act along with aggressive conservation actions has brought this majestic bird back; it was reclassified from Endangered to Threatened status in 1995.

IDENTIFICATION The adult Bald Eagle has a prominent white head and tail; the remainder of its plumage is dark brown. The heavy bill is yellow, as are the legs. Adult plumage is not reached until the bird is over five years old. The body plumage of immature birds varies considerably during this time in the amount and distribution of white mottling over the base of dark-brown feathers. First-year birds tend to be dark overall, with some white in the wing linings and at the base of the tail. As the birds age, white feathers molt into the plumage, particularly on the underparts.

SIMILAR SPECIES The adult Bald Eagle is unlike any other species that occurs in Texas and is unlikely to be misidentified. Immature Bald Eagles can be confused, at certain ages, with the Golden Eagle (*Aquila chrysaetos*). Immature Golden Eagles have a white patch at the base of their primaries and a white base to the tail. First-year Bald Eagles can also have a white base to the tail and white in the wing linings, but they do not have the white primary bases. After the first year, Bald Eagles start to molt in

Bald Eagle, adult. Photo by Greg W. Lasley.

white feathers to their underparts and are not likely to be mistaken for other species.

HABITAT Most often found around large reservoirs in Texas. Also found in open grasslands. They use coastal habitats as well, although not as commonly in Texas as in other parts of their range.

STATUS AND DISTRIBUTION Rare and local summer resident, primarily in the eastern third of the state. There are currently about 80 breeding pairs in Texas. The westernmost pair is found in the Hill Country; others are found as far south as the central coast. During migration and winter, they are more widely distributed and can be found throughout the northern two-thirds of the state. Migrants begin arriving in the state in mid-October, but they are common only on a few of the large reservoirs in the eastern third.

NORTHERN HARRIER
Circus cyaneus

BACKGROUND

Northern Harriers are a common sight gliding over open habitats in Texas each winter. Adult males are more common in the northern half of the state than in the south, but female and immature birds are far more common than adult males in all areas. Because the overall population is strongly biased toward females, the males often have more than one mate during the nesting season; and although the female broods the eggs, the male is largely responsible for providing food to the two, or sometimes more, females and their nestlings. Unlike most hawks, harriers use the sense of hearing to help locate prey. The feathers on the bird's face are arranged to funnel sounds to the ears, much like an owl's. The harrier's softer plumage allows for quieter flight, which also facilitates hunting by ear. The Northern Harrier feeds primarily on small mammals and birds. but it is known to take larger prey, such as rabbits and ducks.

IDENTIFICATION These slim-bodied hawks have long wings and a long tail. They are strongly sexually dimorphic, and females are generally larger than males. Adult males are light gray above, including the head, and white below. The underparts are mottled with light brown, but the amount of spotting varies considerably among individuals. The wings are gray above, with black tips. The tail is also gray, with a broad black subterminal band. Adult females are brown overall, with buff and brown streaked underparts. The tail is heavily banded with dark brown. Immature birds are similar to the adult female but are darker brown above and more uniform russet below. All plumages have a broad white rump patch.

SIMILAR SPECIES The Northern Harrier is most often observed as it hovers over open habitats. Its long body shape, in conjunction with the prominent white rump, makes it a distinctive species.

HABITAT Most commonly encountered in open wetlands, native grasslands, pastures, and fields.

STATUS AND DISTRIBUTION Common to uncommon migrant and winter resident throughout Texas. Rare summer visitor to most regions of the state, but nesting records are rare. Most breeding records come from native grasslands on the Coastal Prairies, Panhandle, and Trans-Pecos. Migrants begin arriving in Texas in late August, and the last wintering birds have generally departed by mid-May.

Northern Harrier, female. Photo by Greg W. Lasley.

COOPER'S HAWK
Accipiter cooperii

BACKGROUND
This forest bird has short, rounded wings well suited to chasing birds through an obstacle course of limbs and branches. Because of its woodland habitat and somewhat secretive habits, Cooper's Hawk is much more common than is readily apparent. In urban areas in particular, they have adapted to using feeding stations as hunting areas. In Texas, the large populations of White-winged Dove found in most urban areas have become a favored target.

IDENTIFICATION A medium-sized hawk, it has rather short, rounded wings and a long, rounded tail. In adults, the upperparts are blue-gray. The underparts are white and heavily barred with rufous. The face is brownish with a distinct black cap, which contrasts with the lighter nape. The tail is blue-gray, with four darker straight bands. Immature birds are brown overall. The upperparts have some white mottling, particularly on the wing covert. The underparts are white and heavily streaked with brown. The tail is brown with four darker brown bands.

SIMILAR SPECIES The Sharp-shinned Hawk (*A. striatus*) is similar in plumage and structure to the larger Cooper's Hawk. The adult Sharp-shinned has the same basic plumage pattern, but its tail is proportionally shorter, with a square tip. In addition to being smaller, the Sharp-shinned Hawk is less robust overall and has a smaller head. Immature Sharp-shinned Hawks are more heavily streaked below and have the same square-tipped

Cooper's Hawk, adult. Photo by Tim Cooper.

tail. In flight, the larger head of Cooper's Hawk is readily visible and sticks out farther in front of the wings. The Northern Goshawk (*A. gentilis*) is very rare in Texas and unlikely to be encountered. A very large accipiter, it is striped with light gray below and has a strong white eyebrow. Immature Northern Goshawks also have a distinct eyebrow, are heavily streaked below on a buffy background, and have an irregularly barred tail.

HABITAT Primarily woodlands. Found in deciduous, mixed, and evergreen forests and more open woodlands. Somewhat tolerant of human disturbance, it is increasingly seen as a breeding bird in urban habitats. During the winter, found in similar habitats and in urban areas where adequate tree cover is available.

STATUS AND DISTRIBUTION Uncommon to rare migrant and winter resident throughout the state. Rare to uncommon and local summer resident in all areas except the High Plains. Fall migrants begin arriving in Texas in mid-September, and the wintering population has generally departed by late April.

HARRIS'S HAWK
Parabuteo unicinctus

BACKGROUND

Harris's Hawks have a complex social behavior and remain in family groups of up to six birds during the fall and winter. Occasionally the previous year's offspring assist in the care of nestlings. The adult female is typically the dominant member of the group. All members of the group help with obtaining food, protecting the nest, and defending the territory of the breeding pair. These hawks have also been documented to hunt cooperatively, enabling them to capture larger prey. Three basic methods have been observed. In the first, several individuals pounced on a single prey. Using another method, a lead bird would flush the prey item while others waited to attempt to capture the flushed prey. Finally, the hawks would tag-team on long prey chases. Group hunting benefits all of the members and likely increases the probability of survival of each of the members.

IDENTIFICATION This is a medium-sized raptor with long broad wings, long legs, and a long tail. Overall, its coloring is a warm chocolate brown with chestnut upper wing coverts, wing lining, and leggings. The tail is long and dark brown with a white base and terminal band. The cere and legs are bright yellow. The sexes are similar, except that females are somewhat larger, as is the case with most raptors. The underparts of immature birds are light and streaked with brown, and the chestnut coloring on the shoulders is muted. This plumage is held for only a short period as the body plumage begins to darken. During this process, the bird looks more like a brown bird streaked with white on its underparts rather than the opposite.

SIMILAR SPECIES Adults could potentially be confused with other dark-colored raptors, such as the Zone-tailed Hawk (*Buteo albonotatus*) or Common Black-Hawk (*Buteogallus anthracinus*). The white band across the rump and upper tail, however, differs from the more finely banded tails of these species.

Harris's Hawk. Photo by Greg W. Lasley.

HABITAT Most commonly encountered in mesquite savannahs and areas of open thorn scrub in the South Texas Brush Country. They tend to be more common in areas with higher numbers of trees and near open water.

STATUS AND DISTRIBUTION Common to uncommon resident in the South Texas Brush Country north to the Balcones Escarpment. Uncommon to rare resident along the Rio Grande from Big Bend northwest to El Paso County. There is also a resident population from the southern High Plains south to the northwestern Edwards Plateau.

RED-SHOULDERED HAWK
Buteo lineatus

BACKGROUND

The Red-shouldered Hawk has an interesting distribution, being a common hawk throughout the eastern United States with a disjunct population in California. Red-shouldered Hawks are most vocal, and thus more obvious, during the spring when they form pairs. The pair often circles well above the trees, calling almost constantly. For most of the rest of the year, these birds are less conspicuous as they attend to the nest and forage. This forest-dwelling raptor has an unusual hunting behavior in which it sits very still on a perch watching for prey to drop upon. One of the most interesting records of this hawk in Texas involved an individual that successfully nested with a Gray Hawk (*Buteo nitida*) in Big Bend National Park in 1989.

IDENTIFICATION This is a large, long-winged hawk with narrow white barring on dark wings. The shoulders are obviously rusty, contrasting with brown flight feathers. The underparts have rufous barring, although the intensity of the color is quite variable. The tail is moderately long and narrowly banded. In flight, the base of the primaries is pale, showing a translucent window area. Immature birds have brown upperparts and heavily streaked white underparts. There is normally some evidence of the rusty red shoulder.

SIMILAR SPECIES The most similar raptor is the Broad-winged Hawk (*Buteo platypterus*), but it is much smaller and has a more compact body type. In addition, the tail is shorter and widely barred. The wings are more pointed, and from below the light-colored flight feathers are outlined in black. An immature Broad-winged can be identified by the dark whisker streak and the same wing shape and color pattern. The adult Cooper's Hawk (*Accipiter cooperii*) has a similar coloration pattern, but its overall shape is more streamlined and the tail is much longer.

HABITAT Found in mature woodlands near water. Riparian corridors are the primary habitat in many areas of the state, particularly in the western portion of the species range. They seem to be adaptable to human intrusion and can be found in human-altered habitats, including urban areas.

STATUS AND DISTRIBUTION Common to uncommon resident throughout the eastern two-thirds of the state. In the remainder of the state, this hawk is a rare to casual visitor and is found primarily along wooded drainages. In south Texas, this species is primarily a winter resident, although there are records from all seasons.

Red-shouldered Hawk. Photo by Greg W. Lasley.

SWAINSON'S HAWK
Buteo swainsoni

BACKGROUND
Covering one of
the longest migra-
tion routes for a rap-
tor, the northernmost
breeding populations of this hawk are
found in Canada, and most of the population winters in Argentina.

IDENTIFICATION The head and upperparts are
uniformly dark brown. The color of the underparts is quite
variable, but most birds have pale underparts with a reddish
brown chest band, or bib. Some individuals have rufous-brown
barring below the bib. The flight feathers are darker than the
wing lining. The wings are so long and pointed that when a
perched bird folds its wings, the tips of the primaries usually
come to the tip of the tail. The tail is grayish brown with numerous bands. Immature birds are buffy white below with large,
rounded spots on the breast and flanks. There is usually some
streaking on the belly as well. The markings on the underparts
are usually heaviest on the breast.

SIMILAR SPECIES Swainson's Hawks can be confused with other
large buteos that inhabit the grasslands of Texas. The dark bib
of the adult sets it apart from other hawks. The Red-tailed Hawk
(*B. jamaicensis*) has a hooded appearance, and the color of its
underparts is quite variable, but it does not have a complete bib
in any plumage. The White-tailed Hawk (*B. albicaudatus*) has a
conspicuous white tail, but a perched bird can look like a
Swainson's when seen from behind. These hawks are all white
below, however. The underwing pattern of the Broad-winged
Hawk (*B. platypterus*) is similar to Swainson's, but the dark

trailing edge is narrower. The Broad-winged also has prominent tail bands and lacks the dark bib.

HABITAT Nests in open grasslands with scattered yuccas and other woody vegetation. Fairly well adapted to agriculture; known to forage in fields until the crops grow too tall.

STATUS AND DISTRIBUTION Uncommon to common summer resident from the Panhandle south through the Rolling Plains to the northern Edwards Plateau and west through most of the Trans-Pecos. Rare summer resident across north-central Texas and in the western South Texas Brush Country. Common to locally abundant migrant in the western three-quarters of the state. Spring migrants are present in Texas from late March through mid-May, although a few often linger into June. During the fall, migrants are present from early August to early November. Very rare and local in winter, with most records coming from the central coast and Lower Rio Grande Valley.

Swainson's Hawk, adult. Photo by Mark W. Lockwood.

WHITE-TAILED HAWK*
Buteo albicaudatus

BACKGROUND
Found in grass-
land and savannah
habitats from central
Argentina northward, this
hawk reaches the northernmost point
of its rather discontinuous range on the
Coastal Prairies of Texas. An interesting
behavioral trait is the bird's attraction to fires
that maintain its grassland habitat. White-tailed Hawks hunt
along the leading edges of these fires to pick up small mammals
as they scurry away from the flames. Unlike other hawks found
in Texas, the adult White-tailed has long wings and a short tail.
This unexpected combination means that on perched birds the
tips of the primaries extend well beyond the tip of the tail.
Oddly enough, juvenile birds have considerably longer tails
than adults. On these dark-plumaged individuals the wing tips
barely surpass the tip of the tail.

IDENTIFICATION Adults are unmistakable, with a bright white tail
with a black subterminal band. The upperparts are light to
medium gray, with rusty shoulder patches that extend slightly
onto the sides of the back. The underparts are white. The
underside of the flight feathers is darker than the wing linings,
providing some contrast when seen in flight. First-year birds
are dark brown overall. The breast and upper belly are brown
with a tan or whitish patch on the breast that is quite variable in
size. The lower belly is white and heavily mottled with dark
spotting. The tail is pale gray with numerous fine bars.

SIMILAR SPECIES This distinctive hawk is unlikely to be confused
with other hawks found in Texas. The dark bib of the adult sets

White-tailed Hawk, adult. Photo by Tim Cooper.

the light-morph of Swainson's Hawk (*B. swainsoni*) apart. The Ferruginous Hawk (*B. regalis*) is very pale, with a white tail, but its upperparts are a rusty color, and it lacks the black band on the tail. In addition, Ferruginous Hawks do not show contrast between the flight feathers and the wing linings.

HABITAT Open habitats, primarily grasslands and savannahs.

STATUS AND DISTRIBUTION Uncommon to locally common resident along the Coastal Prairies, more common on the central and lower coasts than farther north and east. Very rare away from the normal range. Unexpected records from as far away as Jeff Davis and Uvalde counties to the west and Delta County to the north.

ZONE-TAILED HAWK
Buteo albonotatus

BACKGROUND

Often described as a mimic of the Turkey Vulture, the Zone-tailed Hawk is believed to take advantage of prey that mistakes it for a vulture. This is based on the hawk's shallow dihedral wing configuration in flight, similar to the Turkey Vulture's. An alternative explanation is that the dihedral allows the hawk to fly close to the ground in rough terrain. In any case, Zone-tailed Hawks can be easily passed off as vultures.

IDENTIFICATION Almost entirely black with barred flight feathers that are lighter than the wing linings, these birds are long-tailed raptors with white bands across the tail. Males are noticeably smaller than females and usually have fewer white bands in the tail. There is apparently some overlap in the number of bands, however, so that the characteristic cannot be used to sex individuals with certainty. The legs and cere are bright yellow. Immature Zone-tailed Hawks have scattered white spotting on their underparts and, to a lesser extent, on the back and wing coverts. The tail is narrowly barred with gray.

SIMILAR SPECIES Other than the Turkey Vulture, the species most likely to be confused with the Zone-tailed Hawk is the similarly patterned Common Black-Hawk. Both species occupy similar habitats, but Black-Hawks have a very different body structure with wide wings and a short tail. They also have a prominent white central tail band that differs from the Zone-tailed pattern.

HABITAT Although they nest in heavily wooded canyons and in

Zone-tailed Hawk. Photo by Greg W. Lasley.

riparian corridors, these birds have large hunting territories and wander well away from these somewhat restricted habitats. As a result, they can be seen in almost any open area within their range.

STATUS AND DISTRIBUTION Uncommon and local summer resident in the mountains of the central Trans-Pecos east through the southern Edwards Plateau. Rare summer visitor to the Guadalupe Mountains (but not reported from the El Paso area). Rare migrant and winter resident in the Lower Rio Grande Valley and irregular visitor there during the summer. Rare and local winter visitor, possibly more regularly than is currently known, through much of its breeding range. Interestingly, there have been numerous records from Tom Green and Irion counties southward through east-central Texas.

RED-TAILED HAWK
Buteo jamaicensis

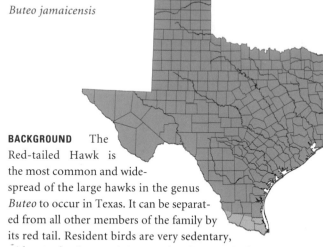

BACKGROUND   The Red-tailed Hawk is the most common and widespread of the large hawks in the genus *Buteo* to occur in Texas. It can be separated from all other members of the family by its red tail. Resident birds are very sedentary, with mated pairs remaining together for years in the same area. One of the more distinctive subspecies of Red-tailed Hawk that occurs in Texas is Harlan's Hawk (*B. j. harlani*). This subspecies nests in Alaska and northwestern Canada and winters in the south-central United States. It was formerly considered a separate species, and in many cases it can be readily separated from the other races of Red-tailed Hawk.

IDENTIFICATION The species is quite variable, with light and dark morphs, although almost all have a red tail as adults. Light-morph birds are characterized by a brown head with a contrasting white throat, white underparts, and brown upperparts. The belly can be clean white or heavily streaked. They have pale underwings that are heavily marked in the wing linings and barred in the flight feathers. The brown back is mottled with white, particularly in the scapulars, forming a V on the shoulders. Dark morphs are generally uniform dark brown. Immature birds are brown and white and usually heavily marked on the underparts. Their tails are barred with tan and dark brown. Harlan's Hawk is a uniform dark brown, with some white streaking on the chest, a dusky white tail spotted with black, and a diffuse black terminal band.

SIMILAR SPECIES The adult is unmistakable if the red tail can be seen. The adult Swainson's Hawk (*B. swainsoni*) can be confusing; however, it has a rufous-brown chest. The immature Red-tailed offers a host of identification problems, but it can normally be identified by the heavily barred tail, whitish mottling on the back and shoulders, heavy brown streaking below, and the heavy-bodied look combined with a medium-length tail.

HABITAT Found in a variety of habitats. Typically, open areas with scattered trees or large shrubs are the best habitats, but they also inhabit open woodlands.

STATUS AND DISTRIBUTION Common to uncommon resident throughout almost all of the state. The exception is the South Texas Brush Country, where they are uncommon, and the Lower Rio Grande Valley, where they are absent as breeders.

Red-tailed Hawk. Photo by Tim Cooper.

Found in all areas of the state during migration and winter. Harlan's Hawks can be found across most of the state east of the Pecos River during migration and winter, but they appear to be most common in the prairies of central Texas and on the Coastal Prairies. They arrive on the wintering grounds in mid-October and most have migrated north by late March.

CRESTED CARACARA
Caracara cheriway

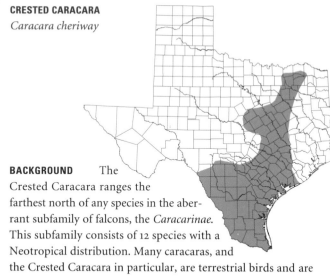

BACKGROUND The Crested Caracara ranges the farthest north of any species in the aberrant subfamily of falcons, the *Caracarinae.* This subfamily consists of 12 species with a Neotropical distribution. Many caracaras, and the Crested Caracara in particular, are terrestrial birds and are often seen walking. The Crested Caracara has a continuous distribution from Texas south to northwestern South America. There is also a disjunct population in Florida and the Caribbean; the U.S. Fish and Wildlife Service considers the Florida population threatened. This species is the national bird of Mexico, and a colloquial name is "Mexican eagle." The Crested Caracara is somewhat of a scavenger and as such probably has the most varied diet of any raptor. These long-legged birds are often seen with vultures at fresh kills or carrion, although they will actively hunt for small mammals and reptiles. Unlike other falcons, caracaras build a nest.

IDENTIFICATION This is a large-headed, long-legged, hawklike bird with rounded wings. The head is white with a black cap and a bare red face. The neck and breast are white, although the breast is heavily barred with brown, eventually blending into the dark brown body plumage. The uppertail coverts are white, and the tail is white, heavily barred with brown, with a black terminal band. The outer primaries are largely white, although barred with brown, and are very evident in flight. Flying caracaras show a distinctive pattern with four areas of white on the head, wing tips, and tail. Immature birds are browner, and the upperparts are heavily spotted with tan. The underparts are also more heavily streaked in young birds.

SIMILAR SPECIES This very distinctive species is unlikely to be confused with other species, both perched and in flight. Black Vultures also have white patches in the primaries; however, their body plumage and tail are uniformly dark.

HABITAT Open rangeland and brush country. Absent in wooded areas.

STATUS AND DISTRIBUTION Uncommon to common resident in the South Texas Brush Country and Coastal Prairies up to the central coast. Occurs irregularly as far up the coast as Chambers County. Uncommon to rare resident in the Blackland Prairies and Post Oak Savannahs north to the eastern counties of north-central Texas. Now a rare and local summer resident on the Edwards Plateau, but appears to be increasing at a steady rate. Casual visitor to the Trans-Pecos at all seasons, although it may be more regular in western Val Verde County. The northern-most populations appear to move southward during cooler winters.

Crested Caracara. Photo by Tim Cooper.

AMERICAN KESTREL
Falco sparverius

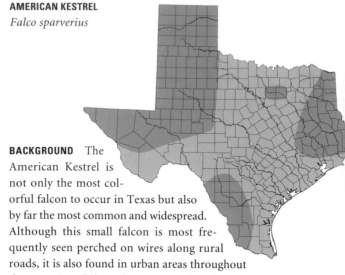

BACKGROUND The American Kestrel is not only the most colorful falcon to occur in Texas but also by far the most common and widespread. Although this small falcon is most frequently seen perched on wires along rural roads, it is also found in urban areas throughout the state. Female kestrels migrate earlier than the males, and it appears that in some areas they set up foraging territories in the prime locations, sometimes forcing the later-arriving males into areas with more trees. These small falcons prey on a wide variety of organisms, ranging from large insects to small rodents and birds.

IDENTIFICATION Very colorful and distinctive, the male has a rusty back that is framed by slaty-blue wings. The tail is rufous with a broad black subterminal band with a white tip. The underparts are pale buff to orangish with black spotting on the flanks and belly. The crown is blue-gray with a small rufous crown patch. The face is white with two black stripes, one through the eye and the other behind the auriculars. The female has rusty upperparts, including the wings. The tail is also rusty, but differs from the male in being much duller and having narrow black bars above the subterminal black band. The face and crown are similar to the male, but not as bright or crisp. The underparts of the female are generally white or washed with buff and heavily streaked with brown.

SIMILAR SPECIES The Merlin (*F. columbarius*) is the only other

American Kestrel, male. Photo by Greg W. Lasley.

small falcon found in Texas. It is easily distinguished from the American Kestrel by the uniform blue-gray (male) or brown (female) upperparts and less distinctive facial pattern. The Peregrine falcon (*F. peregrinus*) and Prairie Falcon (*F. mexicanus*) are considerably larger and more uniform in plumage pattern. In general, American Kestrels are much paler below than other species of falcons found in Texas.

HABITAT Found along borders of woodlands, farmlands, open habitats with scattered trees, and grasslands. The breeding population in the Pineywoods is found in open longleaf forests. They also use urban habitats.

STATUS AND DISTRIBUTION Common to abundant migrant and winter resident throughout the state. Uncommon summer resident in the High Plains and Trans-Pecos. Also rare to uncommon summer resident in the Pineywoods, locally in north-central Texas, and the western South Texas Brush Country. There are isolated breeding records for other areas, but these small falcons are generally absent from the remainder of Texas during the summer.

APLOMADO FALCON*
Falco femoralis

BACKGROUND

A reintroduction program for the Aplomado Falcon was begun in south Texas in 1989, spearheaded by the Peregrine Fund, Inc., and the U.S. Fish and Wildlife Service. More than 700 captive-raised falcons have been released at sites along the coast and in the western Trans-Pecos as of 2005. In 1995, a pair successfully fledged young in Cameron County, in the first nest in the United States since the early 1950s. There have been numerous successful nestings since then, and unbanded birds can now be seen from Brownsville north to Calhoun County. The species is still not considered established, and reintroduction efforts continue with the release of more captive-raised birds. The effort to return these spectacular birds to Texas seems to have cleared its first hurdles.

IDENTIFICATION Adults have a rather sleek body and long tail, which gives them a different look from the other large falcons found in Texas. The upperparts are blue-gray, which extends up through the cap. The face is white with a bold mustache. There is a prominent white eyebrow and a black stripe through the eye. The throat and breast are white bordered by a broad blackish band across the belly. The lower belly, leggings, and undertail are rusty. The tail is long and heavily barred with slaty-blue and white. The feathers of the underparts and face of immature birds are tipped with rufous, which wears off, revealing white. Young birds also have a streaked breast.

SIMILAR SPECIES The Prairie Falcon is similar in total length and shares the prominent mustache, but it has a much heavier build and is brown in overall color. Adult Peregrine Falcons are similar in upperparts color, but they lack the heavily barred tail and distinctive underparts pattern of the Aplomado. The American Kestrel is much smaller and has rufous on the upperparts.

HABITAT Prefers yucca grasslands, where the yuccas serve as favored perches and nesting sites. Also found in a variety of open habitats that mimic this grassland structure.

STATUS AND DISTRIBUTION Almost all Aplomado Falcons found in Texas are the result of Peregrine Fund reintroductions. They are now rare to locally uncommon residents along the Coastal Prairies from Calhoun County southward. There are a few documented records from the mid-elevation grasslands of the Trans-Pecos, where the birds presumably originate from the wild population in northern Mexico. Similar discoveries have also been made in south-central New Mexico. Reintroduction efforts into these same areas of the Trans-Pecos began in 2002. In the 1800s, this falcon was a summer resident from the central Trans-Pecos east to Midland and in the South

Aplomado Falcon. Photo by Tim Cooper.

Texas Brush Country. There were scattered sightings from Cameron County and the western Trans-Pecos until the early 1950s.

KING RAIL
Rallus elegans

BACKGROUND

The King Rail has a broad range through much of the eastern United States. The northern populations are all migratory and have declined dramatically over the past three decades. The resident populations on the Gulf Coast seem to be faring better, and the Texas coast has become a real stronghold for the species. The reasons for its decline are not well understood, but loss of habitat seems to be a primary factor. Newly hatched King Rails are fully feathered and ready to leave the nest. The solid black chicks are occasionally mistaken for the much rarer Black Rail (*Laterallus jamaicensis*). They are, of course, always accompanied by the adults, even if the larger birds are not visible initially.

IDENTIFICATION This large rail has a long, slender bill, which is longer than the head and slightly decurved. The upperparts are olive-brown overall, but the back feathers have tawny edges and black centers. The neck and breast are a rusty cinnamon color, and the flanks are barred with black and white. The bill is dull yellow with a dark culmen and tip. The legs are also dull in color, and the toes are very long.

SIMILAR SPECIES The Clapper Rail (*R. longirostris*) is similar in size and color, but the King Rail can be distinguished from it by the tawny edges of the back feathers, which have black centers. The wing coverts are also tawny. Clapper Rails are generally grayer in overall color, including the face. The Virginia Rail (*R.*

limicola) is considerably smaller, with an obviously gray face and a brighter red bill.

HABITAT Freshwater marshes, rice fields, and other wetlands. Also found, at least occasionally, in brackish marshes.

STATUS AND DISTRIBUTION Common to locally abundant resident in freshwater marshes, irrigation ditches, and weedy lakes on the upper and central coasts. Uncommon on the lower coast and in the Lower Rio Grande Valley. Apparently very rare and local elsewhere in the eastern half of the state during the summer. Rare migrant, or at least seldom observed, through the eastern half of the state. There are a few scattered records from farther west.

King Rail. Photo by Tim Cooper.

AMERICAN COOT
Fulica americana

BACKGROUND
The American Coot has a passing resemblance to a duck. This abundant bird is a member of the *Rallidae* and is one of the most aquatic members of the family. The coot feeds by dabbling on the surface, tipping its tail in the air to reach submerged vegetation in shallow water, diving to the bottom, and grazing along the shore. These are short-winged birds that require a runway to gain speed as they patter over the water before finally becoming airborne. During courtship, the male will chase the female with his head held low and his wings and tail raised. If a female is not interested in the male's advances, she will dive to escape. If she chooses him as a mate, however, she will also display her white undertail feathers.

IDENTIFICATION This coot is gray and ducklike, with a white bill and forehead. Closer inspection shows that the head and neck are dark, almost black, and the outer undertail coverts are white. A reddish brown forehead shield is visible at close range, but this feature can sometimes be very small or absent. The legs and feet are green, and the toes are lobed rather than connected by webbing. Immature birds are similar to adults but are paler overall and have grayish bills. Downy young are black with a bald red head and red-tipped feathers on the remainder of the head and on the neck.

SIMILAR SPECIES They may occasionally be mistaken for a duck, but the white, chickenlike bill separates them from all waterfowl. The species most likely to be mistaken for a coot is the Common Moorhen (*Gallinula chloropus*). The moorhen's body plumage is similar, but it has a bright red bill (with a yellow tip) and forehead and a white line along the flanks. Moorhens do not have lobed toes and are frequently seen walking on lily pads or along the sides of ponds as well as foraging in the water.

HABITAT Found on open bodies of water, including small ponds, reservoirs, and marshes. During the winter it can also be found in brackish marshes and coastal bays.

American Coot. Photo by Mark W. Lockwood.

STATUS AND DISTRIBUTION Uncommon to common summer resident in nearly all regions of the state. Can be found in most areas of the state during the summer, but actual nesting records are only from scattered locations. Common to abundant winter resident statewide.

SANDHILL CRANE
Grus canadensis

BACKGROUND

The Sandhill Crane is one of only 15 species of cranes in the world and is the only common one in North America. They are perhaps best known for their elaborate courtship displays and their trumpeting calls that can be heard from more than a mile away. In Texas, Sandhill Cranes are generally seen in small to very large flocks as they move from roosting areas to feeding grounds. Family groups typically remain together for up to 10 months. Since cranes do not reach maturity until after two years, the immature birds remain with the adults until the young of the year hatch. One of the great avian phenomena, Sandhill Cranes congregate in vast numbers along the Platte River in Nebraska each spring during March and April.

IDENTIFICATION This crane is very tall, with a long neck and legs. The body plumage of adults is a fairly uniform gray. The bare red forehead and crown are diagnostic among long-legged waders. Immature birds are browner, particularly on the head and neck, and they lack the red on the head. Plumage often appears rusty because of iron stains from the water of tundra ponds.

SIMILAR SPECIES The Sandhill is most often confused with the Great Blue Heron. Both are long-legged waders with long necks, but that is where the similarity ends. In flight, herons hold the head and neck tucked back to the shoulders, but cranes fly with the neck outstretched. The crane's body plumage is uniform;

Sandhill Crane. Photo by Tim Cooper.

on close inspection, the plumage of the Great Blue Heron is intricate.

HABITAT Roosts in large flocks in shallow freshwater wetlands as well as open fields and pastures during the winter. During the day, moves out to pastures, open fields, and even cultivated lands for foraging. They congregate in wet meadows and cultivated fields where grains and peanuts are grown.

STATUS AND DISTRIBUTION Uncommon to common migrant throughout much of the state. The High Plains and Rolling Plains in the north and the Coastal Prairies in the south are the two areas in the state where the bulk of the wintering Sandhill Cranes are found. During winter found in almost any area in the western two-thirds of the state. They arrive in mid-October, and most depart by mid-March. Formerly rare resident in the coastal marshes of southeast Texas.

WHOOPING CRANE*
Grus americana

BACKGROUND The effort to protect the endangered Whooping Crane is one of the best-known success stories in conservation. Although it has taken decades, the Whooping Crane has been brought back from the edge of extinction. There were only 14 individuals in the wild in the late 1930s when concerted management activities began. These birds live an astonishing 22–24 years, which allows each pair to raise numerous young during a lifetime. There is only one naturally occurring population, which migrates down a narrow corridor between Aransas National Wildlife Refuge in Texas and Wood Buffalo National Park in Alberta. An experimental migratory flock moving between Wisconsin and Florida was started in 2001 and now includes more than 60 birds. The researchers used ultralight aircraft to train the birds to fly the migration route. The final flock of Whooping Cranes living in the wild, a nonmigratory population of about 80 birds, is found in central Florida.

IDENTIFICATION With the exception of black primaries, the plumage of the adult is totally white. It also has a red cap that extends down the face into a long mustache. This red cap is bare skin with scattered black hairlike feathers. Immature birds can be distinguished by the heavy mottling of reddish brown feathers, particularly on the head and neck. Their heads are entirely feathered, although they begin loosing the feathers of the crown and face before losing the brownish plumage.

SIMILAR SPECIES Although the Whooping Crane is very large and distinctive, it is occasionally confused with the smaller, gray

Sandhill Crane. This happens more often when Sandhill Cranes are in flight; they can look very pale, but they lack the black wing tips. A number of birds have a similar plumage pattern, including the American White Pelican and Snow Goose. The pelican can be eliminated by the black flight feathers, which extend the length of the wings. Snow Geese are much smaller and lack the long bill and long legs. There are also several white egrets, but all are smaller and have completely white wings.

HABITAT The winter habitat consists of estuarine marshes and salt flats where they feed, particularly on blue crabs (*Callinectes sapidus*) and clams.

STATUS AND DISTRIBUTION This critically endangered species is an uncommon winter resident along the central coast. The majority of individuals winter at Aransas National Wildlife Refuge in Aransas and Calhoun counties. They are rarely seen as they migrate along a narrow corridor through the state. Still, migrants are occasionally found with Sandhill Cranes in areas outside the normal migration route. During the winter of 2004–2005, a total of 217 birds wintered in Texas, the first time the population surpassed 200 individuals. Habitat degradation is a serious concern for the continued survival of the species. For any species with such a small population, single catastrophic events such as a chemical spill or storm are always a threat.

Whooping Crane. Photo by Greg W. Lasley.

KILLDEER
Charadrius vociferus

BACKGROUND

The Killdeer is one of the most ubiquitous birds in Texas and is probably our best-known shorebird. Killdeers are the largest of the ringed plovers, the only one likely to be seen well away from water. The other ringed plovers are all small plovers associated with mudflats or coastal shorelines. The loud *kill-dee-dee* call of this species is the origin of its common and scientific names and identifies the species as much as any visual aspect. Perhaps equally well known is the conspicuous broken-wing display, used to distract potential predators from nests and young. The young are precocial, meaning they are fully feathered and ready to leave the nest as soon as they hatch. They almost immediately begin following the parents and searching for food. They are, of course, initially flightless and depend on the parents for protection.

IDENTIFICATION The Killdeer has brown upperparts and is white below. The two prominent black bands across its breast are a key field mark. The relatively long tail is primarily orange with a black subterminal band. Killdeer have long legs and often will run to escape predators or to avoid contact. Downy young have a single breast band, but this plumage is held for a very short time after hatching.

SIMILAR SPECIES The other ringed plovers are the most likely candidates to cause confusion, but all are much smaller and have only one breast band instead of two. Killdeer are often seen in the habitats frequented by these birds. The Piping Plover (*C.*

melodus) and Snowy Plover (*C. alexandrinus*) are sandy gray above and thus are easily eliminated. The Semipalmated Plover's (*C. semipalmatus*) plumage pattern is similar, basically lacking the double breast band and orange tail. Indeed, juvenile Killdeer are occasionally confused with this species. The final ringed plover is Wilson's (*C. wilsonia*). Wilson's is found exclusively along the immediate coast and is similar in overall color, but it also lacks the double breast band and orange tail.

Killdeer. Photo by Tim Cooper.

HABITAT Found in almost all open habitats, including cultivated fields, vacant lots in urban areas, golf courses, pastures, and prairies. Also along shorelines, on mudflats, and other habitats normally associated with shorebirds.

STATUS AND DISTRIBUTION Common to abundant resident throughout the state. During the winter, even more common in the central and southern parts of the state as migrants arrive. Populations fluctuate greatly during the winter in the Panhandle, where it can be common some years and virtually absent in others.

AMERICAN AVOCET
Recurvirostra americana

BACKGROUND The American Avocet has perhaps the most striking plumage of any shorebird in Texas. Avocets feed in a way that is similar to the spoonbill technique; they sweep the bill from side to side along the surface of the water. The bill is very sensitive, and they are able to capture small crustaceans, aquatic insects, and floating seeds. At first glance the sexes appear indistinquishable, but a closer look reveals that the female has a shorter, more curved bill. An interesting behavioral aspect of this species is that females will occasionally lay one to four eggs in another avocet's nest. On rare occasions, they have been found laying eggs in the nests of other species. On the other hand, Black-necked Stilts (*Himantopus mexicanus*) have been known to lay their eggs in avocet nests. In those cases, the avocets have reared the stilts. Avocet young, like most shorebirds, are ready to leave the nest within 24 hours of hatching. They readily follow the adults as they forage for food.

American Avocet, breeding plumage. Photo by Tim Cooper.

Both young and adults are accomplished swimmers and can be seen in deep water resting or feeding.

American Avocet, winter plumage. Photo by Tim Cooper.

IDENTIFICATION This is a large, long-legged shorebird with a slender, upturned bill. The upperparts and wings are boldly patterned in black and white, and the underparts are totally white. During the spring and summer the head and neck are rusty brown, becoming pale gray to white in winter.

SIMILAR SPECIES The boldly patterned plumage makes misidentification unlikely. The Black-necked Stilt has all-black upperparts as well as a black face and back of neck. The Marbled Godwit (*Limosa fedoa*) and Hudsonian Godwit (*L. haemastica*) have recurved bills, but their plumage is more uniform in coloration.

HABITAT Found in freshwater marshes, playa lakes, and other shallow freshwater habitats at inland locations during the breeding season. At breeding sites and in the winter, this species inhabits similar habitats as well as saltwater or brackish marshes and coastal tidal flats for loafing.

STATUS AND DISTRIBUTION Common to locally abundant winter resident on the coast. Wintering birds arrive on the coast in mid-August and most depart by mid-May. Generally absent from the northern half of the state in winter. Uncommon to locally common summer resident on the High Plains and in the El Paso area. Also rare and local summer resident along the coast. Common to uncommon migrant through the western half of the state and uncommon farther east. Migration periods are from early April to mid-May and between early August and late October.

LONG-BILLED CURLEW
Numenius americanus

BACKGROUND The Long-billed Curlew is the largest shorebird found in North America. They were once abundant in the vast prairies of the Great Plains, but they have declined sharply as native grasslands have been converted to agricultural uses; the total population has dropped to close to 15,000 individuals. The Long-billed Curlew is now of very high conservation concern, as are many other grassland species. Curlews use their long bills to probe deeply into damp soil or mud for insects, worms, burrowing spiders, crabs, and other burrowing crustaceans. Young curlews, like other shorebirds, leave the nest within a few hours of hatching. Both parents care for the young for the first few weeks, but then the female leaves the male to continue care until the chicks are about six weeks old. These birds have a relatively low reproductive rate, producing only one brood a year with a maximum of four young in a brood; this makes it more difficult for the population to rebound after dips in overall numbers.

IDENTIFICATION This bird is easily identified by its large size and extremely long, curved bill. The upperparts are sandy brown and heavily marked with dark brown and black. The underparts are buffier and lightly streaked. The underwings are a distinctive bright cinnamon color. The very long bill, up to 8 inches in length, is bright orange near the base and otherwise blackish.

SIMILAR SPECIES The only species that might cause confusion in Texas is the Whimbrel (*N. phaeopus*). The Whimbrel can be

Long-billed Curlew. Photo by Mark W. Lockwood.

distinguished by the boldly striped crown and dark eye line. It is also considerably smaller, with a somewhat straighter bill.

HABITAT Breeds in grasslands. During migration, found on mudflats, along the shores of lakes and ponds, and wet fields. Along the coast it also frequents salt marshes, tidal flats, and beaches.

STATUS AND DISTRIBUTION Common to locally abundant winter resident on the coast, where flocks of several hundred are not unusual. Uncommon to rare winter resident farther inland as far north as Bell County and locally in El Paso and Hudspeth counties. Casual winter visitor in most other areas of the state, although very locally in the Panhandle. Common summer resident in the grasslands of the northwestern Panhandle. There have also been reports of occasional nesting along the upper coast. An uncommon migrant throughout the state, with the exception of the eastern third, where it is essentially absent. Migration occurs from mid-March to mid-May and mid-July to early November. Rare to locally uncommon summer visitor along the coast and inland east of the Pineywoods.

SANDERLING
Calidris alba

BACKGROUND The Sanderling is a very familiar sight along the sand beaches of the Texas coast as they feed along the shoreline, chasing the receding waves and running back as the next wave approaches. This species has an interesting biology, nesting in the Arctic and wintering from Canada to southern Argentina. The Sanderling is also one of the most widespread shorebirds in the world. They are circumpolar breeders and winter on tropical and temperate beaches throughout the world.

IDENTIFICATION Sanderlings are seen in Texas in all plumages. The most commonly encountered are winter-plumaged adults and juveniles. Winter adults are very pale gray on the upperparts and white below. The flight feathers are much darker with pale bases, forming a prominent white stripe in the wing. The bill is black and fairly heavy, and the legs are also black. In late spring, Sanderlings start molting into breeding plumage before departing northward. In this plumage, the upperparts and breast are rusty brown. The belly and undertail remain white, and the bill and legs remain black. Birds remaining in Texas through the summer generally do not molt into breeding plumage. Juvenile birds are similar to winter adults, but they have considerable black marking on the back, nape, and crown. The breast often has a buffy wash, and the remainder of the underparts are white.

SIMILAR SPECIES In winter plumage, the very pale plumage eliminates most species and is the first clue in identifying this shorebird. The white face, black bill and legs, and white wing stripe together eliminate all other species. In summer plumage, the Sanderling looks superficially like Baird's Sandpiper (*C. bairdii*), the Pectoral Sandpiper (*C. melanotos*), or the Red-necked Stint (*C. ruficollis*). Baird's Sandpiper is smaller and slimmer, with no conspicuous wing stripe. The Pectoral Sandpiper has greenish legs and bill and is larger in size. There is only one record of Red-necked Stint in Texas, and this species is considerably smaller as well as having an unmarked face and a shorter bill.

HABITAT Most common in Texas on sand beaches and on salt flats around coastal bays. Migrants, however, can be encountered on sandbars, mudflats, and other typical habitats utilized by shorebirds.

Sanderling, winter plumage. Photo by Greg W. Lasley.

STATUS AND DISTRIBUTION Common to abundant migrant and winter resident along the coast. Common during the summer along the coast, but these birds do not nest. Rare to uncommon migrant away from the coast, although primarily in the eastern two-thirds of the state. Farther west, casual migrant in spring and very rare in fall. Migrants are found between late March and late May and from late July to early November.

LEAST SANDPIPER
Calidris minutilla

BACKGROUND The Least Sandpiper is one of the most common sandpipers found in Texas. It also has the distinction of being the smallest shorebird in the world. Least Sandpipers nest farther south than any other Calidrid sandpiper. Although this species can be seen in Texas during any month of the year, it does not nest in the state. It belongs to a group of very similar small shorebirds frequently referred to as peeps, which includes the Semipalmated (*C. pusilla*), Western (*C. mauri*), White-rumped (*C. fuscicollis*), and Baird's (*C. bairdii*) sandpipers. They are often seen in grassy areas or along the upper portions of mudflats or shorelines in habitats that are drier than those preferred by most shorebirds.

IDENTIFICATION Adults in breeding plumage are dark brown on the upperparts with a pale, indistinct stripe on each side of the back. There is considerable buffy scalloping on the back and shoulders. The head and breast are also brown with dark streaking, particularly on the crown and breast. The belly, flanks, and undertail coverts are white. The bill is black and rather short and thin. A key field mark is the yellow legs. In winter, adults are paler brown overall, with a faint scalloped appearance on the upperparts. The distinct brown breast contrasts with the remainder of the underparts, which are white. Juveniles are more brightly marked with rufous edgings on the feathers of the back and shoulders.

SIMILAR SPECIES This species is smaller and has darker upperparts than the other peeps. Other small Calidrid sandpipers have black legs, but a Least Sandpiper's legs may appear black when they are covered with mud. Semipalmated and Western Sandpipers are grayer above and have a white breast. Baird's Sandpiper is closer in overall plumage pattern, but it is larger, with long wings, black legs, and a longer and straighter bill.

HABITAT Found in freshwater habitats such as playa lakes, sandbars, and mudflats. Also found in coastal tidal flats and open areas in saltwater or brackish marshes.

STATUS AND DISTRIBUTION Common to abundant migrant statewide. Common to locally abundant in winter along the coast, becoming less common inland. In the Panhandle, rare in winter. Nonbreeding birds remain in the state during the summer. They are most common along the coast during this season but have the potential to be found almost anywhere. Migrants of these and many other shorebirds can be found as late as mid-May in the spring and as early as mid-July in the fall.

Least Sandpiper, juvenile. Photo by Greg W. Lasley.

LONG-BILLED DOWITCHER
Limnodromus scolopaceus

BACKGROUND
The Long-billed Dow-
itcher is a common shore-
bird in Texas. Found in freshwater habitats, they are normally encountered in
groups as they feed with a rapid up-and-
down motion reminiscent of a sewing
machine. A close relative, the Short-billed Dowitcher (*L. griseus*), is similar in appearance and was once considered the same species. In winter, the Long-billed favors freshwater habitats, while the Short-billed is found more commonly around salt water, although both species can be seen side by side in both habitat types. During fall migration, the Short-billed Dowitcher arrives in Texas earlier than the Long-billed.

IDENTIFICATION This long-billed shorebird has a white lower back and rump and a black-and-white checkered tail. Birds in breeding plumage have reddish underparts, including the belly and undertail coverts, with considerable black spotting or barring on the breast, flanks, and undertail coverts. The upperparts are brown but have rufous edging and interior markings, giving the birds a rufous cast. Winter birds are gray overall, with a pale eyebrow and white lower back and rump. The undertail coverts are also heavily marked in winter plumage. In all plumages, these birds have long, green legs.

SIMILAR SPECIES Wilson's Snipe (*Gallinago delicata*), formerly known as the Common Snipe, has a similar body shape and structure, but it has a dark rump and tail, golden stripes down the back, and short legs. The Stilt Sandpiper (*Calidris himanto-*

pus) has a shorter, slightly curved bill, longer legs, and a white rump that does not extend up the back. The real identification challenge is separating the Long-billed from the Short-billed Dowitcher. The species are extremely similar and difficult to distinguish in most plumages. Voice is the best tool in identification: the Long-billed has a high-pitched *keek* call, and the call of the Short-billed is a mellow *tu tu tu*. Short-billed Dowitchers are also less heavily marked on the underparts and usually have some white on the belly in breeding plumage. The winter plumage of the Short-billed is generally paler, with less black in the tail, but the birds are often difficult to identify except by voice. The juvenile Short-billed has brighter plumage than the Long-billed and has heavily marked tertials. Despite the common names, bill length overlaps greatly between these species and is most often not a clue to identification.

HABITAT Found on mudflats, shallow marshy habitats, and margins of freshwater ponds.

STATUS AND DISTRIBUTION Uncommon to common migrant throughout the state and abundant on the coast. Common winter resident along the coast as well as locally inland in the southern half of the state. Found during winter farther north, but increasingly less common and casual in the Panhandle. Migrants can be encountered between early March and late May and from late July to mid-

Long-billed Dowitcher, winter plumage. Photo by Tim Cooper.

November. For this and many other species of shorebirds, the time between lingering spring migrants and the arrival of the earliest fall migrants is very short; as a result, Long-billed Dowitchers can be found during every month of the year.

LAUGHING GULL
Larus atricilla

BACKGROUND

The most recognizable and widespread gull along the Texas coast, the Laughing Gull cannot be missed on any beach or bay in the state. Its raucous call is reminiscent of people laughing, which explains the origin of the common name. This is the only species of gull that nests regularly in Texas. Nesting by the very different Herring Gull (*L. argentatus*) has been documented, but only on two occasions.

IDENTIFICATION In breeding plumage, the adult's head is entirely black. The only markings on the head are white crescents above and below the eyes. The mantle is dark gray, and the outer primaries are black, with small white spots at the very tips of these feathers. The remainder of the body, including the tail, is entirely white. The bill is dark red, and the legs are dark with a reddish cast. Nonbreeding adults have a white head with blackish markings on the nape and sides of the head. The body plumage is unchanged, but the bill is black in most individuals. Immature birds are dusky gray-brown overall. The head is gray-brown as well, with paler areas on the forehead and chin. They also have white crescents above and below the eyes.

SIMILAR SPECIES The only other gull with a black hood that most Texas observers are likely to encounter is Franklin's Gull (*L. pipixcan*), an uncommon migrant throughout the state and rare in winter, mostly along the coast. It is slightly smaller, with proportionally shorter wings and a smaller bill. For the two species, the overall plumage pattern of breeding and nonbreeding birds is similar, but Franklin's has a white band that separates the black primary tips and the gray mantle. Franklin's Gull also has much larger white spots at the tips of the primaries. In winter plumage, Franklin's has more extensive black on the head, giving it a more hooded appearance.

HABITAT Most often encountered on sandy beaches, tidal flats, and open water over bays and the Gulf of Mexico.

STATUS AND DISTRIBUTION Abundant resident along the coast. There is a small breeding colony at Falcon Reservoir, Zapata County. It has nested and may still be present at Lake Amistad, Val Verde County. Away from these areas, uncommon to casual visitor inland throughout the state as far north as the southern Panhandle. Most inland records are from late summer and fall. Has become an uncommon visitor to many of the large reservoirs in the eastern half of the state during this time of the year.

Laughing Gull. Photo by Tim Cooper.

RING-BILLED GULL
Larus delawarensis

BACKGROUND

This is the most widespread and common of the white-headed gulls found in Texas, although it is mostly seen only in winter. The species is a typical three-year gull, meaning that individuals reach adulthood in the third year. Immature birds go through numerous molts and plumage changes before reaching adulthood.

IDENTIFICATION In a breeding adult, the entire head, underparts, and tail are white. The mantle is gray, a shade or two lighter than that of a Laughing Gull. The primaries are tipped in black with white spots on the outer two or three feathers. The bill is yellow with a prominent black band, and the legs are also yellow. Nonbreeding birds look very much like those in breeding plumage, except that they have light gray mottling on the head and extending down the nape. Immature birds vary greatly, depending on their age. First-winter birds are heavily mottled with gray and brown on the head and underparts. The pale gray of the mantle is visible on the back, although there can be considerable brown mottling. The wings are also mottled with brown, with a large amount of black on the primaries and some on the secondaries. The tail is whitish with a black band near the tip. The bill is pinkish, with the outer third black. Second-winter birds are similar to adults, with some brown or gray mottling on the head, neck, and underparts. The mantle is light gray with extensive black on the primaries, but they lack the white spots on the outer feathers. The tail is white, with a broken dark band near the tip.

SIMILAR SPECIES The bird most likely to be encountered in Texas that is somewhat similar is the Herring Gull. It is much larger, with a bulkier build in all plumages; the adults have pinkish legs and lack the black ring around the bill. A number of other white-headed gulls are rare to very rare visitors to the state, and some are difficult to identify in immature plumages. One is the California Gull (*L. californicus*), which as an adult has a red and black spot on the lower mandible, greenish legs, and a darker mantle.

HABITAT Found around fresh water, landfills, golf courses, urban parks, and coastal habitats.

Ring-billed Gull. Photo by Tim Cooper.

STATUS AND DISTRIBUTION A common migrant throughout the state. Also common to abundant winter resident along the coast and on inland reservoirs. The most commonly encountered gull on reservoirs in the western half of the state during winter. Fall migrants reach Texas in early September, and spring migrants depart by mid-April. Also uncommon to rare summer visitor throughout most of the state, but does not nest in Texas.

ROYAL TERN
Thalasseus maxima

BACKGROUND This is a large tern with a rather slim build. Like some other terns, this species is in full breeding plumage for a very short time. It holds the full black cap for only two to three months, and many adults will have already molted into nonbreeding plumage by mid-June. Small to even large groups of these birds often loaf together along beaches and tidal flats. Royal Terns can be seen flying over bays and the Gulf of Mexico looking down and then plunging into the water to catch fish.

IDENTIFICATION This large tern has a rather slender orange bill. Bill color ranges from a washed-out orange to nearly red, depending on the time of the year and breeding condition of the bird. The overall body plumage is white. The mantle is light gray with darker tips on the primaries. The mantle contrasts only slightly with the remainder of the body. The species has a short, forked tail. In the spring and early summer during the height of the breeding season, it has a completely black cap with a shaggy crest. During the remainder of the year the cap is reduced to a narrow, shaggy band reaching the back of the head and crest. The forehead and crown are white. Immature birds are similar to adults in winter plumage, with varying amounts of brown mottling on the upperparts and wings.

SIMILAR SPECIES The large size helps to eliminate almost all other species of terns that occur in Texas. The other large terns

Royal Tern, breeding plumage. Photo by Tim Cooper.

found in Texas are the Sandwich (*T. sandvicensis*) and the Caspian (*Hydroprogne caspia*). The Sandwich Tern is more slender, with longer wings, and it has a black bill. The Caspian Tern is larger and heavier, with broader wings. Its bill is thicker, less pointed, and redder, although this color varies depending on the time of the year. In nonbreeding plumage, the forehead and crown are black streaked with white, and there is no shaggy crest. The Royal Tern is very similar to the Elegant Tern (*T. elegans*) of the West Coast, but it is very unlikely that the Elegant Tern would be encountered in Texas.

HABITAT Almost exclusively in saltwater habitats. Found on coastal beaches and tidal flats. Nests on spoil and other similar islands in loose colonies.

STATUS AND DISTRIBUTION Common resident along the coast. Casual to accidental inland visitor, primarily in the eastern half of the state. The majority of inland occurrences are during the summer and fall after the passage of tropical storms.

FORSTER'S TERN
Sterna forsteri

BACKGROUND
Forster's Tern is one
of several medium-
sized terns that are similar in appearance. In winter
plumage, the comma-shaped black ear
patch is distinctive. This species is so similar
to the Common Tern (*S. hirundo*) that it was
not recognized as a distinct species until 1831.
Forster's Tern is the only tern restricted almost entirely to
North America.

IDENTIFICATION Adults in breeding plumage are almost totally
white with a black cap. The cap extends down to the eye, as is
the case with all *Sterna* species in North America. The bill is
orange with a black tip. The wings and mantle are pale gray,
contrasting with the remainder of the body plumage. The upper
surface of the primaries is pale silvery gray and usually lighter
than the mantle. The underside of the primaries has a darker
gray trailing edge and a narrow gray leading edge. The tail is
light gray with white outer edges and is deeply forked. The
white rump contrasts with both the mantle and the tail. Adults
in winter plumage are very similar overall but lack the black cap.
The most prominent feature is the black patch on each side of
the head that includes the eye and auriculars. A gray band across
the nape connects the black mask. The crown and forehead are
white. The bill is totally black in this plumage.

SIMILAR SPECIES Distinguishing among the medium-sized *Sterna* species is a challenge, particularly Forster's Tern, the Common Tern, and the Arctic Tern (*S. paradisaea*). The Common
Tern is an uncommon migrant along the coast and rare inland.

Arctic Terns are accidental migrants in Texas. Forster's Terns are bigger, but with shorter wings than Common Terns. When they perch, the tail extends well beyond the wing tips. Arctic Terns have much shorter legs and an even longer tail, and the trailing edge of the primaries has a sharp black line. In Common and Arctic Terns, the tail has dark outer edges with a white center, the opposite of the Forster's tail.

HABITAT Found in a variety of freshwater habitats, but most commonly seen over reservoirs and lakes. Also present on beaches and tidal flats, feeding in salt water.

STATUS AND DISTRIBUTION Common resident along the coast and common to uncommon migrant in nearly all parts of Texas. Fairly common winter resident on inland lakes and reservoirs east of the Pecos River away from the High Plains. Has been found nesting in small numbers at Choke Canyon Reservoir in Live Oak and McMullen counties, and at Lake Amistad, Val Verde County. The most common species of tern found wintering on inland reservoirs statewide; can be locally abundant along the coast during the winter.

Forster's Tern, breeding plumage. Photo by Tim Cooper.

BLACK SKIMMER
Rynchops niger

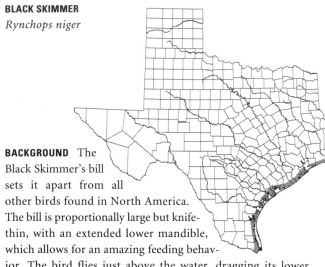

BACKGROUND The Black Skimmer's bill sets it apart from all other birds found in North America. The bill is proportionally large but knife-thin, with an extended lower mandible, which allows for an amazing feeding behavior. The bird flies just above the water, dragging its lower mandible through the water to catch small fish by touch and quick reflexes. Since the hunting strategy relies on touch rather than sight, night feeding is common. The behavior occurs during the day, but activity picks up at dusk and dawn as well as during the night. These elegant birds can be seen feeding in the lights of piers and other structures along the Laguna Madre and elsewhere. During much of the day, large groups loaf on tidal flats and other secluded areas. The Black Skimmer is the only member of its subfamily found in the Americas. The two other members, the African Skimmer (*R. flavirostris*) and the Indian Skimmer (*R. albicollis*), fill similar niches and use the same feeding method.

IDENTIFICATION A rather odd-looking bird that is somewhat ternlike, it has black upperparts that extend up the nape to the crown. The underparts are white. The bill is the most striking feature; this is the only species in North America in which the lower mandible is longer than the upper. The bill is bright orange with a black outer third. The wings are long, slim, and black with a white trailing edge. The tail is white with black central feathers. Adults in winter plumage differ only in having a

Black Skimmer. Photo by Tim Cooper.

white nape, although this feature can be indistinct in some individuals. Females are distinctly smaller than males. Juveniles have shorter bills and brown and white mottled upperparts.

SIMILAR SPECIES There really isn't anything in Texas that is likely to cause confusion. Perhaps when seen from a great distance, a resting American Oystercatcher (*Haematopus palliatus*) could look like a skimmer. American Oystercatchers have a large red bill and are largely dark above, but that is where the similarity ends, as they have sturdy legs, a brown back, and a bold white stripe on the wing.

HABITAT Found exclusively in saltwater habitats. Loafs on coastal beaches and tidal flats. Nests on spoil and other similar islands in loose colonies.

STATUS AND DISTRIBUTION Locally common resident along the coast. A vagrant inland, occurring most often on the Coastal Prairies. Scattered records from farther inland are mostly associated with the passage of a hurricane or tropical storm.

WHITE-WINGED DOVE
Zenaida asiatica

BACKGROUND
Beginning in the early 1970s, the White-winged Dove began its march north-ward. Before this rapid range expansion, it was a bird of the thickets and woodlands along the Rio Grande. The causes of this remarkable change in abundance and range are not known, but the White-winged Dove is now one of the most common urban birds in the southern half of the state. Nesting pairs have been recorded as far north as Amarillo and Denton, and it can't be long before it becomes a common resident in all areas of the state. Perhaps only the pine forests of east Texas will provide a barrier.

IDENTIFICATION This is a large- to medium-sized dove with gray-brown body plumage. In general, these birds have browner upperparts with gray underparts. This dove has prominent blue facial skin around the eye and black crescents on the cheeks. As the name suggests, there are large white stripes on the wings, and they are visible on the perched bird as well as in flight. The tail is short and rounded, with a broad white terminal band that is broken by the brownish central rectrices.

SIMILAR SPECIES Two somewhat similar dove species are found in Texas. The Mourning Dove (*Z. macroura*) is slightly smaller, with a long, pointed tail. It also lacks the broad white wing stripes and does not have the broad white tip to the tail. The second species is the introduced Eurasian Collared-Dove (*Streptopelia decaocto*), which is now a common sight throughout the state. Slightly larger but similar in overall proportion, it has much paler plumage and a thin black band across the nape. The collar may not be easily visible and is missing from immature birds, but the paler plumage and generally more uniform coloration of the wings and tail separate this bird from a White-winged Dove.

White-winged Dove. Photo by Mark W. Lockwood.

HABITAT Found in open woodland habitats as well as open shrublands with dense thickets of brush and small trees. This dove has also adapted well to urban habitats and agricultural areas.

STATUS AND DISTRIBUTION Common to abundant summer resident throughout much of the state and undergoing a range expansion. Now resident north almost to the Oklahoma border and east to Louisiana. An abundant urban species, with the largest population in Texas found within the city limits of San Antonio. Departs from rural areas in the northern portion of its Texas range in winter, but populations appear to remain unchanged in urban areas.

MOURNING DOVE
Zenaida macroura

BACKGROUND
Mourning Doves can
be seen in all areas of the
state except for very dense woodlands.
One reason this species is so common
across its distribution is that although each
nesting includes only two eggs, Mourning
Doves often nest five to six times per year. Occasionally,
clutches of three or four eggs have been noted, but they are the
result of more than one female laying eggs in the nest. The nest
is a flimsy structure, and these doves rarely leave the eggs unat-
tended.

IDENTIFICATION This medium-sized dove with grayish brown
plumage has upperparts that are darker than the buffier underparts. The wing coverts have prominent black spots that are easily visible on perched birds, as they are on many dove species.
Other plumage features include a black comma-shaped mark
on the cheek and an area of iridescent feathers on the side of the
neck. The tail is long and graduated, with white tips except on
the central rectrices. Males have a bluish gray cap and nape, but
this area is more olive-gray in females. Immature Mourning
Doves have a scaly appearance to their body plumage, but they
still have a graduated tail.

SIMILAR SPECIES The White-winged Dove is a larger species and
lacks a long, pointed tail. In addition, the White-winged has a
large white stripe in the wings that is visible perched or in flight.
The Inca Dove (*Columbina inca*) and Common Ground-Dove
(*Columbina passerina*) are smaller and look very scaled. These

species are unlikely to be confused with an adult Mourning Dove, but it might be an issue with an immature bird. The Inca Dove has a long tail with white outer rectrices that are not graduated and has rufous primaries. The Common Ground-Dove has a very short, rounded black tail, and its primaries are rufous as well. The introduced Eurasian Collared-Dove is much larger and heavier bodied, with a long square-tipped tail and much paler body plumage. As the name suggests, these doves have a distinct black line across the back of the neck as adults, but this mark is missing in immature birds.

HABITAT Found in almost all habitats in Texas with the exception of dense woodlands. Indications are that Mourning Doves are being displaced by White-winged and Eurasian Collared-Doves in urban areas.

STATUS AND DISTRIBUTION Common to abundant summer and winter resident throughout the state. Those that nest in Texas largely leave in the fall, only to be replaced by migrants from northern breeding areas. This species is the most abundant game bird in North America.

Mourning Dove. Photo by Tim Cooper.

INCA DOVE
Columbina inca

BACKGROUND The Inca Dove is a common sight in many towns and cities across the state. These small doves have been expanding their range northward and eastward over the past three or four decades. Although common in open habitats in the Southwest, they seem to have adapted well to urban environments, and perhaps that is a key to their continued movement northward. Inca Doves can be rather tame, and their complex social behavior can be readily observed. Males are often very territorial and readily attack other males that enter their territory. This behavior is often carried over to feeding stations, where scuffles are common during the breeding season. In another interesting action, the bird will hold a wing open and pointed skyward while sunning.

IDENTIFICATION This small, slender, long-tailed dove has tan body plumage with a pinkish cast. The most obvious aspect of the plumage is the thin black edge on the body feathers, which creates a scaled appearance. This is most obvious on the belly and upperparts, becoming less obvious on the breast and face. The central rectrices are brown, but the outer tail feathers have broad white tips and a white outer edge. The primaries and outer secondaries are red-brown with black tips. These field marks are readily visible when the birds are in flight. The bill is black, and the legs are pink.

SIMILAR SPECIES The Common Ground-Dove is found in similar habitats in the southern third of the state. This small dove also has a scaled appearance and reddish primaries, but its black tail is short and rounded. The bill of the Common Ground-Dove is pink with a black outer third. The Mourning Dove is considerably larger and gray-brown. It also lacks the prominent white outer tail feathers and reddish primaries.

Inca Dove. Photo by Greg W. Lasley.

HABITAT Found in arid habitats in the South Texas Brush Country and in the Trans-Pecos. Also in open habitats including open oak woodlands. They are, however, encountered most often in urban habitats.

STATUS AND DISTRIBUTION Common resident in the southern two-thirds of the state. Uncommon and generally confined to urban areas north to the Panhandle in Amarillo and east to the Pineywoods. This species, like the White-winged Dove, is expanding its range northward and eastward. It is much more often encountered in cities and towns than in rural areas.

COMMON GROUND-DOVE
Columbina passerina

BACKGROUND

More secretive than its cousin the Inca Dove (*C. inca*), this very small dove is more often seen coming to water or foraging along the edges of brushy areas. It is the smallest dove in Texas, although the Inca is similar in size. Common Ground-Doves form permanent pair bonds, and lone birds are rarely seen. As the name implies, they spend almost all of their time on the ground, foraging almost exclusively on the ground and building a flimsy nest on the ground as well. Their range is restricted to the southern third of Texas, but records indicate that they have wandered as far north as the Panhandle. Their range appears to be slowly expanding northward through the eastern Edwards Plateau.

IDENTIFICATION These are small, somewhat chucky-looking doves with a very short tail. The body plumage is tan with a pinkish cast. Thin black edges on the feathers, particularly on the underparts and head, give these birds a scaled appearance. The tail is short and black. The primaries and outer secondaries are red-brown with black tips, a field mark easily seen when the birds are in flight. The bill is pink with a black tip, and the legs are pink. The female's plumage is duller and less pink than the male's.

SIMILAR SPECIES The Inca Dove is similar but looks more scaled overall. Its primaries are reddish, but it has a long tail with white outer feathers. The Mourning Dove (*Zenaida macroura*) is much larger, with a long, graduated tail.

HABITAT Uses a variety of habitats across its range in Texas. In general, found in relatively dry, open habitats, including woodland edges, open shrublands, mesquite woodlands, thornscrub, and mixed desert scrub.

STATUS AND DISTRIBUTION Uncommon to locally common resident in the South Texas Brush Country, Coastal Prairies, and southern Trans-Pecos. In the Trans-Pecos, much more common along the Rio Grande than away from the river. Uncommon and local summer resident along the southern edge of the Edwards Plateau and on the upper coast.

Common Ground-Dove, male. Photo by Greg W. Lasley.

GREEN PARAKEET*
Aratinga holochlora

BACKGROUND

Green Parakeets add a tropical flavor to the birdlife of the Lower Grande Valley. These slender parakeets are often seen in large flocks during much of the year, but the flocks break up during the breeding season. There has been considerable debate about the origin of these birds, as well as the Red-crowned Parrots (*Amazona viridigenalis*) found in the same habitats. Certainly, parrots and parakeets are popular pets, and it is speculated that these birds were released or escaped during attempts to smuggle them across the border. There are populations of Green Parakeets within 100 miles of Texas, however, and it is certainly possible that some individuals moved north in response to extensive habitat loss in northeastern Mexico. Individuals of the southern red-throated subspecies have been reported, which suggests that they are escapees from captivity. The only species of parakeet that is indisputably native to Texas is the now extinct Carolina Parakeet (*Conuropsis carolinensis*). Once a fairly common resident along the Red River, these yellow and green birds were reported to wander into the eastern third of the state during the winter. The last report of this species in Texas was in 1897.

IDENTIFICATION Bright green with a long, pointed tail. The underparts are slightly paler than the upperparts. The underside of the flight feathers is yellowish, contrasting slightly with the rest of the body. The eye is surrounded by grayish skin,

Green Parakeet. Photo by Greg W. Lasley.

although this is not readily visible except at close range. Some individuals have orange flecks on the throat.

SIMILAR SPECIES No birds are readily confused with the Green Parakeet in the Lower Rio Grande Valley; however, two other Psittacids are found in the state. The introduced Monk Parakeet (*Myiopsitta monachus*) is found in several cities in the eastern half of the state. Monk Parakeets are also largely green, but they have a gray face and chest and contrasting blue flight feathers. The Red-crowned Parrot is also found in the Lower Rio Grande Valley. Considerably larger and chunkier, it lacks the long tail of a parakeet, and although green overall, it has a red crown and secondaries.

HABITAT Found primarily in urban habitats, particularly neighborhoods with large trees. In Mexico, it inhabits deciduous and pine forests.

STATUS AND DISTRIBUTION Uncommon to locally common resident, primarily in urban areas, of the Lower Rio Grande Valley. First reported in the state in 1960; by the early 1990s populations were well established.

YELLOW-BILLED CUCKOO
Coccyzus americanus

BACKGROUND

Although Yellow-billed Cuckoos are common in much of Texas, they are often hard to detect because of their secretive habits. They are also known colloquially as "rain crows," because their loud calls have been associated with coming thunderstorms. Certainly Yellow-billed Cuckoos are heard far more frequently than they are actually seen. A European relative, the Common Cuckoo (*Cuculus canorus*), is well known for laying eggs in the nests of other birds. The Yellow-billed Cuckoo usually raises its own young, but it will on rare occasions lay its egg in the nest of another cuckoo or, even less frequently, that of a different species. Currently, the Yellow-billed Cuckoo is considered monotypic, but some would divide the U.S. population into two subspecies, the western *C. a. occidentalis* and the eastern *C. a. americanus*. This is important because the western populations are declining rather rapidly. Conservation actions could be more easily initiated and funded if the western population were designated a separate subspecies. Migration timing in the eastern population is typically from early April to late May and from mid-August to mid-October, with a few lingering into late November. The western population does not arrive until late May to early June.

IDENTIFICATION This is a slender, medium-sized bird with a long tail. The upperparts are grayish brown, and the underparts are white. The tail is long and graduated, with large white tips on all but the central rectrices. A rufous patch in the primaries is obvious when this species is seen in flight. The bill has a curved culmen, with a black upper mandible and a yellow lower mandible. All cuckoos have zygodactylous feet, meaning that two toes point forward and the outer two point backward. Females are slightly larger than males. Juveniles are similar in appearance to adults, but their tail pattern is less distinct.

SIMILAR SPECIES The closely related Black-billed Cuckoo (*C. erythropthalmus*) has an obvious red orbital ring, a black bill, smaller white tips to the outer rectrices, and lacks the rufous primaries. Another species in the genus that is a very rare visitor to Texas is the Mangrove Cuckoo (*C. minor*). That species has a black mask, buff underparts, and no rufous on the primaries.

HABITAT Found in open woodlands with areas of denser vegetation. Tied to riparian corridors in many areas of the state, particularly true in the Trans-Pecos.

STATUS AND DISTRIBUTION Common migrant and summer resident throughout the eastern three-quarters of the state. Uncommon and local summer resident in the Trans-Pecos, and accidental winter visitor along the coast.

Yellow-billed Cuckoo. Photo by John D. Ingram.

GREATER ROADRUNNER
Geococcyx californianus

BACKGROUND
Perhaps more than any other bird, the Greater Roadrunner is associated with the southwestern deserts. In reality, it is found throughout the state. Where the dense forests of east Texas have been disturbed by human activity in the twentieth century, this species has moved in. These ground-dwelling birds are adept predators, feeding on snakes, lizards, birds, small mammals, and even scorpions and large centipedes. Roadrunners like to sun themselves; in particular, they may be seen turning their back to the sun and fluffing their feathers to expose the black skin and soak up the sun's rays. Roadrunners can run at speeds up to 20 mph when pursuing prey or escaping predators.

IDENTIFICATION The largest cuckoo found in the United States, this bird has powerful legs and feet to accommodate its terrestrial habits. It has a streaked appearance and generally looks brownish in color, but bright sunlight brings out the bird's iridescent olive-green plumage. The shaggy crest is often held erect. A prominent feature is the bare patch of blue and orange skin behind the eyes. It is capable of running at high speeds and has been clocked at close to 20 mph. Roadrunners have zygodactyl feet.

SIMILAR SPECIES No species found in Texas are likely to be mistaken for a roadrunner. The only species that is similar in appearance is the female Ring-necked Pheasant (*Phasianus* *colchicus*). Pheasants are found primarily in the Panhandle and South Plains in Texas; they lack the long, pointed bill of the roadrunner and the orange and blue exposed skin on the sides of the head.

HABITAT Found in a wide variety of habitats from open desert to open woodlands.

STATUS AND DISTRIBUTION Common to uncommon and local resident throughout the state, with the exception of the Pineywoods and northeast sector, where they are rare to uncommon and local.

Greater Roadrunner. Photo by Tim Cooper.

BARN OWL
Tyto alba

BACKGROUND

The Barn Owl is among the most widely distributed birds in the world, found on every continent except Antarctica. A cavity nester, it has adapted, as the name implies, to take advantage of man-made structures; but it is by no means restricted to barns or abandoned buildings and still occupies natural cavities, including caves. Females often have more colorful underparts, with large black spots. Some research has suggested that females with larger spots are more readily selected by potential mates. Barn Owls are largely nocturnal, but on occasion they can be found at dawn or dusk foraging over open habitats. Barn Owls select favored night roosts where they will rest and consume prey items. A peculiarity of the Barn Owl is its appetite for shrews, tiny mammals that hardly seem worth the energy expended to capture them. This has led some to wonder if ultrasonic sounds made by shrews in some way attract the Barn Owl. This owl's knack for catching shrews was discovered by mammalogists who dissected owls' regurgitated pellets looking at the fur and skeletons of small prey items.

IDENTIFICATION This is a large, distinctive owl with dark eyes and large white facial disks. The underparts vary from largely white, particularly in males, to a wash of yellowish brown. The breast and belly are lightly spotted with black, and the spotting is generally heavier in females. The upperparts, including the nape and crown, are golden brown mottled with gray.

SIMILAR SPECIES The only similar owl is the Snowy Owl (*Bubo*

Barn Owl. Photo by Greg W. Lasley

scandiacus), an extremely rare visitor to Texas. Snowy Owls are more uniformly white with yellow eyes.

HABITAT Found in open habitats. Tends to avoid closed-canopy forests.

STATUS AND DISTRIBUTION Easily overlooked, but appears to be a rare to locally common resident throughout most of the state. In particular, rare and local in the forested parts of the Pineywoods region and above 5000 feet in the mountains of the Trans-Pecos.

WESTERN SCREECH-OWL
Megascops kennicottii
and
EASTERN SCREECH-OWL
Megascops asio

BACKGROUND With the exception of the
High Plains, these owls are found throughout the state. Although the ranges of these sister
species overlap in the western Hill Country and the
Concho Valley, they are ecologically separate, with Westerns using more arid areas.
The Eastern Screech-Owl was a resident as
far west as southern Brewster County until
at least the early 1970s, but it is
now found no farther west than
the Devils River. Eastern Screech-
Owls appear to be more tolerant of
urban habitats, at least in Texas.

IDENTIFICATION Eastern and Western Screech-Owls
are very similar in appearance, with only minor
plumage differences. In general, they are small owls with gray
mottled upperparts and white spots on the shoulders. The
underparts are paler, almost whitish, and heavily streaked. The
facial disks have a prominent dark rim. The ear tufts can appear
exaggerated or almost unnoticeable, depending on the posture
of the bird. The eyes of both species are bright yellow. The Eastern Screech-Owl has red and gray morphs; the red morphs are
common only in east Texas. The bill color does differ between
the species; Westerns have a totally black bill, and Easterns have
a greenish bill. More important for identification is the voice.
The primary calls of the Eastern Screech-Owl include a
descending whistled whinny and a whistled trill. The Western
has a series of short whistled hoots that come closer together at
the end of the call, commonly referred to as a "bouncing ball"
call.

SIMILAR SPECIES The only small owl that could be readily confused with a screech-owl is the Flammulated Owl (*Otus flam-*

Western Screech-Owl. Photo by Mark W. Lockwood.

Eastern Screech-Owl. Photo by Mark W. Lockwood.

meolus). The Flammulated has a very different voice and reddish brown plumage, and it is found almost exclusively in the upper elevations of the mountains of the Trans-Pecos in pine-oak forests. It has been seen on many occasions as a migrant in the western third of the state, with scattered records from farther east. The Elf Owl (*Micrathene whitneyi*) is considerably smaller and different in plumage, and pygmy-owls have long tails and are streaked below.

HABITAT Found in a variety of woodland habitats. On the western Edwards Plateau, where the species ranges overlap, the Western Screech Owl occupies mesquite and live oak savannahs, as well as other upland habitats. In these areas, Eastern Screech-Owls are found much more commonly in riparian habitats.

STATUS AND DISTRIBUTION The Western Screech-Owl is a common to uncommon resident in the Trans-Pecos and western Edwards Plateau, found as far east as western Kerr County on the Edwards Plateau and Tom Green County in the Concho Valley. The Eastern Screech-Owl is a common resident throughout the eastern three-quarters of the state and is resident, at least locally, as far west as the Pecos River drainage. It has a less continuous distribution on the High Plains, occupying riparian corridors and urban areas with numerous trees.

GREAT HORNED OWL
Bubo virginianus

BACKGROUND

The Great Horned Owl is easily the most powerful of the owls found in Texas. An aggressive hunter, it is one of the primary avian predators in the southwestern deserts. The diet of these large owls can consist of small rodents up to large mammals such as skunks and raccoons, and they have been known to take even larger prey, such as roosting hawks and even a Great Blue Heron. The reintroduction program for the Endangered Aplomado Falcon (*Falco femoralis*) was hampered by the heavy toll these owls took on the newly released young falcons. Great Horned Owls take up residence in many habitats, including in urban environments. In urban settings they feed primarily on rats, but they have been known to capture domestic animals as well. A Great Horned Owl can lift large prey items, even those that are heavier than its own weight. It will often come out to a prominent perch just before dark and watch for prey. It is a very early nester, starting as early as January.

IDENTIFICATION This is a very large bird, easily the largest owl found in Texas. It has widely spaced ear tufts, but they can be inconspicuous at times. The plumage is heavily barred below and mottled with various shades of brown on the chest and upperparts, with a prominent white throat. The eyes are yellow.

SIMILAR SPECIES There are no widespread owls in Texas that are likely to be confused with this species. The Long-eared Owl (*Asio otus*), however, is similar in coloration and appearance. The Long-eared Owl is much smaller and slimmer, with more-prominent ear tufts that are spaced close together. It lacks the white throat of the Great Horned Owl and has orangish brown patches at the base of the primaries. It is an uncommon to rare winter visitor to the state, with most records coming from the northern third. The Barred Owl (*Strix varia*) has a different pattern to its plumage and is found in dense woodlands. This forest owl also has dark eyes.

HABITAT This very adaptable owl can be found in a wide variety of habitats, in open woodlands, desert scrublands, and riparian corridors. The only habitat where it is not routinely found is dense closed-canopy forest.

STATUS AND DISTRIBUTION Common resident in all areas of the state except the Pineywoods, where it is uncommon. May be most abundant in the deserts and open scrub habitats of the Trans-Pecos.

Great Horned Owl. Photo by Mark W. Lockwood.

FERRUGINOUS PYGMY-OWL*
Glaucidium brasilianum

BACKGROUND The Ferruginous Pygmy-Owl is a common and widespread tropical owl. The northern-most extent of the range barely enters the United States in Arizona and Texas. In Texas, this owl is most common in the open oak woodlands of the Coastal Sand Plain between Sarita and Raymondville. The species has been carefully studied and was at one time considered for listing under the Endangered Species Act in Texas; however, surveys on private ranches determined that it was much more common than originally thought. The discovery of the birds added an attractive ecotourism element on some of the ranches. Unlike most species of owls found in the United States, pygmy-owls are not strictly nocturnal. They are most active at dusk and dawn, but they also hunt during the day. They can also be vocal during the day, often attracting other small birds. Oddly enough, this owl's primary prey seems to be drawn to the owl's calls, responding with aggressive mobbing activity to chase the predator from their feeding or nesting territories.

IDENTIFICATION This is a small, long-tailed owl with a round head, ear tufts, and yellow eyes. The upperparts are rusty brown and spotted with white, and the underparts are white streaked with brown. The crown is finely streaked with white. The tail is long and rusty brown with darker brown bars. The sexes are similar.

SIMILAR SPECIES Two other small owls are found in south Texas. The subspecies of Eastern Screech-Owl that occurs in south

Texas has only a gray morph and is therefore easily distinguished from the rufous-brown pygmy-owl. The Elf Owl is similar in color but is not so prominently streaked below and has a very short tail. The Northern Pygmy-Owl (*G. gnoma*) is very similar, but its crown is spotted, not streaked, and it has different vocalizations. The Northern Pygmy-Owl is accidental in Texas; the state's two records are both from the Chisos Mountains of Big Bend National Park.

Ferruginous Pygmy-Owl Photo by Tim Cooper

HABITAT Found in the open live oak woodlands of Kenedy County and eastern Brooks County. Smaller populations exist in mesquite savannahs elsewhere in Brooks County. In Starr County, found primarily in the riparian corridor of the Rio Grande and the adjacent dense upland woodlands.

STATUS AND DISTRIBUTION Uncommon and local resident on the Coastal Sand Plain. Also a rare resident along the Rio Grande in Starr County. Starting in the late 1990s, appears to be colonizing areas in the Lower Rio Grande Valley where it has not been recorded in decades.

BURROWING OWL
Athene cunicularia

BACKGROUND

This distinctive owl is long-legged and diurnal. When approached, it will make itself less conspicuous by bowing, almost flattening itself on the ground, before deciding to flee an oncoming visitor. When flushed, it often gives a sharp chatter call. Burrowing Owls use existing burrows, most often those created by rodents, for nesting. The owl will scrape the insides of the hole with its bill, feet, and wings to shape the burrow to its needs. The availability of such nesting and roosting sites is a limiting factor in the distribution of this bird in Texas. Burrowing Owls are often associated with Black-tailed Prairie Dog (*Cynomys ludovicianus*) colonies. The decline of the prairie dog and the conversion of much of the prairie habitat to agriculture have caused a decline in this owl species. Burrowing Owls often perch on fence posts or other exposed areas while hunting. When loafing, they are most frequently seen at the mouth of a burrow.

IDENTIFICATION This is a small owl with very long legs. Females are larger than males but are otherwise indistinguishable. The head is rounded and lacks ear tufts. The plumage is sandy-brown, heavily spotted with white over the head and upperparts. The underparts are white with heavy barring and spotting with brown. The face is tan, with the auriculars outlined in white. The throat and chest are white and unmarked, with the exception of a black line like a necklace separating the two areas. The eyes are yellow. Although the feet and legs look naked from a distance, they are covered with hairlike feathers. The tail is very short and narrowly barred. Immature birds have bright buffy underparts that are particularly bright when the young first begin to come out of the burrow. As they mature, this coloration fades, becoming tan.

SIMILAR SPECIES This owl is unlikely to be confused with any other species. The combination of long legs and the habit of standing on the ground near a burrow make it easily recognizable.

HABITAT Open habitats, particularly grasslands. Also found in some desert habitats. Adapted to using farm fields where roosting sites and hunting areas are nearby.

STATUS AND DISTRIBUTION Uncommon to common summer resident in the western half of the state. During the winter, many summer residents depart but are replaced by migrants from farther north, becoming uncommon to rare winter residents. Rare to very rare migrant and winter visitor farther east to the Oaks and Prairies region and south to the Coastal Prairies.

Burrowing Owl. Photo by Mark W. Lockwood.

BARRED OWL
Strix varia

BACKGROUND
This is the forest owl found throughout the east half of Texas. Its call carries a long distance, which is why most owls are more often heard than seen. The typical call of the Barred Owl is often described as "Who cooks for you? Who cooks for you?" The similar call of the White-winged Dove (*Zenaida asiatica*), however, can be heard during the day in almost all areas of the state. As a predator, the Barred Owl is a generalist, feeding on a wide variety of birds, small mammals, amphibians, reptiles, and even invertebrates. One species readily preyed on is the much smaller Eastern Screech-Owl (*Megascops asio*); the Barred Owl homes in on the screech-owl's calls.

IDENTIFICATION This large, gray-brown owl has a round head without extended ear tufts. Like most other owls, it has obvious facial disks around dark eyes. The breast is barred, and the belly is paler and heavily streaked. The head and upperparts are brownish gray and mottled, with whitish to buff bars. The tail is of medium length and barred. The bill is dull yellow.

SIMILAR SPECIES The only other large owl found in the eastern two-thirds of Texas with dark eyes is the very pale Barn Owl (*Tyto alba*). The Spotted Owl (*S. occidentalis*) is similar in overall appearance, but it is heavily spotted rather than barred and streaked like the Barred Owl. The Spotted Owl is rare in Texas, found only in the Guadalupe and Davis mountains of the Trans-Pecos.

HABITAT Found only in forest habitats, but they use a wide variety of areas within those forests, ranging from swamps and riparian corridors to drier upland woodlands. The best-quality habitat appears to be larger, unfragmented blocks of forest. Often associated with old-growth forests.

Barred Owl. Photo by Tim Cooper.

STATUS AND DISTRIBUTION Uncommon to common resident in the eastern two-thirds of the state. Fairly evenly distributed in suitable habitat west to the eastern edge of the Edwards Plateau and Rolling Plains. Farther west, on the Edwards Plateau, in the eastern Panhandle, and in the northern portion of the South Texas Brush Country, found only along riparian corridors.

LESSER NIGHTHAWK
Chordeiles acutipennis

BACKGROUND The Lesser Nighthawk was formerly known as the Texas or Trilling Nighthawk. "Trilling" refers to the bird's distinctive call, somewhat reminiscent of an Eastern Screech-Owl (*Megascops asio*). Lesser Nighthawks deliver this call from a perch on the ground. They feed on whatever flying insects happen to be available on a given evening, apparently roaming over large areas in search of food and water before returning to the nesting or roosting site.

IDENTIFICATION A slender-bodied bird with long wings, it is buffy gray overall and heavily mottled with black, brown, and tan. The upperparts are more heavily mottled and darker than the underparts. The underparts are buffy and heavily barred. The tail is short, with a thin white subterminal band visible only at close range. The primaries have a white (in males) or buffy (in females) patch at about the midpoint. The patch is conspicuous in flight in males. The male also has a bright white throat; in the female the throat tends to be somewhat buffy.

SIMILAR SPECIES Although closely related to and very similar in appearance to the more widespread Common Nighthawk (*C. minor*), the Lesser Nighthawk has several distinguishing characters. The white patch on the primaries is closer to the tip of the wing in the Lesser Nighthawk. In females, this wing patch is usually buffy and inconspicuous. The tenth, or outermost, primary of the Lesser Nighthawk is shorter than the ninth, which makes the wing look rounded. The easiest way to distinguish

Lesser Nighthawk. Photo by Mark W. Lockwood.

these two species, however, is by voice. The low purr or trill of the Lesser Nighthawk is nothing like the nasal *peent* of the Common Nighthawk.

HABITAT Found in arid habitats, most common in open desert and brush country. In more open habitats, they tend to roost along dry washes and riverbeds where the vegetation is denser.

STATUS AND DISTRIBUTION Common to uncommon migrant and summer resident of the South Texas Brush Country north to the southern edge of the Edwards Plateau and central coast and west across the southern Trans-Pecos. Migrants begin to arrive in Texas in early April, and most have departed the state by late October. A locally rare winter resident in the western half of the South Texas Brush Country.

COMMON NIGHTHAWK
Chordeiles minor

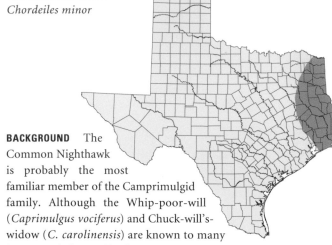

BACKGROUND The
Common Nighthawk
is probably the most
familiar member of the Camprimulgid
family. Although the Whip-poor-will
(*Caprimulgus vociferus*) and Chuck-will's-
widow (*C. carolinensis*) are known to many
because of their calls, fewer people have actually seen the
nighthawk's nocturnal cousins. The Common Nighthawk is
very active in the late afternoon through dusk as it captures flying insects on the wing. It can be seen in flight at any time of the
day; its presence is often first detected by hearing the sharp
peent call given in flight. During the day nighthawks sit motionless, with their eyes closed, on the ground, on tree limbs, fence
posts, or rooftops.

IDENTIFICATION The most conspicuous feature is the long, pointed wings. Overall, the bird is gray and heavily mottled with
black, brown, and tan. The upperparts are more heavily mottled and darker than the underparts. The underparts are white
and heavily barred, most heavily on the breast. The tail is short,
about the length of the closed wings. The tail also has a thin
white subterminal band visible only at close range. A white
patch close to the base of the primaries is conspicuous in flight,
but it can also be seen on roosting birds. Males have a bright
white throat; in females the throat tends to be somewhat buffy.

SIMILAR SPECIES The closely related Lesser Nighthawk (*C. acutipennis*) is very similar to the Common. Found primarily in
the Trans-Pecos and in the South Texas Brush Country, it has

seen elsewhere in the state. The Common Nighthawk has longer, more pointed wings and a longer tail than the Lesser. In the Common, the white patch on the primaries is halfway between the bend of the wing and the tip; in the Lesser, the white patch is much closer to the tip of the wing. The Common Nighthawk flies with slower, deeper wing beats and has a much less fluttery flight than the Lesser. The call of the Lesser Nighthawk is a hollow trill.

Common Nighthawk. Photo by Tim Cooper.

HABITAT Found in a wide variety of habitats, it has adapted well to urban settings. Seen in all areas of the state, except in very dense closed-canopy forests.

STATUS AND DISTRIBUTION Uncommon to common migrant and summer resident throughout most of the state. In the Piney-woods, a common migrant and rare summer resident. Frequently lingers into the winter in urban areas in the southern half of the state. Migrants are seen between early April and late May and again from early August to late October.

COMMON POORWILL
Phalaenoptilus nuttallii

BACKGROUND

Like many goat-suckers, this species is named for its call. At dusk in particular, the Common Poorwill can be heard calling incessantly from the dry hillsides of the Texas Hill Country or from a desert arroyo in the southern Trans-Pecos. A study of these birds discovered their surprising ability to enter a state of torpor under natural conditions. They are the only birds known to spend long periods of time during winter completely inactive, basically hibernating.

IDENTIFICATION The Common Poorwill is a small caprimulgid. It has a large, somewhat flattened head with large eyes and a small bill. The plumage is mottled with gray and brown and, on close inspection, intricately patterned with black, white, and tan. It has a broad white band across the throat. The wings are short and rounded with no white markings. The tail is also short, with broad white tips to the corners in the males and buffy tips in the females.

SIMILAR SPECIES Nighthawks have the same basic body type and coloration, but their wings are longer and thinner, with a white bar across the primaries. Chuck-will's-widow (*Caprimulgus carolinensis*) is found in neighboring habitats on the Edwards Plateau, but it is much larger and more rufescent in color. It is vocally distinctive as well. The Whip-poor-will (*Caprimulgus vociferus*) is found at much higher elevations where its range overlaps the Common Poorwill. Their plumage is similar, but the Whip-poor-will is slightly larger, with much more white in the tail, and is vocally distinctive.

HABITAT Found in open habitats with some woody vegetation: mixed desert scrub in the Trans-Pecos, Tamaulipan thorn-scrub in the South Texas Brush Country, and oak and mesquite savannah farther north. Can be found in areas with considerable brush if there are also ample open areas for foraging.

STATUS AND DISTRIBUTION Common to uncommon summer resident in most of the western two-thirds of the state. Uncommon to rare summer resident on the High Plains and northern Rolling Plains. Rare to locally uncommon winter resident in the southern third of the summer range. Determining the winter status is difficult because they are active only on warm nights.

Common Poorwill. Photo by Mark W. Lockwood.

WHIP-POOR-WILL
Caprimulgus vociferus

BACKGROUND

The plumage of
the Whip-poor-will
(and other nightjars)
is extremely cryptic, which
allows roosting birds to blend in with
the surrounding leaf litter or a tree branch.
The Whip-poor-will is named after its call,
which is often the primary means of detection
and identification as the birds pass through the eastern portion
of the state. Two distinctive subspecies are found in the United
States, and both occur in Texas. The eastern subspecies, *C. v.
vociferus,* is found during migration in the eastern two-thirds
of the state. The western subspecies, *C. v. arizonae,* is a summer
resident in the Trans-Pecos. The two subspecies are easily distinguished by their vocalizations and may represent separate
species.

IDENTIFICATION This medium-sized nightjar has a large, somewhat flattened head with large eyes and a small bill. The
plumage is mottled with gray and brown and is intricately
marked with black, white, and tan. A broad white band across
the throat is bordered by black both above and below. The
wings are short and rounded with no white markings. The male
has broad white tips on the outer three tail feathers. In the the
female these tips are buffy and much narrower.

SIMILAR SPECIES Chuck-will's-widow (*C. carolinensis*) is found
in the same habitats as migrating Whip-poor-wills in the eastern parts of the state, but it is slightly larger, much more rufescent in color, and vocally distinctive. The Common Poorwill is
found at lower elevations where the ranges of the two species

overlap in the Trans-Pecos. The plumage is similar, but the Whip-poor-will is slightly larger, has much more white on the tail, and is vocally distinctive as well. Nighthawks have longer, thinner wings with a white bar across the primaries.

HABITAT In the Trans-Pecos, found in pine-juniper-oak woodlands. More common in more mesic canyons than on the drier hillsides. Migrants can be found in a wide variety of woodland and forest habitats.

Whip-poor-will, eastern subspecies. Photo by Tim Cooper.

STATUS AND DISTRIBUTION Common summer resident at upper elevations in the mountains of the Trans-Pecos. Rare to uncommon migrant in the eastern half of the state west to the central Edwards Plateau. Casual migrant farther west to the High Plains and western Edwards Plateau. Spring migration extends from late March to mid-May, and fall migration occurs from late August to late October. Whip-poor-wills call, although often only briefly, at dusk and dawn during spring migration.

CHIMNEY SWIFT
Chaetura pelagica

BACKGROUND

This is the only swift likely to be seen in Texas, unless you live in the Trans-Pecos. These gregarious birds are a common sight over neighborhoods in the remainder of the state. They are most often seen in small groups, particularly in late summer when the young of the year join the adults in foraging bouts. In the spring and fall, they form enormous flocks that roost together, most commonly in abandoned industrial chimneys and similar structures. As the name suggests, they often use chimneys and other man-made structures for nesting. Natural cavities, such as hollow trees, are also important nesting habitats. The bird uses saliva to attach the nest to the structure and to hold the nest together. Chimney Swift towers are now available to help this species find suitable nesting sites in urban areas, as more chimneys are capped to keep the birds out.

IDENTIFICATION The gray-brown color of this swift is nearly uniform, although it is slightly darker on the upperparts. The lighter underparts are palest on the throat and chest. The tail is very short, with stiff bristles extending beyond the webbing of the feathers. The wings are long and slightly swept back. It is generally seen foraging over towns on rapid wing beats interspersed with long glides. Its presence is often given away by the flight calls, which consist of a rapid series of twittering sounds. The bird is often referred to as a "flying cigar."

SIMILAR SPECIES Only one other swift occurs regularly in Texas, the White-throated Swift (*Aeronautes saxatalis*). It is larger

Chimney Swift. Photo by Greg W. Lasley.

than the Chimney Swift and has a large patch of white that includes the throat and chest and extends down through the center of the belly. There are also white patches on the flanks. The Chimney Swift winters in South America; however, mid-winter *Chaetura* swifts should be carefully documented, since the very similar Vaux's Swift (*C. vauxi*) has been recorded in Louisiana during that season, although not in Texas.

HABITAT Adapted to urban habitats extremely well, and known for nesting in chimneys and other man-made structures. Occurs in natural habitats where hollow trees and other natural cavities with open tops are available for nesting and roosting. Forages over all habitats within the range in Texas.

STATUS AND DISTRIBUTION Common migrant and summer resident east of the Pecos River. In the Trans-Pecos, casual migrant and sporadic summer resident in the eastern half of the region. Rare, but appears to be increasing, during the summer in the Lower Rio Grande Valley. Spring migrants appear in early March, although they are not common until early April. Summer residents and fall migrants are present until mid-October, rarely lingering into November.

BUFF-BELLIED HUMMINGBIRD*
Amazilia yucatanensis

BACKGROUND

This hummingbird is found primarily from the Yucatan Peninsula northward along the Gulf Coast of Mexico to Texas. Unexpectedly, it moves northward along the Gulf Coast during the fall and can be found as far east as the Florida Panhandle in winter. A fairly large tropical species, it is often the only hummingbird found in woodland habitats in the Lower Rio Grande Valley. Other hummingbirds found in the region include migrant Ruby-throated Hummingbirds, a few breeding Black-chinned Hummingbirds, and migrant and winter resident Rufous Hummingbirds (*Selasphorus rufus*).

IDENTIFICATION This hummingbird is larger than the Rufous, Black-chinned, and Ruby-throated Hummingbirds, the other regularly occurring hummingbirds within the Buff-bellied's range. It is bright green on the head, throat, and upperparts, with a buffy belly and rufous tail. The bill is bright red with a black tip. The sexes are similar, but the female has a duller throat and those feathers are often edged with buff.

SIMILAR SPECIES Several species of *Amazilia* share a plumage pattern similar to the Buff-bellied's, and two of them, the Berylline Hummingbird (*A. beryllina*) and Rufous-tailed Hummingbird (*A. tzacatl*), could be confusing. The Berylline has occurred in the mountains of the Trans-Pecos, and the Rufous-tailed has been reported but remains undocumented within the normal range of the Buff-bellied in Texas. The Berylline can be identified by the dark upper mandible and the rufous color of the wings. The Rufous-tailed has a gray belly that contrasts with the rufous undertail coverts and has a more squared tail.

HABITAT A variety of habitats, ranging from city parks and gardens to the dense thorn-scrub of south Texas, but always with trees and dense shrubs.

STATUS AND DISTRIBUTION Uncommon to locally common summer resident in the Lower Rio Grande Valley and along the coast north to Victoria County. Appears to be edging northward up the coast and inland into south-central Texas. Almost annual during spring and summer up the entire coast and inland to Bastrop and Washington counties. Rare to uncommon and very local during winter, primarily at feeders and ornamental plantings in the Lower Rio Grande Valley and along the coast up to Calhoun County. Scattered records on the eastern edge of the Edwards Plateau and one from the Pineywoods.

Buff-bellied Hummingbird. Photo by Greg W. Lasley.

LUCIFER HUMMINGBIRD*
Calothorax lucifer

BACKGROUND
Although common
in portions of north-
ern Mexico, the Lucifer Hummingbird is uncommon and local in Texas
and the United States. Until recently, the
only place in the United States where it was
known to nest was in Texas, although small
numbers are now seen regularly in southeastern Arizona and
southwestern New Mexico as well. The first nesting record for
Texas was not discovered until 1962, despite the species' known
occurrence in the state since 1901. In the spring, this species visits tree tobacco, anisicanth, and ocotillo flowers, but by late
spring and early summer it can be found around the spectacular bloom spikes of century plants (*Agave* sp.). Lucifer and
Black-chinned Hummingbirds are the only species in the desert
foothills in the early summer, and both frequent these plants.

IDENTIFICATION A rather small hummingbird, slightly smaller
than even the Black-chinned, it has a relatively long and
decurved solid black bill. The male has a purple gorget with
extended corners and a green crown. The tail is long and forked,
although the fork is not evident on a perched bird. The green
flanks are often edged with a rich buffy color. The female has a
rich buff color to the underparts, although some individuals are
almost white below. Females have a dusky stripe through the
auriculars as well.

SIMILAR SPECIES Not many birds in Texas could be confused
with this species. The male Costa's Hummingbird (*Calypte
costae*), a very rare visitor to the state, is perhaps the best candidate. It shares the purple extended gorget of the Lucifer, but it

Lucifer Hummingbird, male. Photo by Mark W. Lockwood.

also has a purple crown. The combination of a decurved bill and buffy underparts sets the female apart from all other hummingbirds in the United States.

HABITAT The breeding habitat is the mixed desert scrub found in the foothills of the Chisos Mountains and surrounding area. After breeding, males can be found in the oak woodlands of those mountains, and they wander to similar habitats in the Davis and other mountain ranges in the southern Trans-Pecos.

STATUS AND DISTRIBUTION Locally uncommon summer resident in the Chisos Mountains of Big Bend National Park. Rare and local postbreeding visitor to the Davis Mountains, with the first birds usually arriving in late June. Scattered records from the Chinati and Glass mountains and the Sierra Vieja most likely refer to postbreeding wanderers as well. They arrive on the breeding grounds in early March, and individuals have stayed as late as early November. Elsewhere in the Trans-Pecos, it has been noted in the Guadalupe Mountains and in El Paso County. There are seven records from the Edwards Plateau, five of which involve postbreeding wanderers, and one spring record from the South Texas Brush Country. Also found south through the highlands of central Mexico. The northernmost populations withdraw into the remainder of the breeding range during winter.

RUBY-THROATED HUMMINGBIRD
Archilochus colubris
and
BLACK-CHINNED HUMMINGBIRD
Archilochus alexandri

BACKGROUND The only species in the genus *Archilochus,* the Ruby-throated and Black-chinned Hummingbirds are closely related. They are the common breeding humming-birds in Texas. Between the two of them, they are found in essentially all areas of the state. Spring migrants begin arriving in early March, and the last of the fall migrants are gone by mid-November most years. Although their respective breeding ranges border one another, neither species is known to nest in the other's breeding range.

IDENTIFICATION Males of these species are readily identified by their throat color. When the iridescence of the throat is not visible, however, tail shape is often a first clue. The male Ruby-throated Hummingbird has a longer and more deeply forked tail than a Black-chinned. Females are the real identification challenge, and many individuals may not be identifiable. In general, the best field mark is the shape of the outermost primary. In the Ruby-throated, the primaries are narrower and more tapered; as a result, the wing tip appears to taper to a point. In the Black-chinned the wing tip looks blunt. In addition, the Ruby-throated is brighter green above, particu-larly on the crown, and whiter below.

SIMILAR SPECIES A number of female and immature male hum-mingbirds can be difficult to distinguish from the more com-mon *Archilochus.* The only species that is occasionally confused for a male Ruby-throated is the Broad-tailed Hummingbird (*Selasphorus platycercus*), but it has a magenta throat and the tail shape is very different. Other species that can be confused with the female *Archilocus* are Costa's (*Calypte costae*), very rare in Texas; Anna's (*Calypte anna*), which is much larger and very green below; and the Calliope (*Stellula calliope*), a diminutive bird that has a very short bill and tail.

HABITAT Both species are found in a variety of habitats, ranging from open woodlands to urban environments. During migration, they can be easily enticed to feeders almost anywhere.

STATUS AND DISTRIBUTION As breeding species, these two closely related hummingbirds blanket the state. The Ruby-throated is a common summer resident in the eastern half, and the Black-chinned replaces it in the west.

The western limit of the Ruby-throated range is along the eastern edge of the Rolling Plains and Edwards Plateau southeastward to the Coastal Prairies. Common to abundant migrant across the eastern third of the state and uncommon spring and common fall migrant west through the Edwards Plateau and South Texas Brush Country. Rare to uncommon migrant on the High Plains, and casual spring and rare fall migrant in the Trans-Pecos. Very rare winter visitor along the coast and casual inland in the eastern half of the state.

The Black-chinned is a common to locally abundant summer resident in the western two-thirds of the state. Uncommon to rare summer resident south of the Balcones Escarpment. In migration, found much farther east, and rare to the Pineywoods. Rare in winter along the coast, mainly at feeders, and rare to very rare inland, as far north as the Panhandle.

Ruby-throated Hummingbird, male. Photo by Greg W. Lasley.

Black-chinned Hummingbird, male. Photo by Mark W. Lockwood.

BELTED KINGFISHER
Ceryle alcyon

BACKGROUND

The Belted Kingfisher is the most common and widespread kingfisher in Texas. During the winter it can be seen along rivers as well as around lakes and ponds throughout the state. It is most often seen on high perches watching for prey. Like the other kingfishers found in Texas, it dives headfirst into the water to capture fish just below the surface. It has a distinctive, loud dry rattle when perched or in flight. Belted Kingfishers are solitary, except during the breeding season. Kingfishers nest in burrows that are often in banks along rivers. The burrow is excavated by the pair and can be as much as six feet long. The nesting pair will range up to three miles from the nest when hunting for food for the nestlings. Kingfishers are primarily an Old World family; of the 91 species, only 6 occur in the New World. All of the species that occur in Texas feed primarily on fish, but some members of the family are forest-dwelling species and feed primarily on lizards; still others rely on insects for food.

IDENTIFICATION This is a medium-sized bird with a big-headed appearance, a prominent shaggy crest, and a long, heavy bill. Both sexes are slate blue above with a prominent white collar. The underparts are white, with a single blue breast band in the male. The adult female is similar to the male but has an obvious rufous band across the upper belly that also extends down the flanks. Immature birds are similar to adults but have a tawny breast band. Immature females also have a much-reduced rufous belly band.

Belted Kingfisher, male. Photo by Tim Cooper.

SIMILAR SPECIES This distinctive bird is likely to be confused only with other kingfishers. The Ringed Kingfisher (*C. torquatus*) is found in the South Texas Brush Country and along some rivers on the Edwards Plateau. It is much larger and has rufous underparts. The smaller Green Kingfisher (*Chloroceryle americana*) is found from the Edwards Plateau southward and is green above.

HABITAT Found around almost any freshwater habitat where fish are present. Also along the coast, estuaries, and bays. There are reports of Belted Kingfishers feeding in the open Gulf of Mexico as well.

STATUS AND DISTRIBUTION Uncommon to common winter resident throughout the state. Uncommon and local summer resident across the northern third of the state, becoming rare to very rare and local in summer in the remainder of the state east of the Trans-Pecos.

GREEN KINGFISHER*
Chloroceryle americana

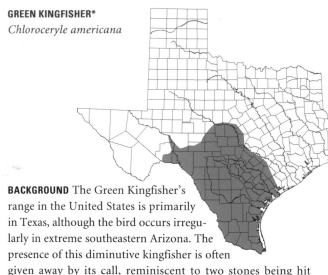

BACKGROUND The Green Kingfisher's
range in the United States is primarily
in Texas, although the bird occurs irregularly in extreme southeastern Arizona. The
presence of this diminutive kingfisher is often
given away by its call, reminiscent to two stones being hit
together, when approached. It is usually seen alone or in pairs.
Green Kingfishers are strongly territorial and usually remain in
the same area year-round. All kingfishers nest in a burrow they
dig themselves.

IDENTIFICATION Compared to the other kingfishers found in
Texas, this species is diminutive, less than nine inches in length.
Both sexes are emerald green above and white below. They also
share a prominent white collar and have considerable white
spotting in the wings. The male has a rufous band across the
breast, and the female has a speckled green band across the
upper breast.

SIMILAR SPECIES In Texas, this species is unmistakable. The
other kingfishers that occur in the state have slate-blue upperparts and are much larger. A tropical species, the Amazon Kingfisher (*C. amazona*), is very similar in color and pattern but is
approximately 1.5 times larger. It occurs as far north as southern Tamaulipas, Mexico, and could potentially occur in Texas.

HABITAT Primarily streams and rivers with low-hanging vegetation. Also resacas and manmade impoundments if there is suf-

ficient vegetation around the water to provide perches.

STATUS AND DISTRIBUTION Uncommon resident from the Edwards Plateau south to the Lower Rio Grande Valley. Rare in the lower Pecos River drainage and upriver along the Rio Grande to Big Bend National Park. Vagrants have been recorded during the summer as far north as Randall County in the Panhandle and east to Washington County. Appears to be sensitive to cold weather. During very cold winters, the northernmost populations retreat well to the south and often do not return for several years.

Green Kingfisher, male. Photo by Tim Cooper.

GOLDEN-FRONTED WOODPECKER*
Melanerpes aurifrons

BACKGROUND
The Golden-fronted Woodpecker is almost a Texas specialty from a United States perspective, although it ranges just into southwestern Oklahoma. This species is, however, widespread in Mexico and is found as far south as northwestern Nicaragua. The Golden-fronted Woodpecker is closely related to the Red-bellied Woodpecker (*M. carolinus*) of the southeastern United States and Gila Woodpecker (*M. uropygialis*) of the Sonoran Desert. The Golden-fronted and Red-bellied ranges overlap in a small area in the vicinity of Wichita Falls and along the Colorado River in the Hill Country. Occasional hybrids are found in these areas, but for the most part the species occupy different habitats. The Gila Woodpecker does not occur in Texas and is an unlikely vagrant as well.

IDENTIFICATION This medium-sized woodpecker has a strongly barred black-and-white back. The underparts are a uniform grayish tan and that color extends up through the unmarked face. The males have a red cap and an orange nape. The females lack the red cap, and both sexes have yellow nasal tufts. Both sexes also have a yellow wash over the belly, but this characteristic can be difficult to see in the field. The Golden-fronted Woodpecker's white rump is prominent in flight and contrasts strongly with the largely black tail. The outer rectrices are white with black markings. Immature birds lack any red or yellow coloration on the head for a brief period after fledging; they closely resemble a female Gila Woodpecker but lack the black-and-white barred central tail feathers of the Gila.

SIMILAR SPECIES The Red-bellied Woodpecker has a similar plumage pattern, but males have a red cap that extends down through the nape. In female Red-bellied Woodpeckers, the red is restricted to the back of the crown and nape. This species also has red nasal tufts. Immature Red-bellied Woodpeckers can look very much like a Golden-fronted, but they have barred central tail feathers like adults of that species. The Ladder-backed Woodpecker (*Picoides scalaris*) is much more common within the range of the Golden-fronted. A small woodpecker, the Ladder-backed has a strongly barred face and spotted underparts, and it lacks the white rump.

HABITAT Found in mesquite woodlands and other open brushy habitats. In the Hill Country, occupies open oak woodlands, but not in closed-canopy forests. On the western periphery of the range, restricted to riparian corridors.

STATUS AND DISTRIBUTION Common resident in the South Texas Brush Country north through the Edwards Plateau and western Rolling Plains to the south-central Panhandle. Also found in riparian habitats in the southern Trans-Pecos. Casual, primarily in winter, just east of the breeding range and on the High Plains.

Golden-fronted Woodpecker, male. Photo by Tim Cooper.

YELLOW-BELLIED SAPSUCKER
Sphyrapicus varius

BACKGROUND
Yellow-bellied Sapsuckers and the other species in the genus are well known for drilling rows of relatively shallow holes in trees for harvesting sap (thus the name "sapsucker"). They drill two basic types of holes: round, deeper holes are made specifically to probe for sap, and shallower holes maintain a continuous flow of sap at the surface.

IDENTIFICATION Yellow-bellied Sapsuckers are medium-sized woodpeckers. Adult males have a prominent red cap and throat. The throat patch is bordered by black, which extends into a bib on the upper breast. The remainder of the head is also largely black with two bold white lines. One line starts at the base of the bill and goes below the eye, and the other is a postocular stripe. The upperparts are mottled brown and white with black wings. The wings have a conspicuous white shoulder patch visible on the perched bird as well as in flight. The rump is white and obvious in flight. The underparts are yellowish with heavy barring on the flanks. The female is similar to the male except that she has a white chin, and some have a reduced crown patch. Immature birds are brownish with a muted pattern of the adults.

SIMILAR SPECIES The Red-naped Sapsucker (*S. nuchalis*) is similar in all plumages. The adult has a red spot in the white stripe across the back of the head, but this can be inconspicuous, and a few Yellow-bellied Sapsuckers have a similar feature. A more consistent field mark is the more extensive red throat in males that blends in to the black outline. The Red-naped also has less white on the back, and the white is restricted to two strips. The

Yellow-bellied Sapsucker, female. Photo by Greg W. Lasley.

female Red-naped has a red throat with a contrasting white chin. Immature birds can be difficult (and in some cases in early fall impossible) to separate. By early winter the plumage pattern of the adult starts to develop, and these birds can usually be identified.

HABITAT A wide variety of woodland habitats in winter. Most common in open woodlands, including in urban settings.

STATUS AND DISTRIBUTION Uncommon to locally common migrant and winter resident throughout most of the state. Rare in the western third of the Trans-Pecos. Fall migrants begin arriving in Texas in early October and are present through March, with a few lingering into April. There are even a few records of individuals staying as late as early May.

LADDER-BACKED WOODPECKER
Picoides scalaris

BACKGROUND
The Ladder-backed Woodpecker, often thought of as a desert bird, is seen in some expected places, such as flying from a cholla to an ocotillo. It is, however, a common woodpecker in woodland habitats in Texas as well. In fact, it is the common woodpecker in the oak-juniper woodlands of the Hill Country. It also occurs in open woodlands at high elevations in the Trans-Pecos.

IDENTIFICATION This is a small black and white woodpecker. Adults are mostly black above, heavily barred with white on the back. The wings are heavily spotted with white as well. The underparts are mostly dull whitish, often tinged with gray, and heavily spotted on the breast and flanks. The face is pale with a broad black eyeline and malar stripes that join around the auriculars. The male has a red crown that extends to the nape. The tail is black with white edges that are barred with black. Immature birds resemble the male, but the red crown is less extensive and spotted with black and white.

SIMILAR SPECIES The Downy Woodpecker (*P. pubescens*) is smaller, and its range overlaps only slightly in Texas, along the eastern Edwards Plateau. The Downy is unlikely to be confused with the male Ladder-backed because of the absence of a red crown. It is more similar to the female, but the Downy has a pure white stripe down the middle of the back and pure white underparts. The Hairy Woodpecker (*P. villosus*) is similar in plumage to the much smaller Downy Woodpecker, and its range overlaps with the Ladder-backed Woodpecker, except in Bastrop County, where the species occupy different habitats. The Golden-fronted Woodpecker (*Melanerpes aurifrons*) is found in many areas with the Ladder-backed, but it is very distinctive, with a plain face and underparts.

HABITAT A wide variety of habitats. Found in desert habitats where there is scattered woody vegetation with some plants large enough to support nesting cavities. Also in a wide variety of woodland habitats, including riparian corridors, pinyon-oak and oak-juniper woodlands, mesquite and oak savannahs, and urban habitats.

STATUS AND DISTRIBUTION Common to uncommon resident throughout the western two thirds of the state, east to the edge of the Blackland Prairies and up the coast to Matagorda County.

Ladder-backed Woodpecker, male. Photo by Tim Cooper.

DOWNY WOODPECKER
Picoides pubescens

BACKGROUND

This is the small-
est woodpecker to
occur in North Amer-
ica. The small size allows it to
feed on small branches and even weed
stems that are not easily exploited by larger woodpeckers. These birds are a classic
example of niche separation between sexes.
Males tend to spend more of their time foraging on smaller
branches, while females concentrate their efforts on larger
branches and trunks of trees.

IDENTIFICATION This small woodpecker has a proportionally
small bill. Adults are primarily black above with a white back
and white spots on the wings. The underparts are white and
unmarked. The head is mainly black with white stripes above
and below the black auriculars. The tail is black with white outer
feathers barred with black. The male has a red patch across the
nape.

SIMILAR SPECIES The Hairy Woodpecker (*P. villosus*) is similar
in plumage and general appearance but is considerably larger
with a proportionally larger bill. One plumage character that
separates these species is a black mark extending down from the
shoulder onto the side of the breast, which is longer and more
distinct on the Hairy Woodpecker. It also has completely white
outer tail feathers. These feathers are barred with black in a
Downy, but this feature is often difficult to see in the field.
Downy Woodpeckers are unlikely to be confused with the male
Ladder-backed Woodpecker (*P. scalaris*) because they have no
red crown. They are more similar to the female, but they have a

pure white stripe down the middle of the back and pure white underparts.

HABITAT In open woodlands and particularly common in riparian corridors. Less common in pure stands of coniferous trees than in more diverse forests. Also found in urban habitats and orchards.

Downy Woodpecker, male. Photo by Mark W. Lockwood.

STATUS AND DISTRIBUTION Common to uncommon resident in the eastern half of the state as far west as the eastern edge of the Rolling Plains and Edwards Plateau. On the Edwards Plateau, found only along the Colorado, Guadalupe, and Medina river drainages. Also a rare to uncommon resident in the eastern Panhandle as far west as Potter and Randall counties. During the winter, rare and irregular west of the normal range in all areas of the state except the Trans-Pecos and the South Texas Brush Country.

RED-COCKADED WOODPECKER
Picoides borealis

BACKGROUND The Red-cockaded Woodpecker is a rare bird over much of its range and is considered endangered by the U.S. Fish and Wildlife Service. In Texas, it is most common within the Sam Houston National Forest. A habitat specialist, it occupies open pine forests that require intensive fire management to prevent the understory and mid-story species, such as yaupon holly (*Ilex vomitoria*), from becoming dominant. This habitat is also important for another species of conservation concern, Bachman's Sparrow (*Aimophila aestivalis*). The Red-cockaded Woodpecker apparently ranged considerably farther west and north in Texas until the early 1900s. Eggs were collected in Lavaca and Lee counties in the late 1800s and early 1900s. In addition to being a habitat specialist, this woodpecker nests in live pines with red-heart disease. It drills wells around the nest opening to drain resin away, causing the area around the nest hole to become caked with oozing resin.

IDENTIFICATION This woodpecker is black and white, with a barred back and wings and largely white underparts. The sides of the chest are spotted with black, a pattern that continues down the flanks. The tail is black with white outer feathers. The forehead and crown are black, extending through the nape. The cheeks have large, unmarked white patches. Black malar stripes extend down the side of the neck. There is a small red patch on the male's head at the sides of the nape near the back of the white cheek, but this feature is rarely visible.

Red-cockaded Woodpecker, male. Photo by Greg W. Lasley.

SIMILAR SPECIES Within the habitat, two other species are similar in appearance, the Downy (*P. pubescens*) and Hairy (*P. villosus*) Woodpeckers. The Hairy Woodpecker is similar in size but has a white unbarred back, and its flanks are unmarked as well. The face of the Hairy has a prominent black bar through the cheek, and the male has a red patch on the nape. The Downy Woodpecker is much smaller, with a proportionally smaller bill. In addition, its plumage pattern is much like the the Hairy's.

HABITAT Open pine forests that contain longleaf (*Pinus palustris*) and loblolly pines (*P. tada*).

STATUS AND DISTRIBUTION Rare to locally uncommon resident in open pine forests in the southern half of the Pineywoods.

NORTHERN FLICKER
Colaptes auratus

BACKGROUND There are two distinct color morphs of the Northern Flicker, those with yellow flight and tail feathers and those with red. Those with yellow feathers were formerly known as Yellow-shafted Flickers, and, of course, those with red were Red-shafted Flickers. Intergrades between the two color morphs are fairly common and can have varying combinations of characteristics. This can include a combination that mimics the plumage pattern of the Gilded Flicker (*C. chrysoides*), which has never been documented in the state and is probably best considered an unlikely vagrant from the Sonoran Desert. Flickers feed mainly on the ground, primarily on ants.

IDENTIFICATION This medium-sized woodpecker has a brown body heavily barred with black above. The underparts are lighter brown and heavily spotted with black. The rump is white and easily seen when the bird is in flight. The upper surface of the tail is black in both morphs as well. In addition to the yellow flight feathers, the yellow-shafted morph has a tan face with a gray crown and nape. The male has a black mustache and a red nape patch. In the red-shafted

Northern Flicker, red-shafted male. Photo by Greg W. Lasley.

birds, the face is gray with a brown crown and nape. The males have a red mustache.

SIMILAR SPECIES The brightly colored flight feathers are unlike any other species that occurs in Texas. The brown body plumage also separates this species from other woodpeckers found in the state.

HABITAT Found in any open woodland habitat, including open oak and even mesquite woodlands.

Northern Flicker, yellow-shafted female. Photo by Tim Cooper.

Also found along edges of closed-canopy forests and in urban areas where large trees and snags are present.

STATUS AND DISTRIBUTION Common to uncommon summer resident in the Panhandle and South Plains and at mid- and upper elevations in the mountains of the Trans-Pecos. Farther east, uncommon to rare summer resident in the Pineywoods, primarily in towns and cities. Common winter resident throughout the northern two-thirds of the state, becoming rare in the southern South Texas Brush Country. The two color morphs have different ranges in the state, with intergrades occurring most frequently from the Panhandle south to the western Hill Country. The yellow morph breeds in the eastern half of the state and is present in winter as far west as the central High Plains and south to the Lower Rio Grande Valley, where it is very rare. Rare and irregular winter visitor west through the Trans-Pecos. The red morph breeds in the Trans-Pecos and in northwestern Texas and is found in winter throughout the western two-thirds of the state, becoming increasingly less common eastward.

PILEATED WOODPECKER
Dryocopus pileatus

BACKGROUND The largest woodpecker found in Texas, this bird is adept at excavating cavities, both for nesting and in search of food. Like many other woodpeckers, it feeds primarily on wood-dwelling ants and beetles. These insects are common in downed trees, and as a result Pileated Woodpeckers are often seen on fallen logs and on the ground. Because of its particular ability to excavate cavities, this species plays an important part in the overall forest ecosystem. Many other birds, mammals, and other organisms use the variety of cavities produced by these birds for shelter and nesting.

IDENTIFICATION This large woodpecker is often compared to a crow in size. Overall the body plumage is black in both sexes. Both sexes also have a white line that extends from the bill across the cheek and down the neck. The female has a white postocular stripe and a white throat. Males have a small white eyebrow, a white throat, and a bright red crest; females, however, have a black forehead and a smaller red crest. The wings are mostly black from above with some white markings at the base of the primaries. From below, the wing linings are white, contrasting strongly with the black flight feathers. The tail is entirely black, and the bill is black on the upper mandible and horn colored on the lower.

SIMILAR SPECIES No other living woodpecker in Texas is similar in size to the Pileated Woodpecker. The Ivory-billed Woodpecker (*Campephilus principalis*) is even larger, but it has not been documented in the state since 1902. With the recent tantalizing reports from Arkansas, the possibility that the Ivory-billed still exists can't be ignored. It differs by having a large whitish bill, a black throat and crown, a white line extending down the side of the neck onto the back, and very large white patches on the wings.

HABITAT Old-growth and otherwise mature coniferous or deciduous forests. Also found in lower densities in younger forests that have scattered older trees and a few large, dead trees.

STATUS AND DISTRIBUTION Uncommon to locally common resident in the Pineywoods and Post Oak Savannahs. Vagrants have been found on a few occasions on the Edwards Plateau and eastern Rolling Plains.

Pileated Woodpecker, male. Photo by Tim Cooper.

VERMILION FLYCATCHER
Pyrocephalus rubinus

BACKGROUND

The Vermilion Fly-catcher is one of the most striking birds found in Texas, and it is unusual among flycatchers as well, because of the striking differences in plumage between the males and females. During the breeding season, the male performs a spectacular courtship display. He will fly as much as 50 feet above the canopy of the woodland and begin a fluttering flight with his head cocked back as he sings a twittering song. After several of these flights, the male then brings a butterfly or other showy insect to the female. During the spring and summer, the male will even perform the courtship flight at night. These birds can be conspicuous and even tame around human habitats, although they can be hard to detect along riparian corridors as they perch high in the canopy. They are most common where water is nearby but are not restricted to such areas. In areas with a low canopy, they will often perch in the shade close to the ground.

IDENTIFICATION This flycatcher is named for its brilliantly scarlet crown, lower face, and underparts. The upperparts are dark brown, as are the nape and a line through the eye. The female has grayish brown upperparts, including the upper half of the head. The underparts are white from the throat through the belly, and the undertail varies from yellowish to pink. The breast, flanks, and belly are streaked with grayish brown. Females also have whitish lores and a weak supercilium. First-fall birds resemble adult females. First-winter males acquire pinkish red coloration on the belly and undertail. Second- and even third-year males resemble fully adult males, but the red portions of the plumage are paler and can look washed out.

SIMILAR SPECIES Say's Phoebe (*Sayornis saya*) is somewhat similar in plumage pattern to a female Vermilion Flycatcher. Its belly and undertail coverts are orangish buff or tawny, but it lacks the whitish, streaked chest and pale supercilium. Although structurally very different, the male Scarlet Tanager (*Piranga olivacea*) shares the scarlet underparts and dark wings. These birds lack the dark back and mask.

Vermilion Flycatcher, male. Photo by Tim Cooper.

HABITAT Found in mixed desert scrub, particularly around water sources. Often found around urban settings and around isolated houses. May also be found in open habitats that are not near water.

STATUS AND DISTRIBUTION Uncommon to common summer resident in the southern Trans-Pecos, Edwards Plateau, and South Texas Brush Country. Farther north, rare summer visitor throughout the High Plains and Rolling Plains. Uncommon winter resident along the Rio Grande in the southern Trans-Pecos eastward through the South Texas Brush Country and along the Coastal Prairies.

GREAT KISKADEE*
Pitangus sulphuratus

BACKGROUND

The Great Kiskadee is a common sight, particularly along watercourses, in South Texas. It is one of those Texas specialties that attract traveling birders, even though the species is common through much of Latin America. The common name comes from the song, a loud *kis-ka-dee*. Kiskadees are omnivorous; in addition to catching insects on the fly, they will eat berries, grab a lizard or other small vertebrate, and are even known to plunge into ponds to catch fish. The distinctive coloration of the Great Kiskadee is unique in Texas, but the plumage pattern shows up in many species of various genera in Latin America. These birds are monogamous and maintain pair bonds as long as both adults survive the rigors of life in the wild. The nest is a basketball-sized structure with an entrance on the side. The young look much like the adults when they leave the nest.

IDENTIFICATION This medium-sized bird has a brown back and rump and bright yellow chest and belly. The head is striped with black and white, with the crown and wide eye line in black. The white stripe extends from the forehead through the eyebrow, and the throat is white. The yellow central crown patch is often concealed, but it can be conspicuous at times. The feathers of the wings and tail are edged in rufous, a feature that is visible and obvious both perched and in flight.

SIMILAR SPECIES The species is unmistakable in the United States, and there are no confusing species in south Texas. Within 200 miles of the Texas-Mexico border, however, are two sim-

Great Kiskadee. Photo by Tim Cooper.

ilarly patterned species: the Social Flycatcher (*Myiozetetes sim-ilis*) and the Boat-billed Flycatcher (*Megarynchus pitangua*). The Social Flycatcher has been documented in Texas, but it is much smaller than the kiskadee, with a small bill and without the rufous coloration of the wings and tail. The Boat-billed Fly-catcher has a much heavier bill and lacks the rufous tones in the upperparts.

HABITAT Found in a wide variety of habitats, including wood-lands, forest edges, brushy watercourses, and urban areas.

STATUS AND DISTRIBUTION Locally common resident in the Lower Rio Grande Valley. Uncommon and local resident northward along the Rio Grande and its tributaries to southern Val Verde County. Also an uncommon and local summer resi-dent along the coast to Calhoun County. Seems to be expand-ing its range farther up the coast and has nested in the greater Houston area. There are isolated records from all of the ecolog-ical regions of the state except the Pineywoods.

WESTERN KINGBIRD
Tyrannus verticalis

BACKGROUND
The Western King-
bird is found in almost
every town as well as around
farm and ranch houses in the western
half of the state. These tyrant flycatchers
loudly defend their territory from other
kingbirds; where multiple pairs are present,
there seems to be a constant battle raging. This continues
through the entire spring and summer, as these birds will
attempt more than one nesting when conditions are favorable.
By late summer, when all of the young have fledged, the population seems overwhelming as they sit in the trees or on power
lines around a rural residence.

IDENTIFICATION This is a large flycatcher with a yellow belly and
light gray breast. The upperparts are olive-brown with contrasting darker wings. The head is light gray, with a slightly lighter
throat and breast. The tail is blackish with bright white margins.
The Western and other kingbirds have a red central crown
patch that is very rarely visible.

SIMILAR SPECIES Three other yellow-bellied kingbirds are found
in Texas. Cassin's Kingbird (*T. vociferans*), found primarily in
the Trans-Pecos, has a darker gray head with a contrasting
white chin. It also has a black tail, which has a thin whitish terminal band. In south Texas, Couch's Kingbird (*T. couchii*) is a
common look-alike. It has a browner tail with a noticeable
notch, a yellow chest, and a longer bill. In the Lower Rio Grande
Valley and locally in the Big Bend area, the Tropical Kingbird
(*T. melancholicus*) is also present. It shares the plumage char-

acteristics of Couch's Kingbird and is indistinguishable except by voice.

HABITAT Found in open habitats with scattered large trees. The planting of trees around rural farm and ranch houses has increased the available habitat and allowed this species to colonize the Great Plains.

STATUS AND DISTRIBUTION Common to uncommon summer resident in the western two-thirds of the state. In the eastern third, uncommon to locally common summer resident, but generally absent from the Pineywoods. In the Trans-Pecos, generally found at elevations up to 5000 feet. Common to uncommon migrant throughout the state west of the Pineywoods, where it is very rare. Western Kingbirds arrive in mid-April, and the breeding population disperses by late August, with few remaining into September. Lingering fall migrants have been noted as late as mid-October and very rarely into November.

Western Kingbird. Photo by Greg W. Lasley.

EASTERN KINGBIRD
Tyrannus tyrannus

BACKGROUND

The Eastern King-
bird is a widespread
and fairly conspicuous
species in the eastern third of the state,
where it basically replaces the Western
Kingbird. This tyrant flycatcher frequently
perches concealed in treetops but also is often
seen on fences and utility lines. Much like the Western Kingbird, during the breeding season these birds are fiercely territorial. They will aggressively defend territories from other kingbirds, and also from much larger species such as hawks and
crows. Eastern Kingbirds feed their young for about seven
weeks, much longer than most passerines of their size. Caring
for dependent young for this long a period generally precludes a
second nesting attempt when the first one is successful. During
the time Eastern Kingbirds are in Texas, they eat primarily flying insects and only small amounts of fruit, in strong contrast
to their winter diet, which consists largely of fruits. During
migration, these birds frequently congregate in large flocks,
sometimes numbering in the thousands. In Texas, this behavior
is most often seen along the upper and central coasts.

IDENTIFICATION This large flycatcher is sharply bicolored. The
head and upperparts are blue-black, and the underparts are
white. The wings are also dark, with some thin white edgings on
the wing coverts and tertials. The tail is black with a wide white
terminal band. Like other kingbirds, the Eastern has an inconspicuous red crown patch that is rarely visible. Immature birds
are similar to the adults, but they are brown on the upperparts

and have wider edgings on the wing feathers. The juvenile is similar but browner.

SIMILAR SPECIES The Eastern Kingbird is unmistakable in Texas. The Gray Kingbird (*T. dominicensis*), an accidental visitor to Texas, has gray upperparts and a much larger bill.

HABITAT Found in open habitats, including open pastures with only scattered trees. Also denser patches of trees and forest edges with surrounding open country, and frequently urban habitats, such as neighborhoods with large trees, parks, and golf courses.

STATUS AND DISTRIBUTION Common to uncommon summer resident in the eastern third of the state. Present more locally as far west as the central Panhandle and the eastern edge of the Edwards Plateau. As a migrant, common to uncommon through the eastern two-thirds of the state. The migration periods are between late March and mid-May and mid-August to early October, with stragglers present into early November.

Eastern Kingbird. Photo by Greg W. Lasley.

SCISSOR-TAILED FLYCATCHER
Tyrannus forficatus

BACKGROUND

With its long forked tail and pink flanks, the Scissor-tailed Fly-catcher is one of the most recognizable birds in Texas. It is common in a wide area between the Trans-Pecos to the west and the Pineywoods to the east. Like other kingbirds, this graceful bird is most often seen on a fence or telephone wire. It was once placed in a separate genus because of its more slender body and long tail, characteristics that make it more aerodynamic and much more aerial than other *Tyrannus* species. It forms large roosts in late summer and fall in preparation for migration. The roosts can contain as many as 1000 birds, and they may gather in towns.

IDENTIFICATION This large, distinctive flycatcher is pearly gray above with a whitish head and breast. The flanks and undertail coverts are salmon pink, becoming very bright under the wings. This bright color is often visible on perched birds around the front of the folded wing. The wings are blackish and contrast strongly with the back. The tail is very long, particularly in adult males. The central rectrices are black, and the outer tail feathers are white with black tips.

SIMILAR SPECIES The pale plumage and long tail set the adult apart from any other regularly occurring birds in Texas. The extremely rare Fork-tailed Flycatcher (*T. savana*) has occurred in the state a few times; it resembles the Scissor-tailed in shape but has a black cap and wings. The Fork-tailed also has a long tail, but the tail is almost totally black and the feathers flutter when in flight. A juvenile Scissor-tailed could be mistaken for a Western Kingbird, but it would have pink rather than yellow on the breast.

HABITAT Found in any open habitat during migration; during breeding season, however, it is a species of savannahs. Also found around farm and ranch houses with large trees, and in urban settings as well.

Scissor-tailed Flycatcher, male. Photo by Tim Cooper.

STATUS AND DISTRIBUTION Common to abundant summer resident throughout the eastern three-quarters of the state. Uncommon to rare in the eastern Trans-Pecos and in the western Panhandle. Spring migrants and residents arrive in southernmost Texas in late February and are present throughout the state by early April. In the fall, a few are often present well into November and occasionally through December, particularly along the coast. Many records of birds overwintering at scattered locations throughout much of the state, most commonly along the coast and particularly in the South Texas Brush Country.

LOGGERHEAD SHRIKE
Lanius ludovicianus

BACKGROUND At first glance, the Logger-head Shrike may not look like a predator, since it looks like many other passerines, but it is well known for its hunting prowess. It does not have strong legs or feet with obvious talons like many other avian predators, but it does have a strong bill with a hook on the upper mandible. The bird uses that bill to immobilize prey items, then employs thorns, yucca leaves, and even barbed wire to impale large prey. Sometimes shrikes leave the item or will ingest it by pulling it into small pieces. The Loggerhead Shrike has declined dramatically in the northeastern portion of its range, but populations appear to be stable in Texas.

IDENTIFICATION This is a medium-sized bird with gray overall coloration. The upperparts are bluish gray with strongly contrasting black wings and tail. The underparts are white and generally unmarked. An obvious field mark is a black mask that extends through the eye and includes the auriculars. The mask also extends over the bill on the forehead. Shrikes have hooked bills, although this feature is not as prominent in the Logger-head as in some other shrikes. Juvenile birds are similar to the adult but are duller gray with faint barring over much of the body.

SIMILAR SPECIES The species most likely to be encountered with potential for confusion is the Northern Mockingbird (*Mimus polyglottos*). It is similarly colored and patterned, but it lacks the black mask and also has a narrow, pointed bill. The North-

Loggerhead Shrike. Photo by Tim Cooper.

ern Shrike (*I. excubitor*) is a rare but regular winter resident in the Panhandle. This related species is larger and is paler in overall coloration, with a larger bill that has a pale base to the lower mandible, a narrower black mask that does not extend across the forehead, and faint barring on the chest. Juvenile Northern Shrikes are similar to adults but are brown. After the post-juvenile molt, they are gray with a brown wash of color remaining on varying parts of the body.

HABITAT Found in open habitats where somewhat concealed perches are available. Often perches on fences and power lines when loafing.

STATUS AND DISTRIBUTION Ranges from a rare to locally common resident in much of the state. Generally absent in summer from much of the South Texas Brush Country and the southwestern Edwards Plateau. Generally more common as a migrant throughout the state. Migrants from nesting areas farther north bolster the more localized resident populations.

WHITE-EYED VIREO
Vireo griseus

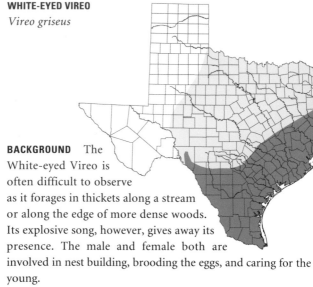

BACKGROUND The White-eyed Vireo is often difficult to observe as it forages in thickets along a stream or along the edge of more dense woods. Its explosive song, however, gives away its presence. The male and female both are involved in nest building, brooding the eggs, and caring for the young.

IDENTIFICATION This vireo is grayish overall with yellow highlights in its plumage. A prominent feature of adults is the white iris, which is obvious when the bird is seen well. Immature birds have brown eyes. These birds have yellow spectacles, although the yellow lores are often the most prominent portion of this feature. The upperparts are greenish gray, and this color extends up through the nape to the crown. The underparts are white with yellow on the side of the breast down through the flanks. The wings are grayish brown with two white or yellowish wing bars. The wing feathers are edged with yellow as well. The bill is black.

SIMILAR SPECIES All other vireos found in Texas have dark eyes. The Blue-headed Vireo (*V. solitarius*) has prominent white spectacles and a slaty blue crown and nape. Bell's Vireo (*V. bellii*) is drab, without the bright yellow plumage features of the White-eyed Vireo. Bell's Vireo does have weak spectacles and a similar color pattern, but the absence of the yellow spectacles and white eyes readily eliminates this species. The Yellow-throated Vireo (*V. flavifrons*) has bright yellow on the throat that extends down through the upper breast.

HABITAT Found in brushy habitats, including scrub in open woodlands, margins of woodlands with closed canopies, overgrown pastures and old fields, and thickets along watercourses. In the western portion of the range, found in open shrublands that have developed in former savannahs and thickets along arroyos.

STATUS AND DISTRIBUTION Common to uncommon migrant throughout the eastern two-thirds of the state, becoming increasingly rare farther west. Common to locally abundant summer resident through the eastern two-thirds of the state west to the central Edwards Plateau. Uncommon and local west through the Concho Valley and western Edwards Plateau. Locally uncommon to rare winter resident from the southern Pineywoods westward to the Balcones Escarpment, and uncommon to common south of the Edwards Plateau.

White-eyed Vireo. Photo by Greg W. Lasley.

BLACK-CAPPED VIREO*
Vireo atricapilla

BACKGROUND The Black-capped Vireo is almost a Texas specialty in terms of its range in the United States. Oklahoma is the only other state where it occurs. The southwestern Edwards Plateau appears to have the largest population in the United States. The Black-capped Vireo is a habitat specialist, requiring open shrublands where foliage is present down to ground level. Heavy browsing by livestock or deer that changes the structure of the vegetation often makes habitat unsuitable for this vireo. Management of Brown-headed Cowbirds (*Molothrus ater*) to reduce the threat of nest parasitism plays an important role in the protection of this endangered species. Cowbirds are known to lay eggs in vireo nests, causing the vireos to spend the nesting season raising cowbirds rather than their own young.

Black-capped Vireo, male. Photo by Greg W. Lasley.

IDENTIFICATION This is the smallest vireo to occur in the United States. The male has a distinctive black cap that contrasts sharply with the olive-green upperparts. The bold white spectacles are broken with black above the red eye. The underparts are white with olive-yellow flanks, and the wings are dark with two pale bars.

Second-year males have a gray nape that separates them from fully adult birds. The female differs from the male by having a slate-gray cap and duller upperparts. Immature birds are similar to the adult female, except that they have brown eyes and a grayish wash to the underparts.

Black-capped Vireo, female. Photo by Mark W. Lockwood.

SIMILAR SPECIES Several other Texas vireos have white spectacles. The species most likely to cause confusion is the Blue-headed Vireo (*V. solitarius;* formerly known as the Solitary Vireo, which is now recognized as three closely related species). The Blue-headed is much larger than a Black-capped and has unbroken white spectacles. Because of its slate-gray cap, it would be confused only with the female Black-capped. Cassin's Vireo (*V. cassinii*), which is very similar to the closely related Blue-headed, occurs regularly in the western extent of the Black-capped Vireo's range.

HABITAT Found in brushy habitats with some open space. In the eastern half of the species' distribution in Texas, these habitats are generally early successional areas. As the habitat continues to mature, it becomes unusable by the vireos.

STATUS AND DISTRIBUTION Rare to locally uncommon summer resident on the Edwards Plateau west to Big Bend National Park and north to Taylor and Palo Pinto/Jack counties. Rarely reported during migration, but a few reports come from outside the breeding range. Nesting birds arrive on the breeding grounds in late March and early April, and most depart by early September.

BLUE-HEADED VIREO
Vireo solitarius

BACKGROUND
The Blue-headed Vireo is one of three species once included under the name "Solitary Vireo." This is the most likely member of the complex to be found east of the Pecos River. The other species are the Plumbeous Vireo (*V. plumbeus*) and Cassin's Vireo (*V. cassinii*). All three species are strongly patterned and generally easily recognizable, although there are some identification issues to be resolved. All three also occur in Texas, but there is not much overlap between the eastern Blue-headed Vireo and the two western species. The Blue-headed Vireo and the White-eyed Vireo (*V. griseus*) are the only vireos likely to be encountered in the winter in Texas. The Blue-headed is deliberate in its movements and can often be easily followed as it forages in the midstory of a woodland. This behavioral characteristic, along with the heavy bill, helps to distinguish it from warblers.

IDENTIFICATION This medium-sized bird is large compared with other vireos. Adults have olive-green upperparts with slightly darker wings exhibiting two bold white or yellowish wing bars. The underparts are white with yellow flanks. They have a blue-gray cap with bold white spectacles and a white throat. Males are generally brighter than females. First-winter birds are similar to the adult, but with slightly duller plumage.

SIMILAR SPECIES Cassin's Vireo is so similar to the Blue-headed that they may not be distinguishable under some circumstances. Fortunately, the ranges of these two birds don't overlap much. Cassin's Vireo is an uncommon migrant through the Trans-Pecos and rare migrant through the western High Plains. It differs from the Blue-headed in having grayish white underparts (including the throat and chin) and lacking a strong contrast between the nape and back. The back half of the crown and nape are olive, which often makes the forecrown and mask appear dull bluish gray. The Plumbeous Vireo has gray upperparts with white edging on the flight feathers. The female Black-capped Vireo is much smaller and has broken spectacles.

HABITAT Found in woodland or forest habitats in Texas, including both coniferous and mixed forests. In the western portions of the winter range in Texas, most frequent in riparian corridors.

STATUS AND DISTRIBUTION Common to uncommon migrant in the eastern three-quarters of the state and rare farther west. Also an uncommon winter resident in much of the eastern two-thirds of the state. Migrants are present from late March to mid-May and late August through most of October.

Blue-headed Vireo. Photo by John D. Ingram.

BLUE JAY
Cyanocitta cristata

BACKGROUND

The Blue Jay is an aggressive and noisy bird and one of the most common urban-adapted birds. This jay, like many other species of birds, hides food for later use, often storing much more than it can possibly eat. Many theories attempt to explain this phenomenon, but perhaps these birds are simply driven by instinct or are removing food from potential competitors. Blue Jays are also at least partially migratory. In the fall large flocks are occasionally encountered in the eastern half of the state. During the winter, invasions westward have been noted, with birds being displaced as far west as El Paso. Perhaps these winter invasions are the origin of the isolated populations in towns along the western edge of the range. In many parts of the Blue Jay's range, populations have declined rather dramatically over the past few decades. This is most frequently tied to habitat loss, in particular the removal of trees, such as oaks, that are used by the birds when foraging.

IDENTIFICATION This large bird has mostly blue plumage and a prominent crest. The upperparts are bright blue, contrasting with the gray-white underparts. The head is mostly blue with a conspicuous crest, and there is a black necklace across the breast that continues up around the back of the head below the crest. It has black-barred wings and tail, with prominent white markings as well.

SIMILAR SPECIES The Blue Jay is fairly unmistakable within its range in Texas. The two other blue-colored jays in the state are easily identifiable. Steller's Jay (*C. stelleri*) is found primarily in the Davis and Guadalupe mountains of west Texas, but occasionally it irrupts into other parts of west Texas in winter. It is similar in size and shape, but the body is a much darker blue and the head and crest are black. The more widespread Western Scrub-Jay (*Aphelocoma californica*) does not have a crest and lacks the black-and-white barring on the wings and tail.

HABITAT Found in woodland and forest habitats. Also common in urban settings, especially where large oaks are present.

Blue Jay. Photo by John D. Ingram.

STATUS AND DISTRIBUTION Common resident in the eastern half of the state. Uncommon and local on the western Edwards Plateau and eastern High Plains. In the western edge of the range, primarily restricted to urban habitats. Very rare south of the Nueces River, although there has been one nesting record in the Lower Rio Grande Valley.

GREEN JAY*
Cyanocorax yncas

BACKGROUND The
Green Jay is one of
the more spectacular birds
found in Texas, providing a tropical
flare to the birds of south Texas. The
species is frequently considered a specialty
of the Lower Rio Grande Valley, but it is actually found far north as Corpus Christi and Eagle Pass. Despite
the flashy plumage, it can be inconspicuous as it moves through
the thorn-scrub. Its presence is often given away by its rather
varied calls. Green Jays are monogamous and retain the pair
bond for life. Only if one of the pair dies will the other adult
search for another mate. Green Jay flocks generally contain the
breeding pair and that year's offspring. Occasionally these
flocks can contain the previous year's offspring that did not
attract mates. These older birds will help in defending the
breeding territory and act as helpers at the nest until the new
fledglings join the flock. The Green Jay occurs through Mexico
into Central America and also in South America. The South
American birds are found in the Andes, and the blue is replaced
with yellow except below the eye. They also have a more prominent frontal crest and yellow eyes. Some authorities have suggested this disjunct population may represent a separate species.
IDENTIFICATION This jay has spectacular plumage with a long tail.
It is similar in size to other jays found in Texas. The fairly bright
green on the upperparts contrasts somewhat with the lighter
yellow-green underparts. The forehead, crown, and nape are
purplish blue, and a crescent of blue is under and just behind

the eye. The throat and breast are black. There is also an area of black in front of the eye, with a short line through the eye. The bird also has blue nasal tufts.

SIMILAR SPECIES No species that occurs in Texas is likely to be confused with the Green Jay.

HABITAT Found in both open and closed-canopy woodlands. Also found in dense secondary growth and brushy Tamaulipan thorn-scrub. Adapted to human disturbance and found in urban areas with large trees and in citrus groves.

STATUS AND DISTRIBUTION Common to uncommon resident from the Lower Rio Grande Valley north through most of the South Texas Brush Country. During the winter, found north of the breeding range to southern Val Verde, Kinney, and Uvalde counties.

Green Jay. Photo by Tim Cooper.

WESTERN SCRUB-JAY
Aphelocoma californica

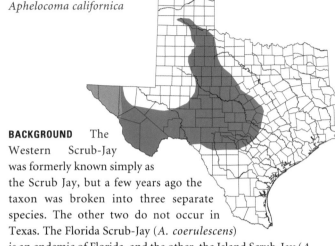

BACKGROUND The Western Scrub-Jay was formerly known simply as the Scrub Jay, but a few years ago the taxon was broken into three separate species. The other two do not occur in Texas. The Florida Scrub-Jay (*A. coerulescens*) is an endemic of Florida, and the other, the Island Scrub-Jay (*A. insularis*), is found on Santa Cruz Island off the California coast. The Western Scrub-Jay can be further divided into three groups, each of which may represent separate species. The birds along the Pacific slope of the United States are much more brightly colored than birds found in the interior. Birds found in Texas can be referred to as Woodhouse's Scrub-Jay and are duller and less well-marked. The third group is found in central Mexico and is whiter below.

IDENTIFICATION Similar in size to other jays that occur in Texas, this species has a long tail that gives it a slimmer appearance than other jays. The head and upperparts, including the wings and tail, are grayish blue with a contrasting dull brown back. The underparts are light gray with a contrasting whitish throat. The whitish eyebrow can be inconspicuous. The auriculars are gray, contrasting somewhat with the surrounding blue. The bill is stout and black.

SIMILAR SPECIES This scrub jay is generally not found with other species of jays, except for Blue Jays on the eastern edge of the Edwards Plateau. It differs from the Blue Jay in its much duller plumage, lack of a crest, and very distinct vocalization. Steller's

Western Scrub-Jay. Photo by Mark W. Lockwood.

Jays can occasionally be found with Western Scrub-Jays during winter irruptions into lower elevations in the Trans-Pecos. Steller's Jay has a prominent crest and blue underparts. The closely related Mexican Jay (*A. ultramarina*) is found in the Chisos Mountains, where this scrub jay does not occur under normal circumstances, although Western Scrub-Jays occasionally wander to the Chisos during winter irruptions. Mexican Jays are more uniform blue-gray and lack the brown back of a scrub jay. They also lack the necklace and white eyebrow.

HABITAT Found primarily in oak-juniper woodlands on the Edwards Plateau and Trans-Pecos. Also in open juniper woodlands on the Rolling Plains and the southeastern Panhandle.

STATUS AND DISTRIBUTION Common resident on the Edwards Plateau west through the mountains of the central Trans-Pecos. Rare to locally uncommon resident in the canyonlands of the southern Panhandle southward through the western Rolling Plains. Irruptive and irregular elsewhere in the Trans-Pecos, Rolling Plains, and High Plains, particularly in winter.

MEXICAN JAY
Aphelocoma ultramarina

BACKGROUND The Mexican Jay has also been known as the Gray-breasted Jay. As the current name suggests, its range is primarily in Mexico, reaching the northern extremes in Texas and Arizona. The distribution resembles a large horseshoe, and the birds on either end are more different than at any other two points in the range. Those in Arizona belong to the subspecies *A. u. arizonae,* and the birds in Big Bend belong to *A. u. couchii.* They are not known to wander away from their feeding territories, which are maintained year-round. In fact, there are only two records in Texas away from the Chisos Mountains, one near Alpine in 1935 and the other just east of El Paso in 2001. The bird from El Paso belonged to the Arizona subspecies. Mexican Jays have rather complex social behavior. They spend the entire year in groups of as many as 25 individuals. A group will maintain several nests within its feeding territory. Only one pair per nest is involved in nest-building, incubation, and brooding, but the entire group may be involved in feeding the young. Genetic studies have shown that not all young in a nest have the same male parent, even though only one male is directly involved in the nesting attempt.

IDENTIFICATION This jay has grayish blue upperparts and grayish underparts. The back is slightly grayer than the remainder of the upperparts. The tail is long and blue. The bill and legs are black.

SIMILAR SPECIES No other jays occur regularly within the Mexican Jay's range in Texas, but the Western Scrub-Jay (*A. califor-*

nica) has occurred on rare occasions. Scrub-jays have a gray-brown back, a gray necklace across the chest, and a white eyebrow. The necklace separates the whiter throat and breast from the grayish white belly.

HABITAT Mixed woodlands at mid and upper elevations of the Chisos Mountains, composed largely of oaks with smaller percentages of other hardwoods and conifers.

STATUS AND DISTRIBUTION Common resident of the Chisos Mountains of Big Bend National Park.

Mexican Jay. Photo by Mark W. Lockwood.

AMERICAN CROW
Corvus brachyrhynchos

BACKGROUND
This crow is the most widespread and probably best-known of the solid-black corvids in Texas. It is much more obvious in winter, when the Texas population is bolstered with migrants from farther north and they congregate in large flocks. American Crows often form large communal roosts, sometimes numbering in the thousands. Young birds do not reach maturity until they are at least two years old, and most do not breed until they are at least four. Young from previous broods sometimes remain with their parents and help with the next year's nesting attempt.

IDENTIFICATION The American Crow is glossy black with a slightly rounded tail.

SIMILAR SPECIES The ranges of three other solid-black corvids overlap with the American Crow in Texas. The Fish Crow (*C. ossifragus*) is the most similar, but it is smaller and its voice is more nasal (usually heard as a double call). The Fish Crow occurs primarily along the Sabine River and the eastern half of the Red River in Texas. The Common Raven (*C. corax*) overlaps with the American Crow in winter on the eastern Edwards Plateau. Larger than crows, it has a wedge-shaped tail, a much heavier bill, shaggy throat feathers, and a deeper and rougher voice. In flight, the primaries of the Common Raven are more distinct and fingerlike, and the tail shape is more readily apparent. The Chihuahuan Raven (*C. cryptoleucus*) is found more commonly with American Crows than the previous species, and it is about the same size. This raven, however, has a wedge-shaped tail, a slightly heavier bill, and a distinctive voice.

HABITAT Very adaptable to a wide range of habitats. Requires open areas for feeding, with scattered trees for nesting and roosting, so the primary habitat type where this species is *not* found is closed-canopy forest. Frequently found in man-made habitats such as agricultural lands, city parks, golf courses, and other urban environments.

American Crow. Photo by Mark W. Lockwood.

STATUS AND DISTRIBUTION Common to abundant resident in the eastern half of the state west to the central Panhandle and to the eastern edge of the Edwards Plateau. Rare to locally uncommon migrant and winter visitor farther west, including the remainder of the High Plains, western Rolling Plains, eastern Edwards Plateau, and eastern parts of the South Texas Brush Country. Also a common to uncommon and local winter visitor in the El Paso area.

COMMON RAVEN
Corvus corax

BACKGROUND

The Common Raven is the largest songbird found in North America. It has an interesting distribution, both in terms of range and ecology. Within its wide distribution, across North America and Eurasia, southward into Central America and northern Africa, it occupies habitats ranging from the high Arctic tundra to low deserts. Through much of the range, however, this is a bird of forests and woodlands. Common Ravens form long-term pair bonds and defend their territory throughout the year. As a result, even small flocks of Common Ravens are seldom seen, other than during the brief time when fledglings are being cared for by the adults.

IDENTIFICATION This very large corvid has glossy black plumage, long pointed wings, and a wedge-shaped tail. The feathers on the throat are elongated and pointed. The bill is heavy and solid black. When seen in flight the primaries are distinct and finger-like.

SIMILAR SPECIES The ranges of two solid-black corvids overlap with the Common Raven in Texas. The Chihuahuan Raven (*C. cryptoleucus*) is the most similar and can pose an identification challenge. Smaller, with a shorter bill and a different voice, it also has longer nasal bristles that extend almost half the length of the bill. It was formerly known as the White-necked Raven because the body feathers are white at the base, rather than gray, a feature most often seen on the longer, more flexible feathers on the neck. Chihuahuan Ravens congregate in large flocks in

Common Raven. Photo by Tim Cooper.

the fall and winter, unlike the Common Raven, which remains in pairs or small family groups year-round. The American Crow (*C. brachyrhynchos*) is considerably smaller, with a rounded, rather than wedge-shaped, tail and a very different voice.

HABITAT In Texas, found primarily in montane habitats in the Trans-Pecos. On the Edwards Plateau, found in oak-juniper woodlands as well as oak and mesquite savannah. Less common at lower elevations in desert habitats in the Trans-Pecos.

STATUS AND DISTRIBUTION Uncommon to common resident in the mountains of the Trans-Pecos and east through the Edwards Plateau. Rare winter and casual summer visitor to the High Plains and southern Rolling Plains.

PURPLE MARTIN
Progne subis

BACKGROUND

One of the best-known birds of the eastern United States, the Purple Martin is so well adapted to human environments that it has become dependent on nest boxes. The reliance on nest boxes appears to be more prevalent in eastern North America than in the West, perhaps because of the higher human population and the greater availability of nest boxes in the East. Purple Martins still use natural cavities to a large extent in the western part of the range.

IDENTIFICATION This is the largest swallow in Texas. The adult male is glossy purplish blue. The female is a duller purplish blue on the upperparts and mostly gray below. The belly is normally paler gray than the breast, almost whitish on some individuals. The female has a prominent grayish collar that can be difficult to see in poor light. The wings are pointed, with the typical swallow shape, and the tail is shallowly forked.

SIMILAR SPECIES The Purple Martin is larger than other swallows. The all-dark plumage, particularly of the male, also separates it from other swallows in Texas. Seen in flight, the European Starling (*Sturnus vulgaris*) can be confused with Purple Martins. The introduced starling is similar in shape, but its flight is not as buoyant or acrobatic as the swallow's. On closer inspection, the black plumage and long bill also easily separate this species.

HABITAT Well adapted to human-altered habitats, to the point that the species seems increasingly dependent on nest houses in urban environments. In general, requires large open areas and is more frequent near water.

STATUS AND DISTRIBUTION Common to uncommon summer resident in most of the state east of the Pecos River. Rare and local to absent on the western High Plains. Common to locally abundant migrant in the eastern two-thirds of the state, becomes less common farther west. Very rare to casual migrant in the Trans-Pecos. Spring migrants start arriving in Texas early in the year, with the first birds appearing in early January. Migrants are still moving through the state into early April, and most fall migrants have departed Texas by early October. There are a few records of birds lingering along the coast and in the Lower Rio Grande Valley into the early winter.

Purple Martin, male on left and female on right. Photo by Greg W. Lasley.

CAVE SWALLOW*
Petrochelidon fulva

BACKGROUND
The Cave Swallow is a fairly recent coloniz-er in the United States. The species was first found in the United States in Florida in 1890 and in Texas in 1910. That marked the beginning of a range expansion that continues today. The monitoring of the occurrence of this species at Carlsbad Caverns National Park in New Mexico provides an excellent example of the change in status of the Cave Swallow. The first two nesting pairs of Cave Swallows were found in Carlsbad Cavern in 1966. In the late 1990s the cavern population had grown to more than 2500 pairs. During that time, the population in Texas expanded from a few caves and sinkholes on the southwestern Edwards Plateau to most of the state, with only the Panhandle and Pineywoods remaining uncolonized. In natural caves, these birds nest in the twilight zone, often placing their nests in areas with minimal light. Cave Swallows nest in colonies and are most often found in single-species groups.

IDENTIFICATION This swallow is similar in size to the Barn and Cliff (*P. pyrrhonota*) Swallows. It is a stocky swallow with a dark, square tail. The upperparts are blue with an obvious buffy rump. The underparts are grayish white with a buffy throat. The crown is blue-black with a chestnut forehead. The buffy throat expands into the collar.

SIMILAR SPECIES The Cliff Swallow is closely related and in many areas occurs with the Cave Swallow. They are very similar in appearance, but the Cliff Swallow has a cream-colored forehead and dark throat. Some individuals will also have a chestnut forehead, but they still have the dark throat.

HABITAT Formerly restricted to nest sites in natural caves. In recent decades it has adapted to man-made structures such as bridges and culverts and has even begun to use buildings. During the day, it forages over nearby open areas.

STATUS AND DISTRIBUTION Common to locally abundant summer resident in the southern half of the state, north through the Edwards Plateau to the southern Rolling Plains and west through the Trans-Pecos. Uncommon, but increasing, in the southern Post Oak Savannahs. Rare to very rare north to the South Plains and north-central Texas. Also rare and local during the summer on the upper coast. During the winter, rare to uncommon in the southern third of the state north to Bexar and Val Verde counties. Migration ranges from early February to mid-April and from mid-August to late October.

Cave Swallow. Photo by Mark W. Lockwood.

BARN SWALLOW
Hirundo rustica

BACKGROUND
The Barn Swallow is the most abundant and widespread swallow in the world. In the New World, this species breeds throughout the vast majority of North America and winters mostly in the southern hemisphere. Before European colonization of the New World, Barn Swallows nested in caves and other natural features that provided overhead protection for the nest. With the spread of buildings across what is now the United States, these birds rapidly adapted to structures that provided the same quality as their natural nesting sites. The conversion is so complete that the species is very rarely found nesting in caves. Barn Swallow populations found across Eurasia are different in plumage coloration: generally white below rather than the continuum of cinnamon to pale buff seen in North America. Research on this species suggests that tail length and symmetry are indicators of the reproductive quality of the bird. Females appear to prefer males that have the longest and most symmetrical tails. These traits seem to be transmitted directly to the offspring.

IDENTIFICATION The Barn Swallow is similar in size to other swallows found in Texas. It looks more slender than Cliff and Cave Swallows, and its build is more similar to that of a Tree Swallow (*Tachycineta bicolor*). It has deep blue upperparts and cinnamon to pale buff underparts. The forehead and throat are reddish brown, and the throat is bordered by a dark breast band. The tail is deeply forked, with long outer rectrices. Males have much longer tails than females and juvenile birds. Female and juvenile birds are similar in coloration and generally have duller plumage than males.

SIMILAR SPECIES No other swallow with a long forked tail occurs regularly in the United States. Cliff and Cave Swallows are different in structure and color, but they could be confused with a short-tailed juvenile Barn Swallow. Both species have a square tail, pale collar, and buffy rump.

HABITAT Found in a variety of open habitats. Since it has adapted extremely well to human habitation, structures for nesting must be in the general area during that season. During migration, any open habitat can be utilized, including agricultural areas, urban areas, and natural savannahs.

STATUS AND DISTRIBUTION Locally uncommon to common summer resident throughout the state. Common to abundant migrant throughout. Migrants pass through Texas between mid-March and mid-May and from mid-August to late October. Very rare winter straggler along the coast and in the South Texas Brush Country, but unlikely that any actually overwinter in these areas.

Barn Swallow. Photo by Greg W. Lasley.

CAROLINA CHICKADEE
Poecile carolinensis

BACKGROUND

The Carolina Chickadee is the most common chickadee that occurs in Texas. The only other chickadee found in the state is the Mountain Chickadee (*P. gambeli*), which occurs regularly only in the Guadalupe and Davis mountains in the Trans-Pecos. The Carolina Chickadee is an endemic species in the southeastern United States, although wandering individuals have been found only a few hundred feet from Mexico in the Lower Rio Grande Valley. Wandering outside the normal range appears to be fairly rare, although there are several records from the South Texas Brush Country. The species is a prominent part of winter feeding flocks within its normal range. These chickadees are often found in small flocks of up to eight birds, serving as leaders of these flocks, helping to alert other species to potential threats. Research has shown that the dominant pair in these flocks is the first to establish breeding territories in the summer. Pairs of these chickadees appear to form long-term bonds.

IDENTIFICATION This small, agile bird has a distinct black cap and bib contrasting sharply with the white sides of the face. The upperparts are gray and the underparts are white, with a tinge of rusty brown on the flanks. It has short wings and a moderately long tail.

SIMILAR SPECIES Although the Carolina Chickadee is extremely similar to the Black-capped Chickadee (*P. atricapillus*), it is not an identification problem in Texas; the Black-capped has been documented in the state on only one occasion. In general, the Black-capped Chickadee is slightly larger and has more white in its wings, especially on the edges of the greater wing coverts and outer secondaries. The Black-capped has a slightly larger black bib that is more ragged on the edges. The song of the Carolina Chickadee consists of four to six whistled notes, *fee-bee-fee-bay*. The Black-capped Chickadee has a shorter song, of two or three whistled notes, *fee-bee* or *fee-bee-bee*.

Carolina Chickadee. Photo by Greg W. Lasley.

HABITAT Deciduous and mixed deciduous-coniferous woodlands. Suitable woodlands can be found in uplands as well as in swamps, along riparian corridors, and in urban habitats.

STATUS AND DISTRIBUTION Common resident in the eastern half of the state west to the west-central Edwards Plateau and south to the Nueces River at Nueces County on the Coastal Bend. Uncommon to common in the eastern Panhandle and along the Canadian River valley as far west as Oldham County.

TUFTED TITMOUSE
Baeolophus bicolor
and
BLACK-CRESTED TITMOUSE
Baeolophus atricristatus

BACKGROUND These noisy birds are a common sight in woodland habitats in most of the state. They are usually seen in pairs, or in family groups during the summer and early fall. Although they can be hard to find at times during the spring and summer as they forage silently, more often they announce their presence by their harsh calls. During the winter, titmice are a frequent component of foraging flocks and are often the first to announce the presence of a potential predator. Titmice are early nesters, often having fledglings out of the nest at the height of migration in April and early May. They nest in cavities, using old woodpecker nests, nest boxes, or natural cavities. Tufted and Black-crested Titmice were formerly considered one species. In a narrow area where the ranges of these species come together, hybrids outnumber the parental types. The hybrids most commonly have a dark chestnut patch on the forehead with a crest that varies from light to charcoal gray.

IDENTIFICATION These small, agile birds have a long tail, prominent crest, and gray overall plumage with orange-buff flanks. The underparts are generally paler gray than the upperparts. The Tufted Titmouse has a gray crest with a black forehead. The Black-crested has a black crest with a pale gray forehead, often with a brownish wash. The Black-crested Titmouse is typically smaller than its eastern counterpart. Juveniles of both species are similar to adults with short crests. Young Black-crested Tit-

Tufted Titmouse. Photo by Mark W. Lockwood. Black-crested Titmouse. Photo by Greg W. Lasley.

mice, however, often have a gray crest for a short period of time.

SIMILAR SPECIES Within their range, there are no other species that can be confused with these titmice. A juvenile with a gray crest could be confused with the Juniper Titmouse (*B. ridgwayi*), which occurs in Texas only in the Guadalupe Mountains. The Black-crested juveniles, however, normally have some hint of buffy coloring on the flanks.

HABITAT Both species inhabit woodlands. Tufted Titmice are found primarily in deciduous forests as well as urban areas and parks. Black-crested Titmice are found in the oak woodlands of the Hill Country and Trans-Pecos and scrub habitats of the South Texas Brush Country and Rolling Plains.

STATUS AND DISTRIBUTION Both species are common, with the Tufted found in the eastern third of the state and the Black-crested in the west. The Tufted Titmouse range is east of a line from the eastern edge of the Rolling Plains and Edwards Plateau south to Refugio County. The Black-crested Titmouse range is west of that line south to the Lower Rio Grande Valley and north to the northern Rolling Plains. In the Trans-Pecos, the Black-crested is more localized and restricted to the larger mountain ranges. It is an irregular visitor to the High Plains and the Guadalupe Mountains.

BUSHTIT
Psaltriparus minimus

BACKGROUND

Bushtits are very acrobatic and are most often encountered in family groups. Very vocal, they are often first detected by their almost constant calls as they move, one after another, from tree to tree. Bushtits exhibit polymorphism within their range in Texas. First-year males frequently have black auriculars and were formerly considered a separate species, the Black-eared Bushtit. This plumage feature is the result of intergradations between the brown-eared populations of the interior of the United States and the black-eared populations of the highlands of Mexico. Black-eared birds are much more common in populations in the Trans-Pecos than on the Edwards Plateau. The Bushtit is the only member of its family to occur in the New World. The other six species are primarily Asian, and one also occurs in Europe.

IDENTIFICATION One of the smallest songbirds found in Texas, the bushtit is gray overall with a long tail and short wings. The upperparts are slightly darker than the underparts. Adults have a brown mask that covers from the base of the bill through the auriculars and contrasts with the gray cap. Males have dark eyes, and females have pale or yellowish eyes. In the Trans-Pecos and Edwards Plateau, immature males can have a black mask, and they are typically lighter gray in plumage. In all ages and sexes, the bill is small, conical, and black. The legs are long and black.

SIMILAR SPECIES The immature Verdin (*Auriparus flaviceps*) is possibly the most likely species to be confused with Bushtits.

Similar in size, with gray plumage, it has a more pointed bill and a shorter tail. Perhaps more obvious is the lack of contrast in the plumage on the Verdin's head. The auriculars of the Bushtits found in Texas are brown. The immature Black-crested Titmouse (*Baeolophus atricristatus*) is a larger, stockier bird with a short tail and a small crest. Gnatcatchers (*Polioptila* sp.) have longer, black tails and prominent eye-rings.

HABITAT Open mixed woodland, typically with at least some junipers. Found in cedar breaks on the Edwards Plateau where few other species of birds are present. Also along riparian corridors where there are at least some evergreen trees and shrubs.

STATUS AND DISTRIBUTION Uncommon to common resident from the southern Panhandle south through the Edwards Plateau and west into the Trans-Pecos.

Bushtit. Photo by Mark W. Lockwood.

CACTUS WREN
*Campylorhynchus
brunneicapillus*

BACKGROUND

The Cactus Wren
is fairly common in
the southwestern por-
tion of the state, another of those
species considered characteristic of the
desert. It is also found in the oak savannahs
of the Edwards Plateau and Tamaulipan
thorn-scrub of the South Texas Brush Country. It
nests in cholla and other very thorny plants, which is thought to
provide another layer of defense from predators. The male Cactus Wren will often build several additional nestlike structures
that may ultimately be used for second broods or as a roosting
site by the male. The large domed nests, made of grasses and
other plant material, are easily recognizable. Cactus Wrens
occupy the same territories all year round; as a result, they are
rarely documented as vagrants outside the normal range.

IDENTIFICATION This large wren has a dark brown crown and a
gray-brown back that is heavily mottled with black and white.
The face is pale gray with a distinctive white eyebrow and mottled auriculars. The chin is white and heavily spotted with black
that extends through the breast. The spotting becomes less
prominent on the belly, which is washed with buffy brown. The
wings and tail are dark with light barring. The bill is long and
slightly decurved.

SIMILAR SPECIES The size and structure of the Cactus Wren easily separates it from any other wren that occurs in the United
States. The Sage Thrasher (*Oreoscoptes montanus*) is somewhat
similar in coloration and occurs in similar habitats in Texas
during the winter, but it lacks the heavy barring on the wings

and tail, the streaking on the back, and the prominent white eyebrow. The Curve-billed Thrasher (*Toxostoma curvirostre*) is more commonly encountered in areas where the Cactus Wren is present, but this species is even less likely to be misidentified. It is a uniform tan in color, with less prominent spotting on the underparts, and it has bright yellow eyes.

HABITAT Often associated with desert habitats and areas with cholla and other succulents in particular, but it occupies a much larger sample of habitats found in the southwestern United States. Found in open thorn-scrub and even brushy areas in oak savannahs. Has adapted well to urban habitats where open plantings with native desert vegetation are available.

STATUS AND DISTRIBUTION Uncommon to locally common resident from the Lower Rio Grande Valley north to the southeastern Panhandle and west through the Trans-Pecos.

Cactus Wren. Photo by Mark W. Lockwood.

CAROLINA WREN
Thryothorus ludovicianus

BACKGROUND The Carolina Wren is a common sight in urban habitats with large trees and some understory. It is generally considered a cavity nester, but it will frequently nest in hanging baskets that provide protection for the nest. The Carolina Wrens in the southern half of the South Texas Brush Country and the Lower Rio Grande Valley are classified as a separate subspecies. They are smaller and less rufous in coloration, but they have a slightly larger bill. In the 1960s, it was feared that they were on the way to extirpation, but now they appear to have made a remarkable comeback. The Carolina Wren is the northernmost member of a genus of tropical wrens. Unlike most members of this genus, only the male Carolina Wren sings. In the majority of the other species, both sexes sing slightly different songs in duets.

IDENTIFICATION This medium-sized wren is larger than most of the other wrens found in Texas. The upperparts are deep rusty brown, and the underparts are washed with cinnamon and are not barred. The wings and tail are barred with black, and there are some white markings on the wings. The throat is white, and the sides of the face are mottled with gray. There is also a prominent white eye stripe.

SIMILAR SPECIES The Carolina Wren's range overlaps considerably with that of Bewick's Wren (*Thryomanes bewickii*). Bewick's Wrens found in the western two-thirds of the state are considerably grayer and lack the rusty color so prominent on the underparts of the Carolina Wren. Bewick's Wrens also have much longer tails that are tipped in white. There are Bewick's Wrens that have more rufous tones to their plumage present during winter in the eastern third of the state. These birds still lack the rufous tones characteristic of a Carolina Wren.

HABITAT Found in a variety of mostly woodland habitats. Most common in mesic woodlands with a patchy deciduous understory. Common in riparian corridors throughout their range in Texas.

Carolina Wren. Photo by Greg W. Lasley.

STATUS AND DISTRIBUTION Common to abundant resident in the eastern two-thirds of the state. Along the western edge of the range, most often found along riparian corridors. Found with increasing regularity in the southern Trans-Pecos close to the Rio Grande, and may be resident now in southern Brewster and Presidio counties.

BEWICK'S WREN
Thryomanes bewickii

BACKGROUND
A common bird through much of its range in Texas, Bewick's Wren can be locally abundant on the Edwards Plateau and in the Trans-Pecos. For reasons that are not well understood, the species has declined precipitously in the eastern United States over the past several decades. Competition for nesting cavities and direct competition with the House Wren (*Troglodytes aedon*) have been proposed as possible explanations. A House Wren will remove eggs from a cavity it finds suitable for nesting, and the two species would be in direct competition for nesting holes of a certain size. Bewick's Wren has an impressive vocal range, and there is considerable variability between individuals. These birds learn their songs as fledglings from, oddly enough, the neighboring territorial males.

IDENTIFICATION This is a medium-sized gray-brown wren with a conspicuous white supercilium. The upperparts are uniform gray-brown for the resident population in the western two-thirds of the state. In the winter, individuals of the eastern subspecies can be recognized by their reddish brown upperparts. In all populations, the long tail is heavily barred with black and has white outer tips. The underparts are grayish white, becoming grayer on the sides and flanks. The bill is fairly long and gray.

SIMILAR SPECIES The Carolina Wren (*Thryothorus ludovicianus*) is similar in several plumage characteristics. Found in the eastern two-thirds of the state, it is considerably more rufous in color and larger. Its tail is shorter and lacks the white outer markings of Bewick's. There are Bewick's Wrens that have more rufous tones to their plumage present during winter in the eastern third of the state, but they lack the rufous tones on the underparts found in a Carolina Wren. The Marsh Wren (*Cistothorus palustris*), found primarily in reed beds, is more intricately patterned on the upperparts.

HABITAT Open, brushy habitats. Also open oak-juniper woodlands, desert scrub along arroyos, riparian woodlands, and urban habitats.

STATUS AND DISTRIBUTION Uncommon to common resident in the western two-thirds of the state, east through north-central Texas, and south along a line to the mouth of the Colorado River. During the winter, rare to very rare winter visitor eastward except in areas of heavy forest in the Pineywoods.

Bewick's Wren. Photo by Tim Cooper.

MARSH WREN
Cistothorus palustris

BACKGROUND A vocal inhabitant of marshy habitats during the winter in Texas. The Marsh Wren often announces its presence by a raspy trilling call used to alert other birds to danger. Close observation and patience are required to get a good look at this skulking. Wintering Marsh Wrens will start to sing before departing as spring migrants. There are two distinct groups within the species. Eastern birds, like those that breed along the upper coast of Texas, have brighter plumage overall, and their songs are more musical than those in the west. The differences in plumage are subtle, and it is difficult to determine the relative abundance of the western population in Texas.

IDENTIFICATION A small passerine of wetland habitats, the Marsh Wren has a dark crown that contrasts strongly with the white supercilium. The remainder of the face is dull brown, and the throat is whitish. The back is black and striped with white. The wings, rump, and tail are cinnamon-brown. The underparts are mostly whitish, with a buffy cinnamon color on the sides and flanks. The wings and tail are barred with black.

SIMILAR SPECIES Both the Carolina Wren (*Thryothorus ludovicianus*) and Bewick's Wren (*Thryomanes bewickii*) have a bold white supercilium. In general, the upperparts of the Marsh Wren are more ornate than the plumage of the other species, and the Marsh Wren is the smallest of these birds. The Carolina is considerably more rufous in color, and Bewick's is uniform gray-brown above. The Sedge Wren (*Cistothorus platensis*) can be found in similar habitats, although usually in grassier areas. It is small, with a streaked back, but it is more tan in overall color. Its crown is paler and streaked, and the supercilium is much less distinct.

Marsh Wren. Photo by Greg W. Lasley.

HABITAT A variety of wetland habitats with abundant emergent vegetation, particularly cattails. More habitat-specific during the breeding season. Known to use both freshwater marshes with cattails and saltwater cordgrass marshes for nesting habitat.

STATUS AND DISTRIBUTION Common winter resident in the marshes of the coast and rare to locally common winter resident elsewhere in the state. Common to uncommon summer resident along the upper and central coasts. Isolated nesting records show this species along the Red River east of the Panhandle and along the Rio Grande in the Trans-Pecos. Fall migrants begin to arrive in Texas in mid-September, and most have departed by mid-May.

RUBY-CROWNED KINGLET
Regulus calendula

BACKGROUND At a scant 4.25 inches in length and only about one-quarter of an ounce in weight, the Ruby-crowned Kinglet is one of the smallest birds in Texas. These tiny birds are a common component of winter feeding flocks in Texas. Kinglets are also seen foraging alone in urban habitats or in any other habitat with woody plants. Ruby-crowned Kinglets can be recognized by their almost constant movement from branch to branch and their almost constant wing-flicking. They are very vocal, and their frequent *did-it* calls often give their presence away in dense thickets. The species is a rather early fall migrant, arriving in the state in September and remaining through the winter.

IDENTIFICATION This very small bird is very active, with rather drab olive-green plumage. It has two bold white wing bars and white to greenish yellow edges on the flight feathers and tertials. The prominent eye-ring thins on the top and bottom and is sometimes broken. Birds with fresh plumage in the fall are brighter and less gray than worn birds seen in the spring. The male's fairly large scarlet central crown spot is mostly concealed, but the crown patch is displayed when the bird is agitated.

SIMILAR SPECIES The Golden-crowned Kinglet (*R. satrapa*) is a common winter resident in Texas, although it is not as wide-spread in distribution. The Golden-crowned is very similar in size and has two prominent wing bars; on its head, however, is a

Ruby-crowned Kinglet. Photo by Greg W. Lasley.

white eyebrow and a yellow central crown stripe. Hutton's Vireo (*Vireo huttoni*) is also similar in plumage pattern and coloration, but it is heavier bodied with a larger head and a heavier bill. *Empidonax* flycatchers share a similar plumage pattern; they can be recognized by their upright posture, longer tail, and the very different shape of the bill. The active behavior of kinglets brings to mind warblers, but warblers have larger bills and longer, heavier bodies.

HABITAT Found in a wide variety of habitats, present in almost all types of woodland and forest habitats as well as brushy areas and savannahs. Also commonly encountered in urban habitats.

STATUS AND DISTRIBUTION Common to abundant migrant and winter resident in all areas of the state. Normally arrives in mid-September and departs by early May.

BLUE-GRAY GNATCATCHER
Polioptila caerulea

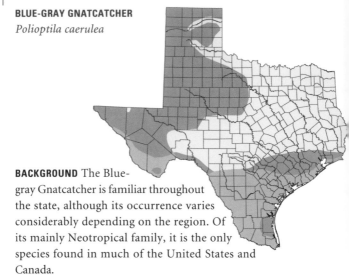

BACKGROUND The Blue-gray Gnatcatcher is familiar throughout the state, although its occurrence varies considerably depending on the region. Of its mainly Neotropical family, it is the only species found in much of the United States and Canada.

IDENTIFICATION This is a very small passerine with blue-gray plumage. Males in breeding plumage have a thin black eyebrow that extends to just behind the eye. The face is bluish with a prominent white eye-ring and a white throat. The crown and upperparts are also bluish, and the underparts are white. The wings are darker than the back and do not have wing bars. The tail is long and black with white outer rectrices. The underside of the tail is white, with some black visible down the center. During the winter, the male loses the black eyebrow. The female is similar to the male but is duller in overall plumage, therefore looking paler gray, and never has a black eyebrow.

SIMILAR SPECIES One other species of gnatcatcher occurs in Texas. The Black-tailed Gnatcatcher (*P. melanura*) is a resident in the Trans-Pecos, southwestern Edwards Plateau, and southward in the western South Texas Brush Country. At all seasons it has mostly black undersides to the tail feathers and grayer plumage. During the breeding season, the male has a black cap. Kinglets are also very small passerines, but they have greenish plumage and short tails.

HABITAT Found in a wide range of woodland habitats, including riparian corridors. Also found in shrublands and dense thickets.

STATUS AND DISTRIBUTION The distribution, on a seasonal basis, is rather complicated. Rare to locally common summer resident in the eastern half of the state and on the Edwards Plateau. Generally absent during the summer from all but the northernmost portions of the Rolling Plains and from the South Texas Brush Country except in the oak mottes of the Coastal Sand Plain. Also common to uncommon summer resident in the Guadalupe and Chisos mountains, but strangely absent from the Davis Mountains. Common to uncommon migrant throughout the state. In winter, uncommon to rare on the Coastal Prairies and in the southern Trans-Pecos and common in the South Texas Brush Country. During winter, also rare and irregular in the floodplains of rivers in the southern Hill Country. Occurs irregularly farther north than the described winter range, particularly in the eastern half of the state.

Blue-gray Gnatcatcher, male in breeding plumage. Photo by Greg W. Lasley.

EASTERN BLUEBIRD
Sialia sialis

BACKGROUND
Eastern Bluebird populations have declined in recent decades. The reasons behind this decline are not well understood, but habitat changes because of human actions and pesticide use are believed to have played important roles. Some authorities also blame competition for nesting sites by increasing numbers of European Starlings (*Sturnus vulgaris*) and, to a lesser extent, House Sparrows (*Passer domesticus*). The development of elaborate nest-box trails for Eastern Bluebirds in many areas of the eastern United States has greatly benefited this species and other cavity nesters.

IDENTIFICATION This medium-sized songbird is structurally similar to other thrushes. The male has a bright blue head, upperparts, wings, and tail. The throat, chest, and flanks are reddish orange, and this color extends up the sides of the neck behind the auriculars. The lower belly and undertail coverts are white. Females are much duller in color, with bluish gray plumage on the upperparts and the brightest blue restricted to the wings and tail. The upperparts are blue-gray with a brownish wash across the upper back. The throat and chest are dull reddish orange, and the belly and undertail coverts are white. Juvenile birds are very different from adults, with a heavily spotted chest and back. After the post-juvenile molt, the immature birds look much more like adult females.

SIMILAR SPECIES Two other species of bluebirds are found in the western portions of the state. The species most similar is the

Western Bluebird (*S. mexicana*). The male Western Bluebird is a darker blue overall with a blue throat. The chestnut on the breast also extends down the flank and onto the back. The belly and undertail are gray. The female is similar in appearance, but the Western female can be identified by her gray throat and chin. The underparts on a female Western are duller, including the breast, with much less contrast between the breast and belly. The male Moun-tain Bluebird (*S. curru-coides*) is easily separated, since it lacks any rufous on the underparts. The female also lacks any rufous on the underparts and is largely gray with light blue wings and tail.

Eastern Bluebird, male. Photo by Tim Cooper.

HABITAT Found in open habitats with little or no understory, including manicured woodlands such as those found in parks, orchards, around golf courses, and pastures.

STATUS AND DISTRIBUTION Uncommon to locally common sum-mer resident in the eastern half of the state west through the eastern half of the Edwards Plateau and along the Concho River drainage. Also common summer resident in the eastern Pan-handle and along the Canadian River drainage. Irregular nester elsewhere east of the Pecos River and very occasionally in the southern Trans-Pecos. Common to uncommon migrant and winter resident east of the Trans-Pecos. West of the Pecos River they are more irregular and local in winter.

HERMIT THRUSH
Catharus guttatus

BACKGROUND The Hermit Thrush is a common migrant through Texas and is the only *Catharus* thrush expected to occur in the state during the winter. It breeds from Alaska to New England and throughout the Rocky Mountains as well. Through this wide range, the Hermit Thrush exhibits considerable variation. The many described subspecies fall generally into three groups: those nesting east of the Rocky Mountains, those nesting in the interior mountains of the West from Alaska south through the Rockies, and birds from the Pacific Coast. Subspecies from the first two groups are seen in Texas. The largest and grayest of the birds found in the state are from the mountain west. Birds from the eastern populations are much more rufous on their upperparts. Individuals from both populations can be seen over much of Texas.

IDENTIFICATION The Hermit Thrush is shaped like an American Robin (*Turdus migratorius*) but is considerably smaller. In general, depending on which subspecies is involved, Hermit Thrushes are grayish brown to reddish brown on the upperparts, contrasting with a reddish rump and tail. They have a distinct white eye-ring, and the lores are usually lighter in color than the forehead. The underparts are grayish white with distinct spotting on the breast, becoming less distinct on the flanks and upper belly.

SIMILAR SPECIES The similar Wood Thrush (*Hylocichla mustelina*) and three other *Catharus* thrushes also occur in

Texas. The Wood Thrush is reddish brown above, from the crown to the lower back, and heavily spotted with black throughout the breast and belly. Similarly, the Veery (*C. fuscescens*) has reddish upperparts and speckling on the breast that is covered by a wash of rufous. The Gray-cheeked Thrush (*C. minimus*) lacks the strong eye-ring seen in the Hermit Thrush, and it is uniform in color on the upperparts through the tail. Finally, Swainson's Thrush (*C. ustulatus*) can be identified by its buffy spectacles and wash over the breast, as well as its concolored back, rump, and tail.

HABITAT Dense woody underbrush in forests and open woodlands. In the western portions of the state, more restricted to riparian corridors and thickets along changes in terrain.

STATUS AND DISTRIBUTION Common migrant and winter resident throughout most of the state. Rare to uncommon winter resident in the Trans-Pecos, Panhandle, and South Plains. Uncommon summer resident in the upper elevations of the Davis and Guadalupe mountains of the Trans Pecos. Fall migrants reach Texas in mid-September; wintering birds and spring migrants have departed by mid-May.

Hermit Thrush. Photo by Mark W. Lockwood.

WOOD THRUSH
Hylocichla mustelina

BACKGROUND
The beautiful, liquid song of this thrush is a favorite sound at dawn and dusk in the mixed deciduous forests of east Texas. Perhaps the easiest place to observe these trans-Gulf migrants in Texas is in various woodlots and other stopover habitats along the Gulf Coast in late April and early May. The species has become a symbol of declining Neotropical migrant birds. The population declined seriously over much of its range during the past 25 years. The bird appears to be particularly susceptible to nest parasitism by the Brown-headed Cowbird (*Molothrus ater*).

IDENTIFICATION The posture of this medium-sized thrush is similar to that of an American Robin (*Turdus migratorius*). The upperparts are reddish brown and brightest from the crown through the upper back. The rump and tail are more olive-brown. The underparts are white with conspicuous black spots on the breast, sides, and flanks. The face is heavily marked black and white, with a dull white eye-ring. The bill is dark with a horn-colored base. The legs are pinkish.

SIMILAR SPECIES The Wood Thrush is occasionally confused with *Catharus* thrushes and the Veery (*Catharus fuscescens*) in particular. The Veery has reddish upperparts, but they are not as bright rufous as a Wood Thrush's. The Veery has indistinct brownish spots on the chest. The Gray-cheeked Thrush (*C. minimus*) and Hermit Thrush (*C. guttatus*) are both plainer gray-brown above, with spotting on the underparts restricted to the breast. The Brown Thrasher (*Toxostoma rufum*) is similar

Wood Thrush. Photo by Mark W. Lockwood.

in plumage pattern, with rufous-brown upperparts and white underparts marked with black, but it has a long tail, wing bars, and black streaks rather than spots on the chest.

HABITAT A wide variety of woodland and forest habitats during migration, including small woodlots and thickets. For breeding habitat, deciduous and mixed forests. More common in forests with a high diversity of deciduous tree species with a well-developed subcanopy. A fairly open forest floor with abundant moist leaf litter appears to be important.

STATUS AND DISTRIBUTION Uncommon to locally common summer resident in the Pineywoods and locally uncommon to rare west Bastrop County. Uncommon to common migrant in the eastern half of the state and rare to casual in the western half.

CLAY-COLORED ROBIN*
Turdus grayi

BACKGROUND The Clay-colored Robin is a new bird to Texas in many ways. This Neotropical thrush was first discovered in the United States in the Lower Rio Grande Valley in 1959. It remained a rarity in Texas until the late 1980s, when the first nesting pair took up residence at Bentsen–Rio Grande Valley State Park. That was the beginning of an influx of birds into south Texas that continues today. There are now multiple pairs of Clay-colored Robins at all of the major preserves and sanctuaries in the Lower Valley, and they continue to be found with increasing abundance wherever native vegetation remains. This species is much like the American Robin (*T. migratorius*) in its habits and behavior in much of Latin America, although in Texas it is much more secretive and often remains at least partially hidden in the undergrowth.

IDENTIFICATION This bird resembles a pale, tawny-colored American Robin. The head and upperparts are a brownish olive to tawny brown, as are the wings and tail. The underparts are a paler buff, contrasting with the darker wings. The bill is dull yellow and often has a darker brown base. The throat is paler than the remainder of the underparts, but not white, with brownish olive streaking. Juvenile birds are spotted below, as are other *Turdus* thrushes, and the upperparts are speckled with reddish brown.

SIMILAR SPECIES Although similar in structure to the American Robin, this species is slightly smaller in size. The Clay-colored

Robin also differs in plumage; it lacks the black head, broken white eye-ring, and rufous underparts. The only other species that could potentially be confused with it is the White-throated Robin (*T. assimilis*), a very rare visitor to the Lower Rio Grande Valley (to date, all records are from the winter months). The White-throated Robin has a dark brown head and upperparts; its very white throat is streaked with black and has a prominent white crescent across the bottom. Overall, the White-throated Robin is darker in overall plumage and has a buffy eye-ring.

Clay-colored Robin. Photo by Mark W. Lockwood.

HABITAT Riparian corridor of the Rio Grande, including refuge woodlands from the middle and western Valley. Prefers dense woodlands, where it may be found in trees or on the forest floor.

STATUS AND DISTRIBUTION Rare, but increasing, resident in the Lower Rio Grande Valley. Scattered records north of the Valley along the Coastal Prairies to the upper coast and inland to Huntsville in Walker County and Gonzales in Gonzales County.

AMERICAN ROBIN
Turdus migratorius

BACKGROUND The American Robin is one of the most familiar birds in North America. Though it is thought of as a harbinger of spring, it is present throughout most of the United States year round. The appearance of robins in spring is perhaps tied to the dispersal of large flocks found primarily in woodlands during the winter into the urban habitats used during the breeding season. The occurrence and abundance of American Robins at any given location varies greatly from year to year. Environmental conditions in the northern portions of the United States have a large effect on how far south migrating birds must go to find favorable conditions. In the winter enormous flocks of robins may be seen going to roosting sites in dense woodlands, including juniper thickets in the Hill Country and mixed coniferous-deciduous woodlands in other areas of the state.

IDENTIFICATION This is a medium-sized bird with brown upperparts and reddish underparts. The head is largely black with a broken white eye-ring and throat. The throat is heavily streaked with black. The lower belly and undertail coverts are white. Females generally have paler or duller plumage than the males. Birds from the eastern portions of the range tend to have brighter plumage than those from the mountain west. Immature robins are heavily spotted below with black and have white streaking in the upperparts.

SIMILAR SPECIES This robin is unlike any other normally occur-

American Robin, male. Photo by Mark W. Lockwood.

ring species in Texas. The only species that could be confused with it is the Rufous-backed Robin (*T. rufopalliatus*), an extremely rare visitor to the state that has been documented in Texas on only 12 occasions. This species is grayer overall than an American Robin and, as the name suggests, has a rufous back and wing coverts that are easily observable.

HABITAT A wide array of habitats from forests and woodlands to parks and urban lawns. During the breeding season, found in open habitats and seems to prefer areas of open ground or short grass for foraging. During the winter, more commonly encountered in large flocks in woodland habitats, including juniper thickets.

STATUS AND DISTRIBUTION Common to abundant migrant and winter resident throughout the state. Presence and abundance can vary greatly from year to year, particularly in the southern third of the state. Common summer resident in the northern half of the state, particularly in urban environments. Rare to uncommon summer resident farther south to the central coast; however, is increasing along the southern edge of the breeding range.

GRAY CATBIRD
Dumetella carolinensis

BACKGROUND
The Gray Catbird
is secretive, spending
most of its time in
thickets. Like other thrashers, it
is able to mimic the songs of other birds,
but the call note that gives it its common
name sounds only vaguely like a cat. This
species is seen much more frequently as a
migrant in Texas than as a breeding bird; it can be common at
stopover habitats along the Gulf Coast in particular. Gray Catbirds have been shown to be very intelligent. Their ability to
recognize their own eggs protects them from brood parasitism
by Brown-headed Cowbirds (*Molothrus ater*); they can quickly
recognize a foreign egg and remove it from the nest. Very few
catbirds have been found raising cowbird fledglings, which suggests that they have an effective defense for the species.

IDENTIFICATION The body plumage of this small thrasher is uniform medium to dark gray, looking very dark in poor light.
There is no contrast between the upperparts and underparts.
The wings are slightly darker and short, with no contrasting
markings. The tail is dark gray to blackish and long without any
markings. The crown, including the forehead, is black. The
undertail coverts are chestnut.

SIMILAR SPECIES The uniform dark gray plumage of the Gray
Catbird sets it apart from other species found in Texas. The
Northern Mockingbird (*Mimus polyglottos*) is similar in structure, but its plumage is much paler gray, with large white patches on the wings and tail. The female Brewer's Blackbird (*Euphagus cyanocephalus*) is uniform in color, but browner, and it

lacks the contrasting black crown and chestnut undertail coverts.

HABITAT Dense, shrubby habitats, including forest edges, woodlots, fencerows, riparian corridors, and urban habitats.

Gray Catbird. Photo by Tim Cooper.

STATUS AND DISTRIBUTION Uncommon to common migrant through the eastern half of the state west to the central Edwards Plateau, becoming increasingly less common westward. Spring migrants are present in Texas from mid-April through May, and fall migrants can be seen between early September and late October. Locally uncommon to rare winter resident along the coast and in the Lower Rio Grande Valley, with scattered winter records from all other areas of the state. Locally uncommon to rare summer resident across the northeastern half of the state. Very rare and local breeders southward in the Pineywoods.

NORTHERN MOCKINGBIRD
Mimus polyglottos

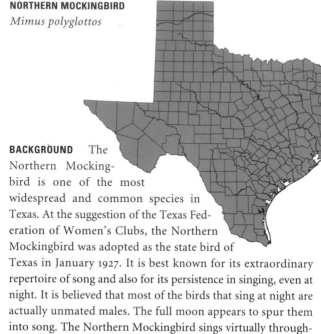

BACKGROUND The Northern Mocking-bird is one of the most widespread and common species in Texas. At the suggestion of the Texas Federation of Women's Clubs, the Northern Mockingbird was adopted as the state bird of Texas in January 1927. It is best known for its extraordinary repertoire of song and also for its persistence in singing, even at night. It is believed that most of the birds that sing at night are actually unmated males. The full moon appears to spur them into song. The Northern Mockingbird sings virtually throughout the year, with the most consistent and varied singing between February and September. The female also sings but is not as persistent or as loud. Females rarely sing in the summer, when the male is particularly vocal in defending the breeding territory. During the breeding season, these birds are often seen flashing their wings to show the large white patches. Whether this is a territorial display or a hunting technique is unknown.

IDENTIFICATION This bird has gray upperparts with grayish white underparts. The wings are also gray, with two white wing bars and a large white patch that is prominent when the wing is spread. The tail is long and edged with white. Immature birds are similar to adults, with faint gray streaks on the underparts.

SIMILAR SPECIES The Loggerhead Shrike (*Lanius ludovicianus*) has a similar plumage pattern, with a prominent black mask, smaller white patches on black wings, and greater contrast between the upperparts and underparts. Townsend's Solitaire

(*Myadestes townsendi*) is darker gray overall and lacks the large white patches in the wing and tail. The Gray Catbird (*Dumetella carolinensis*) has much darker gray plumage and also lacks the white in wings and tail. The Sage Thrasher (*Oreoscoptes montanus*) could be confused with the immature Northern Mockingbird, it likewise lacks the distinctive plumage pattern of the Northern Mockingbird.

HABITAT Found in open areas and along forest edges. This makes this species well adapted for using urban habitats. Males normally use higher perches for singing their advertising song and later for territorial defense. Northern Mockingbirds are also found in meadows and other opening in forests.

STATUS AND DISTRIBUTION Abundant to common resident throughout the state. One of the most widespread and common birds in Texas, they are conspicuous by their song. Seasonal movements are suspected in Texas, and individuals from northern migratory populations may account for apparent influxes of mockingbirds during the winter.

Northern Mockingbird. Photo by Tim Cooper.

BROWN THRASHER
Toxostoma rufum

BACKGROUND
Thrashers have a large vocal range. Although the Brown Thrasher can't compete with the Northern Mockingbird (*Mimus polyglottos*), it does mimic other birds' songs and most often sings imitations in groups of three. The Brown Thrasher spends a lot of time foraging on the ground, and like most birds that work through leaf litter, it has powerful legs and feet that allow it to push away the litter and soil looking for insects, seeds, and berries.

IDENTIFICATION The Brown Thrasher is a large songbird, with reddish brown to rufous upperparts, including the wings and tail. The underparts are whitish with prominent blackish streaks; the streaking on the sides and flanks is more brownish. It has two tan or whitish wing bars, and the tail is long. The bill is dark and fairly straight, with a pale base to the lower mandible. The eyes are yellow.

SIMILAR SPECIES The Long-billed Thrasher (*T. longirostre*) is similar in structure and overall coloration, but its plumage is duller brown on the upperparts, and its bill is longer with a more curved culmen. The face is grayer, but this character is quite variable in the Brown Thrasher. The Long-billed Thrasher is a common resident in the southern third of the state, and there is not much overlap in range between these species. The Wood Thrush (*Hylocichla mustelina*) also has a similar plumage pattern and coloration. Its primary differences are the round spots on its breast, its short tail, and the absence of wing bars.

HABITAT A wide variety of woodland and brushy habitats used during migration and winter. During the breeding season, found in brushy habitats with some open space and along riparian corridors. Also in urban habitats where thickets are available for nesting cover.

Brown Thrasher. Photo by Tim Cooper

STATUS AND DISTRIBUTION Uncommon to locally common resident in the eastern third of the state and westward across north-central Texas to the eastern Panhandle. Very rare and local summer resident across south-central Texas to the eastern edge of the Edwards Plateau. A common migrant and winter resident in the eastern half of the state westward to the eastern Edwards Plateau, becoming increasingly uncommon farther west.

CURVE-BILLED THRASHER
Toxostoma curvirostre

BACKGROUND The
Curve-billed Thrasher
is widespread in the
Southwest and is probably the
most recognizable of the thrashers that
are restricted to that part of the United
States. There are two fairly distinctive groups
of Curve-billed Thrashers. The birds from the
Sonoran Desert of Arizona and northwestern Mexico look
somewhat different from those found in the Chihuahuan
Desert of Texas and northeastern Mexico. Some researchers
have concluded that they may actually be two species. The birds
of Texas are lighter in color and have more distinct spotting on
their underparts. They also have more prominent wing bars and
white tips on the tail. The western birds are grayer, with indistinct spots on the underparts and small, gray tips on the tail.

IDENTIFICATION The Curve-billed Thrasher is slightly larger than
a Northern Mockingbird (*Mimus polyglottos*) and more
robust. Its plumage is gray-brown, with the underparts lighter
than the upperparts. Indistinct spots mark the breast and sides,
and the belly is lighter tan. The two thin wing bars are tan or
whitish, and the tail is long, with conspicuous whitish tips. The
bill is dark and curved. The eyes are yellow.

SIMILAR SPECIES In Texas, only a couple of thrasher species
might be confused with the Curve-billed Thrasher. The Crissal
Thrasher (*T. crissale*) is another large thrasher found primarily
in the Trans-Pecos. Its bill is much more strongly curved, it has
a plain breast, and the undertail coverts are dark rufous. The
Sage Thrasher (*T. montanus*) is considerably smaller. An irrup-

tive winter resident in the western third of the state, it is similar in color on the upperparts, but whitish on the underparts with small black streaks. It also has white wing bars. Immature Northern Mockingbirds have gray mottled underparts, but are much lighter gray in color and have the characteristic white patches in the wings and tail of that species.

HABITAT Found in open brushy habitats, including mixed desert scrub, open shrublands, oak and mesquite savannah that has some brushy understory, and urban habitats.

STATUS AND DISTRIBUTION Common to uncommon resident in the western half of the state. Occurs east through most of the Rolling Plains and Edwards Plateau and north along the Coastal Prairies to the upper portion of the central coast.

Curve-billed Thrasher. Photo by Mark W. Lockwood.

CEDAR WAXWING
Bombycilla cedrorum

BACKGROUND

The Cedar Waxwing is normally a common winter bird in Texas, although the number of birds present at a given location can vary tremendously from one year to the next. The name refers to the waxy red tips of the secondary feathers of the wing. The function of these tips is not known. The Cedar Waxwing feeds largely on fruit, both in the winter and the summer. It is particularly attracted to fruits with high sugar content. These birds are most often seen in Texas in large flocks moving around an area looking for fruiting plants. The flocks often contain as many as 50 to 100 individuals. Juniper fruit makes up a large portion of the diet in areas where these trees are available; as a result, the Texas Hill Country usually attracts high numbers of these birds. As ornamental plantings of trees and shrubs that produce sugary fruit have increased in recent decades, urban areas have supplied the foraging needs of these birds. Cedar Waxwings are well known for gorging themselves when fruit is abundant a practice that has led to the occasional discovery of drunken waxwings that have fed on fermented fruits. Of course, this dependence on a diet of fruit also makes these birds very nomadic, and they will remain in a certain area only as long as food is available.

IDENTIFICATION This is a slender buffy-brown bird with a crest. The brown of the breast fades into pale yellow on the belly. The lower back and rump are gray, as is the tail, except for a terminal band of yellow. It has a black mask, outlined in white, that

Cedar Waxwing. Photo by Mark W. Lockwood.

extends well behind the eye and a small black patch on the chin. At the end of the secondaries is a red waxlike projection to the feather. Juvenile birds are grayer and heavily streaked below.

SIMILAR SPECIES The only similar species is the Bohemian Waxwing (*B. garrulus*), which is extremely rare in Texas. It is larger with grayer plumage and has a prominent white wing bar and cinnamon undertail coverts.

HABITAT Winters in areas with fruit-bearing trees and shrubs, especially open woodlands, parks, gardens, and forest edges.

STATUS AND DISTRIBUTION Uncommon to abundant winter resident and migrant. Considered an uncommon winter resident in the Lower Rio Grande Valley. Common to uncommon migrant and winter resident in the Trans-Pecos. The number present in a given area fluctuates greatly from year to year. Typically present from mid-October to late May.

PHAINOPEPLA
Phainopepla nitens

BACKGROUND

The Phainopepla belongs to a small family of Neotropical birds known as silky-flycatchers. One of the other members of this family, the Gray Silky-flycatcher (*Ptilogonys cinereus*), is widespread in Mexico and has been documented in Texas on two occasions. The remaining two species are found in the Chiriqui highlands of Costa Rica and Panama. All members of this family are particularly fond of the fruits of mistletoe. Studies have shown that a single Phainopepla will consume more than 1,000 mistletoe berries in a single day, when they are available. These berries are where this species gets most of its water. The name is Greek for "shining robe," referring to the glossy plumage of the adult male.

Phainopepla, male. Photo by Mark W. Lockwood.

IDENTIFICATION The Phainopepla is a slender, elegant-looking songbird. The adult male has glossy black body plumage. The wings are also black, with the exception of the inner webbing of the primaries, which forms a prominent white patch in the wing visible only in flight or if the wing is extended. The male has a slender, erect

Phainopepla, female. Photo by Greg W. Lasley.

crest, a long black tail, and bright red eyes. The adult female is similar in structure and plumage pattern but is grayish overall. The wing patch on the female is pale gray and thus does not stand out as dramatically.

SIMILAR SPECIES The Phainopepla, particularly the male, is a distinctive species unlikely to be confused with other birds when seen well. The Northern Mockingbird (*Mimus polyglottos*) is paler gray overall, and although it has white wing patches, the size and shape of the patches are quite different. Mockingbirds also have extensive white markings in the tail. The Cedar Waxwing (*Bombycilla cedrorum*) has a sleek body shape with a tall crest, but otherwise it does not resemble a Phainopepla. The Cedar Waxwing is tan with a yellow belly, and its short tail has a yellow terminal band.

HABITAT Found in open oak and mixed woodlands. Often attracted to areas where mistletoe is common. Also found in riparian corridors and, less commonly, in mixed desert scrub.

STATUS AND DISTRIBUTION Rare to locally uncommon resident throughout most of the Trans-Pecos. Common in the foothills of the Davis Mountains. A casual visitor, at all seasons, to the western Edwards Plateau and southern Rolling Plains.

ORANGE-CROWNED WARBLER
Vermivora celata

BACKGROUND The Orange-crowned Warbler is one of the most common western warblers found in Texas. It is rather uniform in color, and the lack of conspicuous field marks is actually a clue to its identification. As the name suggests, it has an orange crown patch, but the patch is rarely seen, normally only when the bird is alarmed. The four subspecies of Orange-crowned Warbler differ in plumage color and size. As a result, there is some variation in the birds observed in Texas, with some being very gray and dull and others being rather bright, bordering on yellow in color. This species nests in the boreal forests of northern North America and is among the latest of the warblers to migrate south in the fall. The majority of birds do not leave the breeding grounds until late September or October. Reports of Orange-crowned Warblers made in early fall are most likely actually dull Tennessee Warblers (*V. peregrina*) or immature Yellow Warblers (*Dendroica petechia*).

IDENTIFICATION Both sexes are dull grayish olive. Key field marks include a split eye-ring, dark eye line, and weak yellowish supercilium. The upperparts are generally grayish olive, contrasting slightly with the yellowish underparts. The underparts are lightly streaked with olive, and the undertail coverts are brighter yellow. The concealed orange crown patch is visible only when the crown feathers are raised. Males have a larger crown patch than females.

SIMILAR SPECIES The Tennessee Warbler can look very similar, particularly in the fall. The key field mark is the Tennessee Warbler's white undertail coverts. Other features to look for are faint streaking on the breast and a split eye-ring; the Tennessee has neither. The plumage of the Philadelphia Vireo is not as dull, it has a thicker bill, and it has a prominent whitish stripe over the eye. Immature Yellow Warblers, particularly the very plain first-fall female that can be washed with gray and have yellow undertail coverts, are also confused with the Orange-crowned Warbler. These birds are generally more yellow in overall coloration, with a plain face and yellow tail spots.

Orange-crowned Warbler. Photo by Mark W. Lockwood.

HABITAT Seen in many habitats as a migrant, including almost any woodland habitat and even places with tall weeds. In the winter, found in a variety of woodland habitats.

STATUS AND DISTRIBUTION Common to abundant migrant throughout the state. Uncommon to common winter resident south of the South Plains and Panhandle. Especially common in winter in the southern third of the state and along the coast, where it can be locally abundant. Uncommon and local summer resident in the higher elevations of the Davis and Guadalupe mountains of the Trans-Pecos. In general, fall migrants begin arriving in early September and have departed by mid-May.

NASHVILLE WARBLER
Vermivora ruficapilla

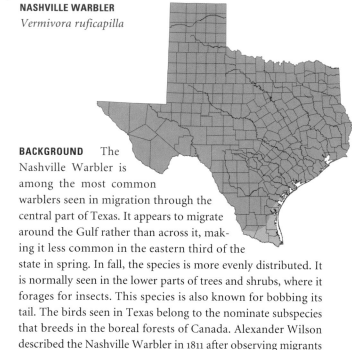

BACKGROUND The Nashville Warbler is among the most common warblers seen in migration through the central part of Texas. It appears to migrate around the Gulf rather than across it, making it less common in the eastern third of the state in spring. In fall, the species is more evenly distributed. It is normally seen in the lower parts of trees and shrubs, where it forages for insects. This species is also known for bobbing its tail. The birds seen in Texas belong to the nominate subspecies that breeds in the boreal forests of Canada. Alexander Wilson described the Nashville Warbler in 1811 after observing migrants as they passed through Nashville, Tennessee.

IDENTIFICATION This warbler has a conspicuous white eye-ring that contrasts strongly against the gray head. The upperparts are olive-green, and the underparts are bright yellow. This yellow extends from the throat to the undertail coverts, but frequently the belly is white. The scientific name refers to the inconspicuous patch of rust on the crown. Immature birds are duller than adults, with weaker contrast between the gray cheeks and dull yellow throat.

SIMILAR SPECIES Virginia's Warbler (*V. virginiae*) has a gray head with a prominent white eye-ring, but the body is gray with yellow on only the breast, rump, and undertail coverts. The Connecticut Warbler (*Oporornis agilis*) is a casual visitor to Texas and is very unlikely to be encountered. It is much larger and heavier than the Nashville, and its gray hood extends all the way through the throat and upper breast. It spends most of its time on the ground, unlike the more arboreal Nashville Warbler. The Orange-crowned Warbler is duller in overall color and has a split eye-ring with a dark eye line. It also lacks the contrast between the upperparts and underparts.

HABITAT Seen in many habitats as a migrant, including almost any woodland habitat and even places with tall weeds. In the winter, found in the thick natural woodlands of the Lower Rio Grande Valley as well as urban areas with large trees.

STATUS AND DISTRIBUTION Uncommon to abundant migrant throughout most of the state. Usually more common in fall than in spring. Rare to very uncommon migrant in the western half of the Trans-Pecos. Rare winter resident in the Lower Rio Grande Valley and very rare farther north. Average migration dates are from early April to mid-May and from early September to late October.

Nashville Warbler, immature (first-fall). Photo by Mark W. Lockwood.

COLIMA WARBLER*
Vermivora crissalis

BACKGROUND

Like several other warblers, the Colima Warbler is named after the place where it was first recorded. In this case, it was discovered along the west coast of Mexico in the state of Colima, which is part of the winter range. The Colima Warbler rivals the endangered Kirtland's Warbler (*Dendroica kirtlandii*) as the warbler with the smallest range in the United States. In this country, the Colima Warbler is restricted to the Chisos Mountains of Big Bend National Park, where it was first discovered in 1928 and was confirmed nesting in 1932. It nests on the ground in small depressions or cavities that most often concealed by overhanging vegetation or rocks. The Colima Warbler is by far the most common nesting warbler in the Chisos Mountains, with only the Painted Redstart (*Myioborus pictus*) also nesting there. This warbler attracts birders from all over the United States, if not worldwide, to make the hike to the upper elevations of the Chisos. Although the bird is fairly common, some familiarity with its song, a musical trill,

Colima Warbler. Photo by Mark W. Lockwood.

greatly increases the probability of finding this rather drab-colored warbler.

IDENTIFICATION This large *Vermivora* warbler has a golden yellow rump and undertail. Close inspection shows a brownish gray back and flanks that contrast with the gray head and belly. A chestnut crown patch is often visible, particularly on males. This species also has a prominent, but narrow, white eye-ring.

Colima Warbler, adult on nest. Photo by Mark W. Lockwood.

SIMILAR SPECIES Virginia's Warbler is similar in overall appearance, although it is considerably smaller and more uniformly colored, lacking brownish tones on the back and flanks. The undertail coverts and rump are a brighter yellow than the golden cast of the Colima.

HABITAT In Texas, found in mixed deciduous woodlands in the upper elevations of the Chisos Mountains. This habitat is generally found in more mesic areas, including maple-oak woodlands in canyon bottoms, as well as oak woodlands in canyons that are drier.

STATUS AND DISTRIBUTION Uncommon and extremely localized summer resident in the Chisos Mountains of Big Bend National Park. Very small numbers apparently overshoot during spring migration and arrive in the Davis Mountains. There have been no nesting records of this species in the Davis Mountains, but apparent hybrids with Virginia's Warbler have been documented. Colima Warblers arrive in Big Bend National Park in early April, and most depart by early September.

TROPICAL PARULA*
Parula pitiayumi

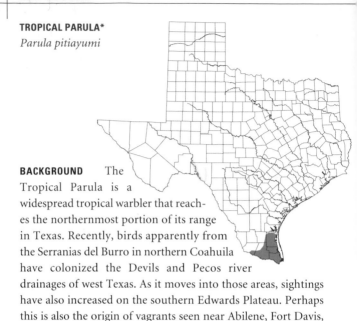

BACKGROUND The Tropical Parula is a widespread tropical warbler that reaches the northernmost portion of its range in Texas. Recently, birds apparently from the Serranias del Burro in northern Coahuila have colonized the Devils and Pecos river drainages of west Texas. As it moves into those areas, sightings have also increased on the southern Edwards Plateau. Perhaps this is also the origin of vagrants seen near Abilene, Fort Davis, and Lubbock.

IDENTIFICATION It is blue-gray above with an obvious yellow-green patch covering the back. The underparts are bright yellow from the throat to the upper belly, becoming white through the undertail coverts. There is often an orangish band of varying intensity across the breast. There are two wide white wing bars on the otherwise blue-gray wing. The tail is short and has white spots in the inner webbing of the outer two or three feathers. The lores are black, and that coloration extends to below the eye. Normally there are no white markings around the eye. On average, males have brighter plumage than females, and immature birds have the dullest plumage.

SIMILAR SPECIES This species is most likely to be confused with the closely related Northern Parula (*P. americana*). The Northern has similar plumage characteristics but lacks the black mask and has white eye crescents. In addition, the male has a dark breast band. Also, the yellow on the throat of a Tropical Parula is much more extensive, bordering the lower edge of the auriculars. Apparent hybrids between the Tropical and the Northern have been noted in the Devils River population as well as in south Texas. Features suggesting hybridization are partial eye crescents and an intermediate border in the yellow on the throat.

HABITAT Breeds in open live oak woodlands on the Coastal Sand Plain and in emergent trees in Tamaulipan thorn-scrub in the Lower Rio Grande Valley. In the winter, uses a wider variety of woodland habitats, including urban settings.

STATUS AND DISTRIBUTION Rare to uncommon resident along the lower coast and in the Lower Rio Grande Valley. Most common in the live oak woodlands of the Coastal Sand Plain in Kenedy and Brooks counties. Increasingly rare and local during the summer north along the coast to Calhoun County. A separate population has become established along the Devils and Pecos rivers in Val Verde County. During the summer of 2001, a pair nested unsuccessfully at Davis Mountains State Park, Jeff Davis County.

Tropical Parula, male. Photo by Mark W. Lockwood.

YELLOW WARBLER
Dendroica petechia

BACKGROUND

The Yellow War-
bler is a common
sight during migration
throughout the state. It breeds
throughout most of Canada and the
northern two-thirds of the United States.
One of the outstanding ornithological finds
in Texas in recent years was a population of Mangrove Yellow Warblers in the Lower Laguna Madre in 2005. Presumably belonging to the subspecies *oraria,* these birds are different in appearance from the Northern Yellow Warblers seen
elsewhere in the state. The Mangrove Yellow Warbler has been
considered a separate species in the past and may be elevated to
species status again.

IDENTIFICATION The male is bright yellow with reddish streaks in
the breast and yellow tail spots. The upperparts usually have a
greenish wash. The female is considerably duller overall, but
still yellow with greenish yellow upperparts. Females generally
lack the reddish streaking below, but a few will show a reduced
pattern of red on the breast. First-fall birds are quite variable,
depending on the subspecies, ranging from fairly bright yellow
overall to heavy greenish or even gray tones above. All ages are
plain-faced and have a complete yellow eye-ring. The Mangrove
subspecies is similar, but adult males have a chestnut head.
Females and immature birds tend to be grayer overall and have
short primaries. Some adult females will have chestnut on the
cap and elsewhere on the face.

SIMILAR SPECIES The Orange-crowned Warbler is occasionally
mistaken for the Yellow Warbler, particularly brightly

plumaged males. The Orange-crowned has a split eye-ring with a dark eye line and a supercilium, along with indistinct olive streaking on the breast. Wilson's Warbler (*Wilsonia pusilla*) is also bright yellow with relatively few markings. The male has a distinct black cap, and all plumages lack yellow tail spots and yellow edgings on the wing feathers. The female Hooded Warbler (*W. citrina*) is larger with white tail spots.

Yellow Warbler, male. Photo by Tim Cooper.

HABITAT Almost any brushy or woodland habitat during migration. The same is true of the very few that occasionally winter in the Lower Rio Grande Valley. The Mangrove Yellow Warbler is restricted to mangrove thickets.

STATUS AND DISTRIBUTION Common to abundant migrant statewide, particularly in fall. Formerly a rare summer resident in the state; territorial males are still occasionally encountered, but nesting has not been confirmed. Rare to very rare winter visitor in the Lower Rio Grande Valley and in El Paso. The migration period is from early April to late May and from late July to mid-October. The Mangrove Yellow Warbler is currently a common resident, although the population is small, in the mangroves surrounding the South Bay of the Laguna Madre at Port Isabel.

YELLOW-RUMPED WARBLER
Dendroica coronata

BACKGROUND The Yellow-rumped Warbler has two distinctively plumaged populations, which were formerly considered separate species. Hybrids of the two populations are known only from a small area in the Canadian Rockies. The population known as Audubon's Warbler nests in the Rocky Mountains and has a yellow throat and darker underparts. The Myrtle Warbler nests from Alaska east to New England and is paler with a white throat. The two forms may be elevated to species status again, and both commonly occur in Texas.

IDENTIFICATION Both forms have a bright yellow rump and crown, broken white eye-rings, and large white tail spots. The adult male Myrtle has a white throat and a black mask including the lores through the auriculars. The mask is bordered above by a thin white supercilium. The upperparts are blue-gray with black streaking on the back. The underparts are white with

a band of black streaks across the breast and down the flanks. The flanks are largely yellow, bordered by the broken streaks of black. The female is similar to the male, but with brown upperparts. First-fall birds are brownish with a brownish white throat and indistinct markings on the body. Audubon's Warbler has a

Yellow-rumped Warbler, breeding plumage, Myrtle form. Photo by Tim Cooper.

yellow throat and generally much more black on the underparts. Its plain blue-gray face has a broken white eye-ring. The female is much duller, with brownish upperparts and more mottled underparts. First-fall birds are brownish with a plain face and a dull yellow throat.

Yellow-rumped Warbler, winter plumage, Myrtle. Photo by Greg W. Lasley.

SIMILAR SPECIES These birds are very distinctive and unlikely to be confused with other warblers. Dull female Cape May Warblers (*D. tigrina*) also have a yellow rump, but they are more evenly streaked below and usually show some yellow behind the auriculars. The Magnolia Warbler (*D. magnolia*) also has a yellow rump, but it has yellow underparts in all plumages. Separating first-winter birds of the two forms can sometimes be challenging. In most cases, Audubon's has some yellow in the throat and a darker, plainer face. The Palm Warbler (*D. palmarum*), particularly the duller plumaged birds from the western populations, can be confusing, but its supercilium and yellow undertail coverts should be more distinct. In addition, it habitually wags its tail as it forages.

HABITAT Found in brushy and woodland habitats throughout the state. The breeding Audubon's Warblers in the Trans-Pecos are found in mixed deciduous woodlands.

STATUS AND DISTRIBUTION Common to abundant migrant over the entire state. Common to abundant winter resident in all areas of the state except the Panhandle, where it is rare to uncommon. Audubon's Warbler is a rare to locally uncommon summer resident in the higher elevations of the Davis and Guadalupe mountains of the Trans-Pecos. It begins to appear in the state in early September, and spring migrants are gone by mid-May. The Myrtle Warbler is more common in the eastern two-thirds of the state, although it is present in all areas. Audubon's Warblers are uncommon in the Trans-Pecos, Panhandle, and South Plains, becoming scarce farther east and south.

GOLDEN-CHEEKED WARBLER*
Dendroica chrysoparia

BACKGROUND

The Golden-cheeked Warbler is the quintessential Texas specialty, since it nests only in Texas. It is an Endangered species because of its strict habitat requirements and small breeding range. Henry Attwater wrote of his concern about the long-term survival of this species in 1892.

IDENTIFICATION The combination of the bright unmarked yellow cheek and black upperparts makes the plumage of the adult male unique among North American birds. The female has dull olive upperparts streaked with black. The key feature in identifying this species is the prominent black eye line that cuts through the yellow cheek. This feature eliminates all other similar species. First-fall females are similar to Black-throated Green Warblers of the same age, but generally they have a dull eye line and otherwise yellow auriculars. Identification of out-of-range Golden-cheeked Warblers should be undertaken with great caution.

Golden-cheeked Warbler, male with juvenile Brown-headed Cowbird. Photo by Mark W. Lockwood.

SIMILAR SPECIES The closely related Black-throated Green Warbler (*D. virens*) looks very similar, but it lacks the all-important black eye line (although it often has a prominent olive line through the eye). Other features that distinguish the Black-throated Green are its unmarked bright olive-green upperparts and the tinge of yellow on the thighs and vent. The Hermit Warbler (*D. occidentalis*) also has an unmarked yellow cheek, but it lacks the bold eye line.

HABITAT Restricted to Ashe juniper–oak woodlands. This warbler depends on Ashe juniper because it builds its nest solely out of the bark of this tree. As a result, at least some mature Ashe junipers must be present for the bird to occur. The highest-quality habitat contains a mixture of oaks and other hardwoods with the junipers; the higher the

Golden-cheeked Warbler, female with fledgling. Photo by Mark W. Lockwood.

percentage of hardwoods, the better the habitat. Lost Maples State Natural Area near Vanderpool in Bandera County is a great example of such habitat; it is home to a large population of the warbler. Winter habitat is montane pine-oak woodland.

STATUS AND DISTRIBUTION Locally uncommon to rare summer resident in the Hill Country northward to north-central Texas. Arrives on the breeding grounds in early March and departs by early August. Fall migration begins as early as late June, with almost all of the population gone from Texas by the end of July. Most common in the Balcones Canyonlands subregion of the Edwards Plateau. Found locally northward to Dallas, Palo Pinto, and Somervell counties. Rarely seen in migration, although, amazingly, there are documented late fall records from California and Florida. In Texas, there are records from as far west as Big Bend National Park and as far east as Galveston. Winters in extreme southern Mexico south to Nicaragua.

BLACK-AND-WHITE WARBLER
Mniotilta varia

BACKGROUND

The Black-and-white Warbler has a unique feeding strategy among wood warblers. It is reminiscent of a nuthatch as it creeps along limbs or tree trunks looking for insects and other arthropods, and its relatively short legs and long bill seem to assist in this feeding style. Black-and-white Warblers occasionally catch insects on the wing as well, and will hover briefly in vegetation to pick off prey items.

IDENTIFICATION This warbler is entirely black and white. Both sexes have a white central crown stripe that is bordered by black, a characteristic not shared by any other warbler. The male has a black cheek patch bordered by a white supercilium and malar stripe. The remainder of the body is heavily streaked. The female has a white face with a thin black postocular stripe and dusky auriculars. The white throat and less heavily streaked underparts give the female a much whiter overall appearance. First-fall birds are similar to adult females. Birds of all ages have broad white wing bars.

SIMILAR SPECIES The male Blackpoll Warbler (*Dendroica striata*) is similar in overall coloration to the Black-and-white, but the Blackpoll has a solid black cap and a large white cheek patch. The streaking on the underparts is also less extensive, and the upperparts are a more uniform brownish gray. The adult female is similar in overall pattern to a female Black-and-white. Blackpolls have gray crowns and upperparts and lack the white central crown stripe. The Black-throated Gray Warbler (*D.*

nigrescens), another similar bird, has uniformly gray upperparts with only fine black streaking on the back. It lacks the white central crown stripe and does have a yellow spot on the lores. Both species are more like typical warblers in behavior and would not be seen gleaning insects from bark for any extended period of time.

HABITAT Migrant and wintering birds are found in open wooded habitats, including urban areas. Breeding birds are found in mixed deciduous and pine-oak woodlands.

STATUS AND DISTRIBUTION Uncommon to common summer resident in the eastern half of the state west through the southern Hill Country. Uncommon to common spring and fall migrant throughout most of the state, although rare in the western Trans-Pecos. Migrants arrive in early March, and spring migrants are present until mid-May. Fall migrants are in the state from late July to early November. Rare to uncommon winter resident in the southern third of the state and along the coast. Very rare to casual elsewhere in the state.

Black-and-white Warbler, male. Photo by Tim Cooper.

COMMON YELLOWTHROAT
Geothlypis trichas

BACKGROUND
This is a common warbler of marshy habitats in many areas of the state. Its skulking behavior often makes it hard to detect.

IDENTIFICATION The male has a prominent black mask with a bright yellow throat, breast, and undertail coverts. The upperparts are olive, and the tail is often held pointing upward. The female is much duller and often lacks any hint of the black mask. It also has a complete eye-ring.

SIMILAR SPECIES The black mask of the male separates this species from almost all other warblers in Texas. The Kentucky Warbler (*Oporornis formosus*) has something of a black mask, but it also has a yellow supercilium that wraps behind the eye. The first-fall female Mourning Warbler (*O. philadelphia*) is rather drab and could be confused with a female Common Yellowthroat. It has a brownish breast band forming the lower edge of the hood seen in the adult, and it is chunkier with a shorter tail. The final similar species is the Gray-crowned Yellowthroat (*G. poliocephala*), a very rare visitor to the Lower Rio Grande Valley in the United States and unlikely to be encountered. It is larger and has only black lores; the forehead and crown are gray.

HABITAT Found primarily in marshy habitats, most often in cattails. In mesic areas in the eastern part of the state, also found in damp habitats with dense vegetation. Migrants can be encountered in other habitats, such as woodland edges and brushy areas.

STATUS AND DISTRIBUTION A rather complex distribution in

Common Yellowthroat, male. Photo by Tim Cooper.

Texas. For the most part, very local as a breeding species in all of the summer range except along the Coastal Prairies. Rare to locally common during summer in the northeastern part of the state and the Panhandle. Uncommon to locally common during this season in the remainder of the eastern third of the state and along the Coastal Prairies to the central coast. Along the Rio Grande, uncommon and very localized. Isolated nesting records from virtually all of the remaining areas of the state, and a common to uncommon migrant throughout the state. In winter, uncommon to locally common across much of the southern half of the state, but generally rare to locally uncommon in the Trans-Pecos and Edwards Plateau. In the northern half of Texas, winters locally, but is absent from most of the Panhandle. The migration timing is often hard to discern and is complicated by the presence of resident birds; however, it generally falls from mid-March to mid-May and from early September to late October.

WILSON'S WARBLER
Wilsonia pusilla

BACKGROUND
Wilson's Warbler is one of the migrant warblers that can be seen in all areas of the state. In the western third of the state it is second only to the Yellow-rumped Warbler in terms of relative abundance. This small, bright yellow bird is extremely active as it gleans insects. In addition to foraging in vegetation, Wilson's Warbler will also make sallies after flying insects and will hover over vegetation to pick off prey items.

IDENTIFICATION The male is bright yellow with a distinctive black cap. The upperparts are tinged with green to olive, giving them a darker appearance. Adult females have the same plumage pattern, but the head markings can range from a smaller, lighter cap to an olive crown similar in color to the upperparts. Females from the Rocky Mountain population tend to have more of a capped appearance. Their small black eyes in particular seem to stand out against the unmarked yellow face.

SIMILAR SPECIES The female Hooded Warbler has a similar overall color pattern, but usually with some remnant of the hooded pattern of the male. In addition, the Hooded Warbler has large white spots on the inner webbing of the outer tail feathers. The Yellow Warbler has yellow tail spots and edgings on the wing feathers that Wilson's lacks, and its tail is much shorter. The Orange-crowned Warbler is much greener in plumage and has conspicuous olive streaking in the underparts; it also has a split eye-ring and black eye line.

HABITAT Found in almost any brushy or woodland habitat during migration. During the winter, most often found in open woodlands, riparian thickets, and other mesic habitats.

STATUS AND DISTRIBUTION Uncommon to common migrant throughout the state. Most common in migration in the western third of the state, where it can be abundant. Generally less common in the spring than in the fall. Uncommon winter resident in the southern third of the state, ranging north to near the Balcones Escarpment and Matagorda Bay; elsewhere, rare to very rare. Migration runs from early April to mid-May and from late August to mid-October.

Wilson's Warbler, male. Photo by Greg W. Lasley.

SUMMER TANAGER
Piranga rubra

BACKGROUND
The Summer Tanager is one of those species routinely referred to as "red bird" across the state. In fact, the male is the only entirely red-plumaged bird in North America. This species specializes in eating bees and wasps, both during the summer in Texas and in the winter in Central and South America. Despite the bright color of the male Summer Tanager, it is the frequent *ki-ti-kuck* calls that most frequently give away his presence.

IDENTIFICATION The male is bright red with a yellowish bill. He retains this coloration year round, so fall migrants are red as well. The female has golden yellow underparts and slightly darker, and browner, upperparts. Birds in the Trans-Pecos tend to be a little paler than the remainder of the population. Occa

sionally there are females with a reddish wash on the plumage, but they are rare. First-spring males are often blotched with red and yellow; the pattern and amount of red varies among individuals.

SIMILAR SPECIES The breeding plumage of the male Scarlet Tanager (*P. olivacea*) is also brilliant red, but the wings and tail are jet-black. The

Summer Tanager, male. Photo by Greg W. Lasley.

Scarlet Tanager female is brighter in overall plumage and is more greenish yellow. A diagnostic difference is the white wing lining of the female Scarlet. The male Hepatic Tanager (*P. flava*) is more brick-red in color and has a considerable amount of gray in its plumage. In addition, the Hepatic Tanager has a dark-colored bill and dusky gray auriculars. The female Hepatic Tanager also has a darker bill and gray auriculars. The female Western Tanager (*P. ludoviciana*) has prominent white wing bars on blackish wings. Female orioles have white wing bars and more-pointed bills. The male Northern Cardinal (*Cardinalis cardinalis*) is also bright red but has a distinctive crest and a black mask.

Summer Tanager, female. Photo by Mark W. Lockwood.

HABITAT Breeds in deciduous woodlands and forests, often in areas where the forests are not as dense, including pine oak forests in the eastern part of the state and juniper-oak woodlands farther west. In the Trans-Pecos and other arid areas, more restricted to riparian corridors.

STATUS AND DISTRIBUTION Rare to locally common summer resident in most of the state. Absent for the most part as a summer resident from the High Plains, Rolling Plains, and the southern South Texas Brush Country. In the Trans-Pecos, only along rivers and creeks with woodland habitat. Uncommon to common migrant in all parts of the state. Rare to very rare winter resident along the coast and in the Lower Rio Grande Valley. Migrants are present in the state between early April and mid-May and from mid-August to late October.

SCARLET TANAGER
Piranga olivacea

BACKGROUND

Although the Scarlet Tanager is well known in the eastern United States, it can be difficult to see in Texas away from migrant traps on the immediate coast. The spectacular plumage of the spring males makes them a favorite among birders. The presence of fruiting mulberry trees in these stopover habitats has a tendency to hold birds as they gorge on the fruit after making the long flight across the Gulf of Mexico. This tanager is much less common in the fall and more difficult to detect. It molts on the breeding grounds before migrating and is in a basic, or nonbreeding, plumage by the time it reaches Texas in the fall. The male Scarlet Tanager is one of only two species of tanagers that undergo this dramatic seasonal plumage change. This bird also undertakes a very long migration route, breeding in temperate North America and wintering in the extreme western side of the Amazon basin. Recent genetic studies have strongly suggested that the tanagers in the genus *Piranga* are more closely related to the grosbeaks than to other tanagers.

IDENTIFICATION The breeding plumage of the male is bright scarlet with black wings and tail. The bill is a pale horn or whitish color. Nonbreeding plumage of the male is bright olive-green, retaining the black wings and tail. Migrating first-year males can be seen molting in Texas in the spring and therefore show a mixture of red and green body feathers. The females are olive-green to yellowish green, generally brightest on the throat and undertail coverts. The wings are slightly darker than the body and have white wing linings.

SIMILAR SPECIES The male Summer Tanager (*P. rubra*) is entirely red, including the wings and tail. It is also a different, duller, shade of red. The female Summer Tanager is a darker, more mustard yellow, particularly on the upperparts, with yellow wing linings. Female orioles have white wing bars and more pointed bills.

Scarlet Tanager, male in breeding plumage. Photo by Greg W. Lasley.

HABITAT Most frequently seen in Texas in woodland habitats along the Coastal Prairies. These migrant stopover habitats are important for trans-Gulf migrants as they first make landfall. Farther inland, these birds might be found in any wooded habitat.

STATUS AND DISTRIBUTION Uncommon to locally common spring and rare fall migrant in the eastern third of Texas, by far most frequently encountered along the coast. Very rare to casual migrant in the western two-thirds of the state. Migration periods are between early April and mid-May and from early September to mid-October.

SPOTTED TOWHEE
Pipilo maculatus

BACKGROUND
The Spotted Towhee was formerly considered conspecific with the Eastern Towhee (*P. erythrophthalmus*), under the name "Rufous-sided Towhee." This large sparrow is attractive, but it can be difficult to observe of its skulking habits. Its presence is often given away by its method of foraging. It searches for food in leaf litter by kicking both feet backward to toss leaves aside and reveal seeds and insects. During the winter, it calls frequently; these *meow* calls are very distinctive and are given to alert other birds to possible predators. During the breeding season the male perches on the top of a shrub or small tree to sing. The song is a burred version of the classic *drink your tea* song of the Eastern Towhee. In general, the Spotted Towhee is the more common and widespread of these sister taxa.

IDENTIFICATION The male has a black hood and upperparts with rufous flanks and a white belly. The tail is black with broad white sides and corners. There is considerable white spotting on the scapulars, tertials, and wing coverts. The female Spotted Towhee is browner than the male but is still best described as blackish brown. Juveniles are brown and heavily streaked.

SIMILAR SPECIES The primary species that could cause confusion is the Eastern Towhee, which can be identified by the lack of white spotting on the upperparts. These two taxa have been known to hybridize, and hybrid females can have brown upperparts similar to an Eastern's with some amount of spotting. The

Eastern Towhee is an uncommon to rare migrant and winter resident in the eastern third of the state.

HABITAT Found in brushy habitats and woodlands with sufficient undergrowth. Tangles in riparian areas and along arroyos are also prime habitat. During the breeding season, found in mixed coniferous-deciduous woodlands with scattered areas of dense undergrowth.

STATUS AND DISTRIBUTION Uncommon to locally common summer resident in the mountains of the Trans-Pecos. Common migrant and winter resident throughout the western two-thirds of the state east to the Blackland Prairies region. Becomes increasingly rare farther east, primarily as a winter visitor. Migrants and wintering birds are present between early October and early May.

Spotted Towhee, male. Photo by Greg W. Lasley.

CHIPPING SPARROW
Spizella passerina

BACKGROUND

The Chipping Sparrow is a small, slender sparrow that is often seen in small to large flocks during the winter in open woodland as well as along roadsides, old fields, and other habitats with lush herbaceous vegetation. It typically forages on the ground in areas with some grass cover. Its small size and habit of squatting close to the ground when feeding make it easy to overlook. It is somewhat more arboreal than other sparrows and will usually retreat to nearby trees when flushed. In winter it often joins mixed feeding flocks with other sparrows.

IDENTIFICATION In breeding plumage, this small sparrow is identified by the bright red cap, white supercilium, and black eye stripe. In winter plumage, the cap is duller and streaked with black. Adult birds have a gray collar, underparts, and rump with a brown back that is heavily streaked with black. First-winter birds have a brownish wash over the head and underparts and often lack any rufous in the crown, making them more difficult to separate from other species of *Spizella*. Juvenile birds are heavily streaked with brown.

SIMILAR SPECIES Several species in the genus *Spizella* can pose identification problems. The Field Sparrow (*S. pusilla*) has a reddish cap but lacks the black line through the eye and is browner in overall plumage. Brewer's Sparrow (*S. breweri*) lacks the reddish cap, white supercilium and black eye line. When in flight it has a brown rump, rather than gray. The Clay-colored Sparrow (*S. pallida*) lacks the same features as Brewer's

Chipping Sparrow, winter plumage. Photo by Mark W. Lockwood.

and has a brown cheek patch that is bordered above and below with brown stripes. It also has a brown rump.

HABITAT During the breeding season, found in open woodlands: oak-juniper on the Edwards Plateau, pine in east Texas, and mixed coniferous-deciduous in the Trans-Pecos. During the winter, found in a wide variety of habitats with some brushy or lush herbaceous vegetation component, as well as the open woodlands occupied in the breeding season.

STATUS AND DISTRIBUTION Their breeding distribution forms a patchwork pattern in the state. Common resident on the Edwards Plateau and abundant in the upper elevations of the Guadalupe and Davis mountains. In the Pineywoods, uncommon summer resident. Common to abundant migrant and winter resident in the state away from the High Plains. Uncommon and local winter resident on the South Plains, and irregular in the Panhandle. Migrants are generally present between mid-March and late April and from late September to mid-November.

LARK SPARROW
Chondestes grammacus

BACKGROUND

The Lark Sparrow is a boldly marked sparrow found in savannahlike habitats throughout most of Texas. It is frequently seen sitting on fences or singing from low trees or shrubs. Its song is exceptionally musical, which is why this sparrow is named "lark." During courtship, the male struts on the ground and sings with its wings slightly open and the tail spread to show off the white markings. It sings from perches above the ground as well.

IDENTIFICATION The Lark Sparrow has a distinctive face pattern, with a white central crown stripe that is bordered by wide chestnut bands. Below the chestnut is a wide white supercilium. A black line runs through the eye, the auriculars are chestnut, and there is a broad black malar stripe as well. The underparts are grayish brown, with a black central breast spot. The upperparts are brown and heavily streaked. The tail is bordered with white and has broad white corners. Juvenile birds are heavily streaked on the face and underparts. They share the facial pattern of the adults but lack the chestnut coloration. First-winter birds lose the streaking, but the facial pattern is still considerably duller than adults.

SIMILAR SPECIES This species is so distinctive that it is rarely confused with other sparrows. The Sage Sparrow (*Amphispiza belli*) has a similar face pattern, but it lacks the chestnut patches on the face and crown. The Vesper Sparrow (*Pooecetes gramineus*) has white outer tail feathers but is heavily streaked on the body.

HABITAT Found in open habitats including oak and mesquite savannah, juniper woodlands, and open brushlands, also hedgerows or fence lines along pastures.

STATUS AND DISTRIBUTION Common to uncommon migrant and summer resident throughout most of the state. Absent as breeder from the most arid habitats in the Trans-Pecos. Rare and very local in summer in the Pineywoods. Locally uncommon winter resident on the Blackland Prairies and Post Oak Savannahs, Coastal Prairies, and in the South Texas Brush Country. During winter, rare to casual in the remainder of the state north to the southern Panhandle.

Lark Sparrow. Photo by Greg W. Lasley.

BLACK-THROATED SPARROW
Amphispiza bilineata

BACKGROUND
The Black-throated Sparrow is often the most common bird in the open desert. In creosote bush flats, it sometimes appears to be the only bird present. Some reports indicate that extensive brush clearing has reduced the abundance of this species; it is, however, still very common in most of its range in Texas. These birds, like other *Amphispiza*, spend a lot of time on the ground. They are often seen hopping, and occasionally running, as they forage. Black-throated Sparrows join mixed flocks during the winter; in the open desert such flocks often include Sage (*A. belli*) and Brewer's Sparrows (*Spizella breweri*).

IDENTIFICATION This gray, medium-sized sparrow has two white facial stripes, one a supercilium and the other a mustache. The throat and upper breast are black. The crown nape and auriculars are gray, as is the upper back. The remainder of the upperparts is grayish brown. The wings are also grayish brown and do not have wing bars. The outer tail feathers are edged in white, and the corners of the tail are white. The underparts are white, becoming gray on the sides. The lower flanks are usually brown. Immature birds lack the black throat, giving them a very wide white throat, as the mustache line is not yet easily recognized. They will often have some gray and brown streaking on the sides. These birds molt into adult plumage in the late fall and early winter.

SIMILAR SPECIES Because of its very distinctive plumage, the adult of this species is unlikely to be confused with other birds.

Immature birds might be confused with the Sage Sparrow, but young Black-throated Sparrows have a bold supercilium. Sage Sparrows are generally grayer on the upperparts and have conspicuous white wing bars. The period of possible confusion lasts only briefly, when wintering Sage Sparrows have arrived but first-year Black-throated Sparrows have not yet molted into adult plumage. The adult male House Sparrow (*Passer domesticus*) also has a black chin and throat, but it lacks the bold white stripes on the face. In addition, the male House Sparrow has a chestnut postocular stripe.

Black-throated Sparrow. Photo by Mark W. Lockwood

HABITAT In the Tran-Pecos, in open desert and in mixed desert scrub. Found primarily in oak savannah and brushy habitats were the natural vegetation has been disturbed, making for a more open habitat on the Edwards Plateau. Also open brushlands in south Texas.

STATUS AND DISTRIBUTION Common to abundant resident in the Trans-Pecos, western Edwards Plateau, and through the South Texas Brush Country. Uncommon and more localized on the eastern Edwards Plateau and in the southern Rolling Plains.

SAVANNAH SPARROW
Passerculus sandwichensis

BACKGROUND The Savannah Sparrow is often the most abundant winter sparrow in native grasslands, pastures, and other open habitats in Texas. It is quite variable in the amount of yellow in the lores, and sometimes face, and the amount and darkness of streaking on the underparts.

IDENTIFICATION This small sparrow has a short, slightly notched tail. The upperparts are brown and heavily streaked with darker brown and black. The underparts are white with a wide band of streaks across the breast that continues along the sides. There is usually a central breast spot. A white central crown stripe is bordered by brown stripes. The lores are yellow, and the intensity and extent of the yellow is quite variable, sometimes including much of the face. There is a light supercilium, darker auriculars, and a dark malar stripe. The legs are bright pink, and the bill is often pink with a duskier culmen.

SIMILAR SPECIES Several species of sparrows are similar to the Savannah Sparrow in that they are brownish in overall color and streaked below. The Vesper Sparrow (*Pooecetes gramineus*), frequently found in the same habitats, differs in being larger with a longer tail that is bordered with white, and it has a thin eye ring and a rufous shoulder. It also lacks the pale central crown stripe and yellow lores. The Song Sparrow (*Melospiza melodia*) is typically found in brushier habitats and is also larger with a longer, rounded tail. It lacks the yellow lores of the Savannah and is normally much darker brown in

Savannah Sparrow. Photo by Greg W. Lasley.

plumage color, although both species are quite variable. Baird's Sparrow (*Ammodramus bairdii*) is very rare in Texas and appears to be a regular winter resident only on the Marfa Plateau of the Trans-Pecos. Although it is quite similar in appearance to the Savannah, it has a buffy central crown stripe, the auriculars are outlined in black, and the head is buffy overall. Its underparts are largely white, but the band of streaks across the chest is narrow and washed in buff.

HABITAT Most abundant in native grasslands, but also found in weedy habitats such as along fences, along roads, in pastures, and in cultivated fields where grains have been grown.

STATUS AND DISTRIBUTION Abundant to uncommon migrant and winter resident throughout the state. Fall migrants arrive in mid-September; the bulk of the winter population is present by early November. Wintering birds begin to depart in early April, and migrants are present as late as mid-May.

HARRIS'S SPARROW
Zonotrichia querula

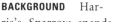

BACKGROUND Harris's Sparrow spends the summer in the High Arctic along Hudson Bay and westward across northern Canada, and it winters primarily on the Great Plains from North Dakota to Texas. Despite this narrow wintering range, the species has been found along both coasts and many places in between. Upon reaching Texas, these birds join mixed feeding flocks and often feed on the ground adjacent to thickets and woodlands. When flushed, they will often fly up into a tree, which provides excellent opportunities to study them. The amount of black on the male's face is controlled by hormone levels. It appears that the more black present, the greater the male's dominance and the higher the probability that he will successfully attract females.

IDENTIFICATION Adults have a full black crown, face, and upper breast. The upperparts are brown with darker streaking on the back. The underparts are whiter with black streaking on the sides of the breast and down the flanks. The wing feathers are edged in brown or reddish brown, and there are two thin white wing bars. The tail is long and brown. The sides of the head are buffy brown and the bill is pinkish. The amount of black on the face varies considerably among winter-plumaged individuals. First-winter birds lack the black face and have a white throat that is bordered below by a necklace, of varying thickness, of dark brown or black feathers. The crown is heavily barred with black. These birds are generally a little buffier overall, including on the flanks, which are heavily streaked with brown.

SIMILAR SPECIES Adults that retain the black face and upper breast are unmistakable. The large size of immature birds and the lack of a striped crown also make these birds unlikely to be confused with other species. The House Sparrow (*Passer domesticus*) has a black face and throat, but its gray crown and brown postocular stripe are distinctive.

HABITAT Found in old fields, along fencerows and low brush that is adjacent to thickets and deciduous woodlands. Also in thickets in riparian corridors.

STATUS AND DISTRIBUTION Common to uncommon and local winter resident in the central portion of the state. Found from the central Panhandle and eastern Edwards Plateau east through the Blackland Prairies and Oak Savannahs. Generally found between early November and late March; however, a few individuals routinely linger as late as early May in north-central Texas and in the Panhandle.

Harris's Sparrow, winter plumage. Photo by Mark W. Lockwood.

WHITE-CROWNED
SPARROW
Zonotrichia leucophrys

BACKGROUND

The adult White-
crowned Sparrow is
one of the most readily
identifiable sparrows in Texas. This
attractive bird has been studied closely
over the years and has provided important
information about song development. Its
abundance and wide distribution have made it
an ideal candidate for such studies. Some populations are fairly
long-distance migrants, and others are sedentary, but all of the
birds in Texas are migrants. Two identifiable subspecies groups
are found in Texas. White-lored individuals (*Z. l. gambelii*)
breed in the northern Rocky Mountains and occur with greater
frequency in the western half of the state. Most of the black-
lored individuals found in the state belong to *Z. l. leucophrys*,
which breeds in the boreal forest of Canada. Another black-
lored subspecies, *Z. l. oriantha*, breeds in the southern Rocky
Mountains and occurs in the Trans-Pecos as a migrant.

IDENTIFICATION Adults of this fairly large sparrow have a boldly
patterned crown, with a broad white central crown stripe bordered by black lateral stripes. Depending on the subspecies, the
lateral stripes either include the lores or meet across the forehead. If the lores are black, a white supercilium begins just
before the eye. Below the supercilium is a thin, black postocular
stripe. The nape and underparts are gray, with a slightly paler
throat and belly. The back is brown streaked with black, contrasting with the brown rump and tail. The wings are also
brown, with two white wing bars. First-winter birds have brown
crown stripes in the same pattern as the adults: the black stripes

of an adult are replaced with dark brown and the white stripes with pale tan. These immature birds molt into adult plumage just before migrating in the spring.

SIMILAR SPECIES The White-throated Sparrow (*Z. albicollis*) shares the black-and-white crown pattern but differs in having a bright white throat and yellow lores. The Golden-crowned Sparrow (*Z. atricapilla*) is a casual visitor to Texas and therefore unlikely to be encountered. It is similar in plumage to an immature White-crowned but has some yellow in the central crown stripe and lacks the brown postocular stripe.

White-crowned Sparrow, adult. Photo by Mark W. Lockwood.

HABITAT Found in brushy habitats, including the understory of open woodlands. Frequently found in urban habitats and visits feeding stations readily.

STATUS AND DISTRIBUTION Abundant to uncommon migrant and winter resident throughout the northern two-thirds of the state. Becomes increasingly uncommon southward. Migrants arrive as early as mid-September and remain as late as late May.

DARK-EYED JUNCO
Junco hyemalis

BACKGROUND The Dark-eyed Junco is an abundant winter bird over much of the northern portion of the state. The species includes several rather distinctive populations that have been treated as separate species at various times. This group continues to be studied, and some populations could be elevated to species status again; however, the various forms freely interbreed where they come into contact. This conspicuous sparrow is often encountered in flocks that move out into open areas to feed on the ground. It does not often forage in leaf litter but typically picks up exposed seeds.

IDENTIFICATION This medium-sized sparrow has white outer tail feathers. The various populations of Dark-eyed Junco are all generally gray or brown in body plumage, contrasting with a white belly, and have a light-colored bill. The Slate-colored population has a dark gray hood and upperparts with no markings on the wings. The female is browner than the male. The White-winged group is similar to the Slate-colored form but is

larger and has paler body plumage and two white wing bars. The Oregon form has a dark hood (black for the male and gray for the female) and brown body plumage. The Pink-sided group is similar to the Oregon form, but with a gray

Slate-colored Junco. Photo by Tim Cooper.

hood with black lores. The Gray-headed group has gray body plumage with a prominent, bright rufous back.

SIMILAR SPECIES The dark body plumage and white outer tail feathers make this species distinctive. The Vesper Sparrow (*Pooecetes gramineus*) is brown and heavily streaked, although it also has white outer tail feathers.

Oregon/Pink-sided Junco. Photo by Greg W. Lasley.

HABITAT Found in woodland or brushy habitats, including patches of brush along arroyos and creeks and open brushlands.

STATUS AND DISTRIBUTION Uncommon to abundant migrant and winter resident throughout the northern two-thirds of the state. Less common and more irregular farther south, including along the coast. Occurs in Texas between mid-October and mid-April, although occasionally individuals may be encountered outside this range. The Slate-colored form is common in the eastern two-thirds of the state, becoming increasingly less common westward. The White-winged variety is a casual visitor to the Panhandle and Trans Pecos. The Oregon group, including the Pink-sided birds, is a common to uncommon migrant and winter resident in the western half of the state. Finally, the Gray-headed

Gray-headed Junco. Photo by Greg W. Lasley.

form is a common summer resident in the upper elevations of the Guadalupe Mountains and a common to rare migrant and winter resident in the Trans-Pecos and Panhandle south to the Concho Valley. This group includes the Red-backed variety, which is the breeding bird in the Guadalupe Mountains.

NORTHERN CARDINAL
Cardinalis cardinalis

BACKGROUND

The North-ern Cardinal is the original red bird. This species has adapted well to human encroachment in natural habitats and is easily recognizable as a common visitor to feeders in urban environments. In recent decades the Northern Cardinal has expanded its range significantly, taking advantage of logging and other practices that create more open habitats. The limiting factor in its expansion to the west seems to be annual rainfall. The common name "cardinal" is derived from the similarity of the bird's plumage to robes worn by Roman Catholic cardinals, but the name has been applied to a variety of other species that have similar body structure and

Northern Cardinal, male. Photo by Tim Cooper.

size. In the late 1800s, it was a popular cage bird, and thousands were trapped for the pet trade and shipped to Europe, as well as being sold in the United States. Although the Northern Cardinal is not known as a migratory bird, some seasonal movements have been noted in Texas. Whether the movements are more local in origin or a larger migration in search of better food resources is not well understood.

IDENTIFICATION The male is fairly bright red overall, with a crest. Its black face extends back just past the eyes. The female is buffy brown overall, with red wings and tail. She also has a black face and a reddish crest. Both sexes have a heavy red bill. Immature birds are similar to the adult female but have a black bill and lack the black face until the post-juvenile molt.

SIMILAR SPECIES The male is unmistakable with its red plumage

Northern Cardinal, female. Photo by Mark W. Lockwood.

and crest. The female, however, is similar to the related Pyrrhuloxia (*C. sinuatus*), which is common in similar habitats in much of the Southwestern portion of the state. In general, the Pyrrhuloxia inhabits more arid habitats, but there are places where the species are seen together. The plumage of the Pyrrhuloxia is grayer overall, and the bird has a yellow bill with a much more strongly curved culmen.

HABITAT Found in woodlands and brushlands. Also common in urban environments.

STATUS AND DISTRIBUTION Common to abundant resident throughout most of the state. In the Trans-Pecos, uncommon to locally common resident in the southern counties, and rare visitor at all seasons in the northern half. In the Panhandle and South Plains, rare and local resident in the western counties.

PYRRHULOXIA
Cardinalis sinuatus

BACKGROUND

The Pyrrhuloxia resembles its close relative the Northern Cardinal (*C. cardinalis*), with its crest and heavy, finchlike bill. These closely related birds are also similar vocally. Their calls and songs can be difficult to separate without some experience where both species occur. In many areas of the state, particularly on the Edwards Plateau and in the South Texas Brush Country, the Northern Cardinal and Pyrrhuloxia occur in the same habitats or in adjacent areas. Unlike most species, the Pyrrhuloxia has a well-established pattern of moving northward and eastward during the winter. These wanderers routinely make their way into the Panhandle, but there are records from much farther north in the Great Plains.

IDENTIFICATION The Pyrrhuloxia is similar in size and structure to the Northern Cardinal. The male is brownish gray with a red face and throat. The red extends down the center of the underparts, and the wings and tail are red as well. The male also has a thin, red crest and a yellow bill with a strongly curved culmen. The female is similar, with more brown tones in the body plumage, but lacks the strong red highlights of the male. There is some red highlight in the wings and tail, but the underparts are uniform in color, with a reddish wash on the chest and belly.

SIMILAR SPECIES The species most likely to be confused with the Pyrrhuloxia is the female Northern Cardinal. These related species are found in similar habitats in much of the southwestern portion of the state. In general, Northern Cardinals occupy

Pyrrhuloxia, male. Photo by Mark W. Lockwood.

more mesic habitats, but in some places the species are seen together. The Pyrrhuloxia has grayer plumage overall and a yellow bill that has a much more strongly curved culmen.

HABITAT Mixed desert scrub and open woodlands. Also open shrublands and mesquite and oak savannahs with some brushy component.

STATUS AND DISTRIBUTION Common to uncommon resident in the southwestern portion of the state. Found throughout the Trans-Pecos, east through the southern High and Rolling Plains, and south through the Edwards Plateau and South Texas Brush Country. Well known for wandering northward after the breeding season. Uncommon winter visitor to the entire South Plains and irregularly to the southern Panhandle.

BLACK-HEADED GROSBEAK
Pheucticus melanocephalus

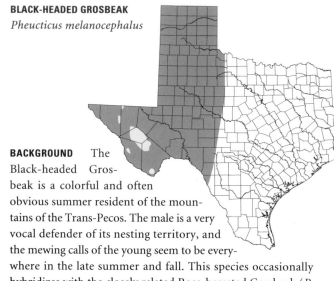

BACKGROUND The Black-headed Grosbeak is a colorful and often obvious summer resident of the mountains of the Trans-Pecos. The male is a very vocal defender of its nesting territory, and the mewing calls of the young seem to be everywhere in the late summer and fall. This species occasionally hybridizes with the closely related Rose-breasted Grosbeak (*P. ludovicianus*) where their ranges overlap, but hybrids are fairly rare and appear to be limited to areas where neither parental type is common.

IDENTIFICATION The male in breeding plumage has a black head. The back is also largely black but heavily streaked with orange. The underparts are yellowish orange with a yellow stripe on the central belly. The wings are black with prominent white markings and yellow wing linings. The tail is black with white inner webbing on the outermost three feathers. The female has a dark brown crown with a white central stripe. A white supercilium separates the crown from a dark brown cheek patch. The upperparts are brown and heavily streaked with darker brown. The underparts are buffy yellow with some darker streaking on the flanks, but not in the breast. The wings have reduced white patches and yellow linings.

SIMILAR SPECIES The adult male is very distinctive and could be confused only with a Baltimore Oriole (*Icterus galbula*), but the body shape and bill structure quickly eliminate that species. The female Rose-breasted Grosbeak is similar, but the Black-headed female is more uniform in color, with less streaking, on the underparts. The underparts are more yellowish buff in color, extending up to the throat and around the nape. A characteristic that is difficult to see in the field is the color of the wing linings. In the Black-headed Grosbeak they are buffy yellow, not the bright yellow of a Rose-breasted.

HABITAT Found in open montane woodlands during the summer. Might be encountered as a migrant in any woodland or urban area with large trees.

Black-headed Grosbeak, male. Photo by Mark W. Lockwood.

STATUS AND DISTRIBUTION Common migrant and summer resident in the mountains of the TransPecos. Very rare to casual summer visitor to the Panhandle and South Plains. During migration, uncommon to rare throughout the western third of the state east to the central Edwards Plateau and south through the Lower Rio Grande Valley. Found annually during migration as far east as north-central Texas and the central coast. Migrates through the state between early April and late May and from early August to late October, although fall migrants are occasionally noted as early as late July. Very rare and irregular winter visitor along the coast and inland as far north as Randall County.

BLUE GROSBEAK
Passerina caerulea

BACKGROUND The Blue Grosbeak was long considered a monotypic genus, but recent studies have shown that it is closely related to the *Passerina* buntings, and the Lazuli Bunting (*P. amoena*) is thought to be its closest relative. It is a rather shy bird, and although it can be locally common on the Edwards Plateau and in the Trans-Pecos, it often difficult to see well.

Blue Grosbeak, male. Photo by Greg W. Lasley.

IDENTIFICATION The adult male is bright blue with two reddish brown wing bars. There are often some reddish brown markings on the back as well. The bill is heavy and two-toned, with a black upper and silver lower mandible. The black of the lores extends around the bill to the chin, forming a small mask. The female is brown overall, with two paler brown wing bars. Some individuals may have a pale blue rump and shoulder or just some scattered blue feathers. First-year males begin to acquire adult plumage with varying amounts of blue. Birds of this age sometimes have a blue head and mostly brown body.

SIMILAR SPECIES The male Indigo Bunting (*P. cyanea*) is a bright blue bird that might be confused with the Blue Grosbeak. The bunting is considerably smaller, lacks rufous wing bars, and has a more diminutive beak. The male Eastern Bluebird (*Sialia sialis*) is bright blue above, but it has red and white underparts. Likewise, the male Western Bluebird (*S. mexicana*) has a rufous-brown back and chest, and the male Mountain Blue-

Blue Grosbeak, female. Photo by Greg W. Lasley.

bird (*S. currucoides*) is sky-blue in color. The female is similar in plumage to the female Indigo Bunting but has prominent pale wing bars and a heavy bill. The female Lazuli Bunting does have thin wing bars, but normally it has a buffy breast contrasting with the whitish belly.

HABITAT A wide variety of habitats, including woodland edge, grasslands and fields with at least occasional woody shrubs, riparian corridors, old fields, and other areas with scattered trees and shrubs.

STATUS AND DISTRIBUTION Locally common to uncommon summer resident through most of the state. Uncommon to rare in the Blackland Prairie and Post Oak Savannah regions and on the upper coast. Common to uncommon migrant throughout the state. Birds arrive in Texas in early April and are present until mid-October, with some lingering well into November. A few individuals may linger into early winter, particularly along the coast and in extreme southern Texas.

INDIGO BUNTING
Passerina cyanea

BACKGROUND

The Indigo Bunting is a familiar bird of the eastern United States. The bright blue male will sing from an exposed perch within the nesting territory. These birds will use early successional habitats, such as old fields and other disturbed habitats.

IDENTIFICATION The breeding plumage of the adult male is bright blue. The head is often darker, sometimes almost purplish, than the rest of the body. The lores are black. The wings are darker than the body, but most of the feathers are edged with blue, making for very little contrast on the folded wing. Males in winter plumage are similar to adult females but often have some patches of blue in the upperparts. First-year males have a variable amount of blue in their plumage. They are often a mix of blue and brown, but a few can be mostly blue with a brown wash over parts of the body. The adult female is brown overall with some indistinct streaking on the underparts and indistinct buffy wing bars. The bill is small and conical, bicolored in adult males with a black upper and silver lower mandible.

SIMILAR SPECIES The male Blue Grosbeak (*P. caerulea*) is larger and heavier bodied, with rufous wing bars and a heavier beak. The male Eastern Bluebird (*Sialia sialis*) is bright blue above but has red and white underparts. The female is similar in plumage to the female Blue Grosbeak but is smaller with less prominent wing bars and a diminutive bill. The female Lazuli Bunting (*P. amoena*) has more noticeable wing bars and a sky-blue rump.

HABITAT Found in brushy and weedy habitats. Also in old fields, open woodlands, and riparian corridors. During the winter, frequents weedy fields, urban habitats, and open shrublands.

STATUS AND DISTRIBUTION Common to locally abundant summer resident in the eastern half of the state. Breeding populations are found west to the western Edwards Plateau, eastern Rolling Plains, and Panhandle. Breeds, in small numbers, along riparian corridors in the Trans-Pecos, particularly in El Paso, Hudspeth, and Jeff Davis counties. Abundant migrant through the eastern half of Texas, becoming increasingly less common westward. Migrants pass through the state between late March and late May and from mid-August to early November. Rare to locally uncommon winter resident in the Lower Rio Grande Valley and, to a lesser extent, along the coast.

Indigo Bunting, male. Photo by Greg W. Lasley.

VARIED BUNTING
Passerina versicolor

BACKGROUND When seen in good light, the male Varied Bunting is strikingly beautiful. The species is wide ranging in Mexico and reaches the northern tip of its range in the southwestern United States. It is most easily seen along brushy arroyos in the southern Trans-Pecos when the males sing from exposed perches. Like the closely related Painted Bunting (*P. ciris*), the male Varied Bunting does not reach adult plumage until its second summer. First-summer males sing and defend territories, but they have brown plumage much like the adult female's. These young males have difficulty attracting mates and thus sing vigorously through much of the summer. They usually

have scattered purple, blue, or red feathers, but these spots of color are seldom visible unless the bird is in the hand.

IDENTIFICATION The male's breeding plumage is dark purple-blue overall. In poor light or from a distance it can look black. The head is largely light blue with a dull red patch on the nape. Its black lores extend into a narrow

Varied Bunting, male. Photo by Greg W. Lasley.

band around the base of the bill. The underparts and back are reddish purple. The rump is light blue, as are the edges of the tail feathers. The female is gray-brown overall and really lacks anything in the way of field marks.

Varied Bunting, immature. Photo by Mark W. Lockwood.

SIMILAR SPECIES

The male is unmistakable. Although in poor light or from a distance the male can look black, its size and bill shape eliminate any confusion with blackbirds. It also lacks the white wing patches of the breeding male Lark Bunting (*Calamospiza melanocorys*). The female might be mistaken for an immature female Painted Bunting that is a dull olive color. The female Indigo Bunting (*P. cyanea*) has some streaking on the underparts. The female Lazuli Bunting (*P. amoena*) has a pale blue rump and wing bars.

HABITAT In the Trans-Pecos, along brushy arroyos, canyon bottoms, and riparian corridors. In the Edwards Plateau and south Texas, in areas of fairly thick brush. On the plateau, this habitat is often found in the upper parts of canyons where the understory is thick and there are only occasional trees.

STATUS AND DISTRIBUTION Uncommon to rare summer resident in the southern Trans-Pecos and eastward to the southwestern Edwards Plateau. Rare and local summer resident in the western half of the South Texas Brush Country and the Lower Rio Grande Valley. Very rare winter resident in southern Brewster and Presidio counties. Very rare spring migrant along the lower and central coast as far north as Corpus Christi.

PAINTED BUNTING
Passerina ciris

BACKGROUND Despite the brilliant colors of the male Painted Bunting, this bird is far more often heard than seen. Territorial males often pick singing perches that are somewhat concealed. Learning the song of this sparrow-sized bird is the first step in discovering how common it actually is in many areas of the state. In brushy habitats in the southwestern Hill Country, it is often the most common breeding bird. Highly territorial, it is very vocal through the spring and much of the summer, particularly from early to mid-morning. Mature plumage is delayed in both the Painted and Varied Buntings. In other words, first-year males retain a plumage that closely resembles that of the adult female.

Painted Bunting, male. Photo by Greg W. Lasley.

IDENTIFICATION The male is brightly colored. The head and nape are blue with a red eye-ring. The throat, rump, and underparts are bright red, and the back is bright green. The wings and tail are dark gray with fine red edgings on all the feathers. The adult female is a rather bright olive-green. The underparts are more yellow-green than the upperparts. First-year males are similar to adult females but usually have many blue feathers in the head and often a reddish wash over the breast. These features, however, are often not detectable in

Painted Bunting, female. Photo by Greg W. Lasley.

the field. First-year females are also similar to the adult female, but considerably drabber. Those with the drabbest plumage are a dull olive overall.

SIMILAR SPECIES The male is unmistakable. The combination of blue head, green back, and red underparts eliminates all other species found in Texas. Female and first-year males are also distinctive because of the uniform green and yellow plumage. A pale female Lesser Goldfinch (*Carduelis psaltria*) can have similar plumage color, but it will be smaller, with wing bars and a smaller conical bill. The plumage of other female *Passerina* buntings is dominated by brown rather than green. The drabbest of the first-year females are the only individuals that may create confusion.

HABITAT Nests in a variety of brushy and savannah-like habitats. Most frequently in brushlands, thickets in canyons, and riparian corridors. Migrants are found in a variety of brushy or open woodland habitats.

STATUS AND DISTRIBUTION Uncommon to common summer resident and migrant throughout most of the state. Migrants begin passing through Texas in early April. Summer residents arrive on the breeding grounds in late April and remain until early September. Fall migrants linger, particularly along the coast, into early November. Very rare winter resident in the Lower Rio Grande Valley and along the coast.

RED-WINGED BLACKBIRD
Agelaius phoeniceus

BACKGROUND The Red-winged Blackbird is one of the most abundant birds in North America. In the eastern two-thirds of Texas, it can be found in very large numbers in wetlands and agricultural areas. In the remainder of the state, where conditions are more arid, the species is still common but does not approach the numbers seen elsewhere. The male can effectively hide his scarlet shoulders when at rest, but moments later he can show them off in a courtship display. Males are very territorial and arrive in breeding areas well before the females. The species is highly polygynous. One male typically has three or four females nesting within his territory, but a male has been found with as many as 15 different females. Although almost all territories have multiple females, the male within a territory is not necessarily the parent to all their off-

Red-winged Blackbird, male. Photo by Greg W. Lasley.

spring. Studies have shown that up to half of the offspring can come from neighboring males.

IDENTIFICATION This is a medium-sized black-bird, smaller than a female Great-tailed Grackle (*Quiscalus mexicanus*). The male is glossy black with prominent red shoulders. The shoulders are scarlet bordered with a thin yellowish or dull band. The bill, eyes, and feet are black. The female is blackish brown overall and heavily streaked below, with a prominent pale supercilium that separates a darker cap and auriculars. The face can have a wash of pink or buff. Males do not attain full adult plumage until their third year. Immature males can look much like a female, with dull red shoulders, or like an adult male.

Red-winged Blackbird, female. Photo by Greg W. Lasley.

SIMILAR SPECIES The male is unmistakable when the shoulder is seen. The female can be distinguished from all other Texas blackbirds by the heavily streaked underparts and mottled upperparts. Immature Brown-headed Cowbirds (*Molothrus ater*) are streaked below but uniform in plumage pattern above.

HABITAT Found in a variety of habitats, but most often in wetlands. Also, sometimes in very large numbers, in agricultural areas, particularly grain and corn fields. Also in open woodlands.

STATUS AND DISTRIBUTION Abundant to locally uncommon resident throughout the state. More localized during the breeding season because of the spotty availability of nesting habitat, particularly in the western half of the state. More widespread and often found in large flocks during the remainder of the year as migrants join the resident population. Some wintering roosts reportedly contain a million or more birds.

EASTERN MEADOWLARK
Sturnella magna
and
WESTERN MEADOWLARK
Sturnella neglecta

BACKGROUND Meadowlarks are almost ubiquitous in grasslands, pastures, and agricultural areas during the winter in Texas. In many places both species are present, which allows study of the minute differences between winter-plumaged birds. Their identity is often given away as they sing on warm winter mornings. During the breeding season, these sibling species are not often found together, with only minimal overlap in nesting habitat in mid-elevation grasslands and agricultural areas in the Trans-Pecos and on the western High Plains. A pale subspecies of the Eastern Meadowlark (*S. m. lilianae*) found in the grasslands of the Trans-Pecos may actually be a separate species. These birds appear to be more closely related to meadowlarks found in northern Mexico than to Eastern Meadowlarks in the United States.

IDENTIFICATION These stocky, ground-dwelling birds have bright yellow underparts and a prominent black V on the breast during the breeding season. The upperparts are brown with buff and black markings. The head has a black and white striped crown and a sharply pointed bill. The tail is brown with white outer edges. Eastern Meadowlarks in the eastern half of the state are considerably darker above than those found farther west.

SIMILAR SPECIES This combination of structure and plumage pattern is seen only in meadowlarks, but separating the two meadowlark species is a real challenge. In many cases, particu-

Eastern Meadowlark, breeding plumage. Photo by Greg W. Lasley.

Western Meadowlark, winter plumage. Photo by Greg W. Lasley.

larly in winter, that can be done only if the bird sings. Eastern Meadowlarks are slightly darker because the dark internal markings of the feathers on the upperparts are more extensive. The yellow on the throat of a Western Meadowlark extends up into the cheeks. In winter plumage, however, this difference is often impossible to discern, particularly in first-winter birds. The Dickcissel (*Spiza americana*) has a similar plumage pattern, including yellow underparts with a black **V** and brown upperparts, but it is much smaller and shaped like a sparrow.

HABITAT Found in grasslands, pastures, agricultural areas, and other open habitats.

STATUS AND DISTRIBUTION The Eastern Meadowlark is a common to locally uncommon resident through the eastern half of the state west to the eastern Panhandle. Also an uncommon resident in the mid- and upper-elevation grasslands of the central Trans-Pecos. During winter, uncommon to rare and more widespread in the western half of the state. The Western Meadowlark is a common to uncommon resident in portions of the western half of the state east through the Rolling Plains and western Edwards Plateau. Common to abundant during the winter through the western half of the state east to the Blackland Prairies and south through the South Texas Brush Country, and locally uncommon east to the Pineywoods, where it is very rare but regular. Winter residents are generally present from October through early April.

YELLOW-HEADED BLACKBIRD
Xanthocephalus xanthocephalus

BACKGROUND

In the western half of the state, a sign of migration season is the appearance of flocks of Yellow-headed Blackbirds in open fields and other agricultural areas. These flocks often include hundreds of individuals. The striking plumage of the male is hard to miss when mixed in flocks of other species of blackbirds. This species winters primarily in Mexico, but a sizable population does spend the winter in the El Paso area. These birds gather in large feeding and roosting flocks, sometimes containing as many as 20,000 individuals. On the nesting grounds, a male Yellow-headed Blackbird will defend a small territory of prime nesting space. Within that area, he may attract more than one female, although he helps feed only the young in the first nest established.

IDENTIFICATION The adult male is distinctive, with a bright yellow head, neck, and breast. The lores are black, contrasting sharply with the rest of the head. The body is entirely black, except for a prominent white wing patch, which is normally visible only in flight. Females and immature males have duller plumage, dull black and brown overall, with a pale yellow supercilium. They also have a yellow throat and breast. Frequently, white streaking emanates from the yellow patch on the breast into the brown sides and belly.

SIMILAR SPECIES The male of the species is unmistakable; there is no other bird in Texas with a bright yellow head and black body. The female Red-winged Blackbird (*Agelaius phoeniceus*) can have a dull yellow wash over the face and throat, somewhat reminiscent of a female Yellow-headed, but these birds are heavily streaked below.

HABITAT Often seen in open fields, pastures, around lakes and ponds, and other open habitats during migration. Nests around small lakes with cattails and other emergent vegetation. In winter, often found in large flocks foraging in agricultural areas and around areas where cattle are present, including feedlots.

STATUS AND DISTRIBUTION Common to uncommon migrant in the western half of the state, becoming increasingly less common eastward. Migrants are seen in Texas between early April and late May and from mid-July through early November. Very local summer resident in the southwestern Panhandle. Rare and irregular in winter in most areas of the state except in the El Paso area, where it is locally common.

Yellow-headed Blackbird, male. Photo by Greg W. Lasley.

BOAT-TAILED GRACKLE
Quiscalus major

BACKGROUND The Boat-tailed Grackle is a common inhabitant of marshes from the Louisiana border south to the central coast, found in many areas with the closely related Great-tailed Grackle (*Q. mexicanus*). The two grackles were long considered the same species, under the name "Boat-tailed." The birds found in Texas have dark eyes, setting them apart from the Great-tailed Grackle, but along the Atlantic Coast the Boat-tailed has yellow eyes. The Boat-tailed Grackle has an interesting nesting strategy. The females nest in large clusters while the males compete to defend the colony. The dominant male gets to mate with most of the females in the colony. Other males will also mate with the females when they are away from the colony, so that the dominate male ends up fathering only about a quarter of the young raised.

IDENTIFICATION The male is a large and conspicuous, glossy blackbird, uniform glassy black with a bluish iridescence. It has a long, somewhat keel-shaped tail, with a black bill and legs. The eyes are brown, often looking black in poor light. The adult female is much smaller than the male and brown overall. They are medium-brown above with contrastingly paler underparts. The female also has dark eyes.

SIMILAR SPECIES The Great-tailed Grackle is the species most similar to the Boat-tailed Grackle. The two species are closely related. The male Great-tailed has a slightly larger and more keel-shaped tail. Its profile is flatter and less rounded. The Boat-

Boat-tailed Grackle, male above two females. Photo by Tim Cooper.

tailed Grackles found in Texas have brown eyes, as opposed to the yellow eyes of the Great-tailed. They also have a different voice. The females of the species are similar and are best separated by eye color. The Common Grackle (*Q. quiscula*) is not so strongly sexually dimorphic. It is distinguished from the male Boat-tailed Grackle by its smaller size, shorter tail, and bronze iridescence of the body.

HABITAT Freshwater and saltwater marshes. Most often in open habitats. Also found in upland habitats, agricultural fields and pastures, and urban habitats. Rarely found more than 50 miles from the coast in Texas.

STATUS AND DISTRIBUTION Uncommon to locally abundant resident along the upper and central coasts. Much more common on the upper coast, becoming very rare south of Rockport.

GREAT-TAILED GRACKLE
Quiscalus mexicanus

BACKGROUND The Great-tailed Grackle is well known to urban Texas residents. Its presence in much of Texas has been chronicled by naturalists over the past century. Before 1910, it was restricted to south Texas. When John James Audubon visited Texas in 1837, he never encountered this bird. The species has readily adapted to, and taken advantage of, human changes in the landscape. By 1960 it had colonized the remainder of the Coastal Prairies and much of the central portion of the state, with breeding documented as far north as north-central Texas and the southern Panhandle. The remainder of the state, west of the Pineywoods, was colonized by the mid-1980s. This bird's adaptability to urban habitats has made it a pest in all of the cities in the state. During the day, flocks spread out over the urban landscape, feeding on lawns, parks, and golf courses. The real problem arises at night, when the birds congregate in very large roosting flocks. They seem to prefer open areas with scattered trees, such as parking lots at grocery stores and malls.

IDENTIFICATION The male

Great-tailed Grackle, male displaying. Photo by Tim Cooper.

Great-tailed Grackle, female. Photo by Mark W. Lockwood.

is unmistakable because of his large size—up to 17 inches in length including the long keel-shaped tail—and vocal manner. The male is black, with iridescent blue on the back and breast. The female is smaller and brown. The underparts are palest on the throat and upper breast. The eyes of both sexes are yellow.

SIMILAR SPECIES The two other species of grackles found in Texas provide the greatest identification challenge. The Common Grackle (*Q. quiscula*), which is common over the eastern three-quarters of the state, is notably smaller, with a much smaller tail. It also has iridescent plumage, but in Texas birds the iridescence is bronzy. The Boat-tailed Grackle (*Q. major*) is very similar to the Great-tailed, but it has brown eyes. The Boat-tailed is common along the Coastal Prairies south to Rockport, Aransas County.

HABITAT Found in disturbed habitats, including agricultural and urban areas. In the southern portion of the state, in open habitats with at least a few scattered trees.

STATUS AND DISTRIBUTION Abundant resident throughout most of the southern half of the state. Common farther north, but largely limited to urban areas. In the Pineywoods, very rare resident, particularly away from urban areas. In the Trans-Pecos, common to abundant in urban areas and rare to absent otherwise.

BRONZED COWBIRD
Molothrus aeneus

BACKGROUND

The Bronzed Cowbird, like its cousin the Brown-headed Cowbird (*M. ater*), lays eggs in the nests of other birds. The larger Bronzed typically parasitizes the nests of larger birds, such as the Northern Cardinal (*Cardinalis cardinalis*), Northern Mockingbird (*Mimus polyglottos*), Green Jay (*Cyanocorax yncas*), orioles, and other species of blackbirds. Environmental changes in northern Mexico and the southwestern United States over the past 130 years have led a northward range expansion of the species. Bronzed Cowbirds reached Texas in the 1950s and continue to move northward today. These birds are being seen with increasing frequency on the High Plains each year.

IDENTIFICATION The male is a heavy-bodied blackbird. The head and body plumage is glossy black with some bronzy iridescence. In good light, the blue iridescence of the wings and tail contrasts with the darker body. The eyes are red. The male has a ruff of longer feathers around the neck that are raised in courtship displays and occasionally at other times. The female is noticeably smaller than the male. Those from south Texas are blackish overall, and those found in the Trans-Pecos and Edwards Plateau are a dark gray-brown. Both populations have red eyes.

SIMILAR SPECIES The male Bronzed Cowbird, when seen well, is fairly unmistakable. The male Brown-headed Cowbird is smaller, with a brown head and less iridescent plumage. It also has a shorter tail and brown eyes. The male Brewer's Blackbird (*Euphagus cyanocephalus*) has a sleeker body, iridescent blue body plumage, and yellow eyes. The female Bronzed Cowbird is darker in plumage than other female blackbirds and is most likely to be confused with the female Brewer's Blackbird. The female Brewer's has duller brown plumage, a sleeker body, and a thinner, more pointed bill.

HABITAT Found in open habitats, including pastures and other agricultural areas, open shrublands, savannahs, and mixed desert scrub.

STATUS AND DISTRIBUTION Abundant to uncommon summer resident in the southwestern part of the state. In summer north through the Edwards Plateau to the southern High and Rolling Plains and east to the central coast. The population in Texas is expanding northward, with reports farther north on the High Plains each summer. The birds withdraw from the northern portion of the range during the winter. Locally uncommon winter resident in the South Texas Brush Country and rare on the Coastal Prairies.

Bronzed Cowbird, male. Photo by Greg W. Lasley.

BROWN-HEADED COWBIRD
Molothrus ater

BACKGROUND The Brown-headed Cowbird is well known for laying eggs in the nests of other birds. That habit has been a major issue in the conservation of several endangered songbirds, such as the Black-capped Vireo (*Vireo atricapilla*) in Texas and Kirtland's Warbler (*Dendroica kirtlandii*) in Michigan. The cowbird eggs hatch faster than other small passerines, and as a result they have a higher survival rate. In many cases the adoptive parents raise only the cowbird chick. For widespread and common birds, such parasitism this does not have any great impact on the overall population, but for limited-range and rare species, it can be detrimental to the long-term survival of the species.

IDENTIFICATION The male Brown-headed Cowbird has a brown hood that extends over the head, down the upper breast, and through the nape. The body, including the wings and tail, is uniform glossy black. The eyes are dark, as are the bill and legs. The female is slightly smaller than the male and is a plain grayish brown overall. Some individuals will have some indistinct streaking on the underparts. Like the male, the eyes and soft parts are dark. Immature birds are similar to the adult female but are heavily streaked below.

SIMILAR SPECIES Seen in good light, the male Brown-headed Cowbird is unmistakable when the brown hood is visible. The male Bronzed Cowbird (*M. aeneus*) is larger, with iridescent blue wings and red eyes. The male Brewer's Blackbird (*Euphagus cyanocephalus*) has an iridescent blue body and yellow eyes.

Brown-headed Cowbird, male. Photo by Mark W. Lockwood.

The female Brown-headed Cowbird is similar to the female Bronzed Cowbird but is smaller, with brown eyes, a longer tail, and a smaller bill. The female Brewer's Blackbird is a grayer brown overall, with a thinner, more pointed bill.

HABITAT Found in almost all open habitats. The only areas rarely occupied are closed-canopy forests. Found in open woodlands and forest edges, and increasingly common in urban habitats and agricultural areas.

STATUS AND DISTRIBUTION Common to locally abundant summer resident throughout the state, except in the southern South Texas Brush Country, where it is uncommon. During the winter, part of the population in the western half of the state withdraws, and the species becomes locally uncommon. In contrast, migrants from farther north bolster the population in the eastern half and the population increases in winter.

BULLOCK'S ORIOLE
Icterus bullockii

BACKGROUND
Bullock's Oriole is the most widespread orange-plumaged oriole in the western half of the state. The species hybridizes extensively with the Baltimore Oriole (*I. galbula*) where their ranges overlap in the Great Plains. As a result, they were once considered conspecific under the name "Northern Oriole." Recent molecular studies of the genus *Icterus* indicate, however, that the two species are not even each other's closest relative.

Bullock's Oriole, immature male. Photo by Greg W. Lasley.

IDENTIFICATION The male is bright orange with a prominent white wing patch. The crown, nape, and back are black, contrasting with an orange rump. The face and undersides are bright orange, except for the prominent black eye line and a small black bib covering the chin and the center of the throat. The central tail feathers are black, and the outer ones are orange with a broad black tip. The wings are black, with a large white patch. The female has yellowish gray upperparts. Her face and breast are a dull yellowish color, and the belly and undertail coverts are gray. The wings are gray-brown, with one or two thin wing bars. Immature males have the basic plumage pattern of the adults but are much duller overall.

SIMILAR SPECIES The Hooded Oriole (*I. cucullatus*) is in some ways most similar to Bullock's. Its crown and nape are orange rather than black, the black of its bib and face is much more extensive, it lacks the large white wing patch, and its tail is all black. The male Baltimore Oriole has an all-black head and two distinct wing bars. The female Baltimore is very similar to Bullock's female, but it has darker upperparts and is more uniform in color on the underparts, including an orangish belly. The

Bullock's Oriole, female. Photo by Greg W. Lasley.

female Baltimore also often has a dusky head, except for the orangish throat. The first-summer male Orchard Oriole (*I. spurius*) is yellow-green with a more extensive mask and bib. The female Scott's Oriole (*I. parisorum*) is more greenish in overall color, and first-summer males often have black extending through the face.

HABITAT Found in woodlands, including mesquite and oak savannahs, and along riparian corridors, particularly in the Trans-Pecos. During migration, it uses any woodland habitat.

STATUS AND DISTRIBUTION Common summer resident in the western half of the state. Irregular breeder east to the Balcones Escarpment and the central coast. Common to uncommon migrant through the western half of the state, becoming very rare east to Bastrop and Tarrant counties. Migration is generally from late March to mid-May and late July to late September. Very rare winter visitor to virtually all areas of the state, including the Pineywoods.

ALTAMIRA ORIOLE*
Icterus gularis

BACKGROUND

Although the Altamira Oriole is now one of those species that gives the Lower Rio Grande Valley a tropical flair, it is a fairly recent development. It was a vagrant to Texas before the 1940s and was not known to nest here until the early 1950s. The Altamira is the largest oriole found in the United States, although Audubon's Oriole (*I. graduacauda*), which also occurs in south Texas, is not much smaller. The Altamira colonized the Lower Valley during the 1960s and reached the abundance levels seen today. Along with Audubon's, it differs from the temperate orioles found in Texas in that the sexes are similar in plumage. It builds a nest similar to those of other Texas orioles, except that it is very long. These basketlike nests, which are built by the female, can be over two feet long from the entrance at the top of the bag to the bottom. They are often placed in open areas to protect the eggs and young from predators. The pairs are monogamous, remaining together throughout the year. This species has been previously known as Lichtenstein's Oriole and the Black-throated Oriole.

IDENTIFICATION The adult is bright orange with a black back, lores, and bib. The wings are black with an orange shoulder and prominent white wing bar. The tail is totally black. The bill is very heavy compared with other orioles. Juveniles are dull yellow-orange overall. The back is usually duskier and often has some mottling. The wings and tail are usually blackish. First-year birds are more like adults, but yellowish orange, with a dusky back.

SIMILAR SPECIES The Hooded Oriole (*I. cucullatus*) is similar in many aspects but is much smaller. Its key characteristics include a much thinner bill, a broad white upper wing bar, and a more extensive black bib and mask. Audubon's Oriole is similar in size but is yellow. The adult also has a black head and a yellow-green back. Immature Altamira Orioles usually have some aspects of adult plumage and are at least orangish in plumage.

Altamira Oriole. Photo by Mark W. Lockwood.

HABITAT Open, arid woodlands throughout its range. In Texas, found primarily in dense Tamaulipan thorn-scrub woodlands, less commonly in urban areas.

STATUS AND DISTRIBUTION Uncommon resident in the Lower Rio Grande Valley upriver to at least northern Zapata County.

BALTIMORE ORIOLE
Icterus galbula

BACKGROUND

The Baltimore Oriole is the most common orange-plumaged oriole found in the eastern half of Texas. With the exception of the occasional migrant Bullock's Oriole (*I. bullockii*), it is the only orange oriole likely even to be encountered. The Baltimore Oriole was formerly considered conspecific with Bullock's Oriole under the name "Northern Oriole." The two taxa interbreed on the Great Plains where habitat has been created with the settlement of the region and the subsequent planting of trees around farmhouses and in urban areas.

IDENTIFICATION The male is a prominently black and orange bird. The head and back are black, contrasting with the bright orange underparts and rump. The wings are black, with an orange shoulder and white wing bars and edges to the tertials and secondaries. The tail has a black base and central rectrices, but the outer three-quarters of the outer feathers are orange. The female is more variable in appearance; females look similar to the male but their plumage is usually duller. Most individuals have dull orange underparts, rump, and face. The crown, nape, and back are olive-brown and mottled with black. The wings are dark with a white shoulder and a prominent white wing bar, and the tail is olive-brown. Immature birds are similar to the adult female. Males do not reach adult plumage until the second year and can show characteristics of the adult.

SIMILAR SPECIES The plumage pattern of the male Orchard Oriole (*I. spurius*) is similar, except that deep chestnut replaces the orange, and the bird is smaller. The female Orchard Oriole is greenish yellow. The male Bullock's Oriole lacks the full black head and has a large white patch on the wings. Bullock's female is similar to the female Baltimore but is grayer on the upperparts and belly.

HABITAT Nests in open woodlands and forest edges, also around farmhouses and other isolated clumps of trees. During migration, will use any woodland habitat and can also be seen in isolated patches of brushy vegetation or trees.

STATUS AND DISTRIBUTION Locally uncommon summer resident in the eastern third of the Panhandle; rare to uncommon at that season in north-central Texas. Common to uncommon migrant in the eastern half of the state, becoming increasingly less common west to the Pecos River and casual farther west. Migrants pass through the state between mid-March and mid-May and from late August to mid-November. Rare winter visitor along the coast; several winter records are from inland locations.

Baltimore Oriole, male. Photo by Tim Cooper.

HOUSE FINCH
Carpodacus mexicanus

BACKGROUND The House Finch is a relatively recent addition to the birdlife for most of Texas. Before the 1950s, this reddish finch was found only in the western third of the state. For reasons that are unclear, it began to expand eastward. During the next thirty years the bird colonized all of the Rolling Plains and Edwards Plateau. At the same time, birds that originated from an introduced population in the eastern United States began colonizing the eastern half of the state. Today, there are House Finches in nearly all areas of the state.

IDENTIFICATION This is a red and brown, sparrow-sized bird with

a conical bill. The male has a red supercilium that meets over the forehead, as well as a red throat and breast. The crown and nape are brown, along with the remainder of the upperparts. These areas are faintly streaked with brown, and the wings have thin wing bars. The belly and undertail coverts are white with indistinct brown streaks. Females and immature

House Finch, male. Photo by Greg W. Lasley.

males are brown overall. Their upperparts are faintly streaked, and the lighter underparts are heavily streaked.

SIMILAR SPECIES The Purple Finch (*C. purpureus*) is an uncommon to rare, and irregular, winter visitor to the northeastern portion of the state. The male has a more pointed bill, unstreaked undertail coverts, dark auriculars, and in general a more wine-red color, including the back. The female Purple Finch also has dark auriculars, with an obvious white supercili-

House Finch, female. Photo by Greg W. Lasley.

um and malar stripes. These birds are more crisply patterned, with unstreaked undertail coverts. Cassin's Finch (*C. cassinii*) is a rare to very rare, and irregular, winter visitor to the western third of the state. The male has a more pointed bill and is rosy pink, including the face, with a much brighter crown. The female has a more defined plumage pattern on the face, sharper streaking on whiter underparts, and an obviously streaked back. The Pine Siskin (*Carduelis pinus*) has a much more pointed bill, heavily streaked upperparts, and prominent yellow patches in the wings and tail.

HABITAT Open woodlands, including savannahs as well as urban habitats. Well adapted to human disturbance, and can be found around farmhouses and similar places where only a few trees may be present.

STATUS AND DISTRIBUTION Uncommon to common resident throughout virtually all of the state. Still rare to very rare along the contact zone, including an area east of the Balcones Escarpment and south to the central coast. Also very rare from Laredo in Webb County, south and east through the Lower Rio Grande Valley.

LESSER GOLDFINCH
Carduelis psaltria

BACKGROUND

Adult plumage is delayed in Lesser Goldfinch males, so the plumage of first-year males is different from fully adult birds. Most adult males found in Texas have a black back, but first-year males have a green back with a black cap. First-year birds resemble the adult males in the western portion of the range; these green-backed adult birds are found in Texas only in the El Paso area. The two color forms were once considered separate subspecies, but recent research suggests that there is a cline where intermediate birds are found from El Paso westward through southern Arizona. An interesting characteristic of this species is that the male will incorporate parts of other species' songs into its own repertoire. The Lesser

Goldfinch is the smallest member of its genus to occur in the United States. Unlike the American Goldfinch (*C. tristis*), it does not go through seasonal plumage changes. It is currently expanding its range to the north in Texas. Although still rare, these birds are now found as far north as Amarillo.

Lesser Goldfinch, adult male. Photo by Greg W. Lasley.

IDENTIFICATION The vast majority of adult males found in Texas are of the black-backed form. They birds have bright yellow underparts that contrast sharply with the black upperparts. The white patches in the wings and tail are also very evident. The green-backed form has yellow underparts, green upperparts, and a black cap. First-year males of the black-backed form

Lesser Goldfinch, female. Photo by Greg W. Lasley.

are similar to the fully adult green-back form. Females are greenish yellow overall, with slightly brighter yellow throat and undertail coverts.

SIMILAR SPECIES Males in breeding plumage are very distinctive and unlikely to be mistaken. During the winter, the most likely species that can be confused with the Lesser Goldfinch in Texas is the American Goldfinch. American Goldfinches are browner in overall plumage, with a contrasting yellow face, a yellowish shoulder, a single whitish wing bar, and white undertail coverts.

HABITAT Brushlands with scattered trees and roadside and hedgerow habitats. Also along riparian corridors. During winter, more commonly encountered in urban habitats.

STATUS AND DISTRIBUTION Uncommon to locally abundant summer resident throughout the western half of the state south to the Lower Rio Grande Valley. Rare and local on the High Plains. Has wandered eastward to the edge of the Pineywoods and to the upper coast. Most individuals retreat from the northern half of the breeding range during winter. Uncommon to rare winter resident in the southern Trans-Pecos and eastward through the South Texas Brush Country.

AMERICAN GOLDFINCH
Carduelis tristis

BACKGROUND The American Goldfinch is normally seen in Texas along roadsides and in hedgerows or at backyard feeders. Its winter distribution is dictated somewhat by food availability. Some winters, if food resources are good farther north, most birds do not reach the state. In other years, feeding stations may be overwhelmed by large numbers of goldfinches. Adult males can usually be identified by their brighter plumage and blacker wings. American Goldfinches are normally seen in flocks, sometimes in fairly large numbers. These social birds are rarely encountered singly. Like all species in the genus, they have an undulating flight. They beat their wings a few times to maintain speed, and this also gives the bird some uplift. The wings are then closed, causing the bird to lose altitude.

IDENTIFICATION Birds in winter plumage are olive-brown above and grayish white below, with white undertail coverts. The face is yellow, being brightest in males. The wings are dark, with two wing bars in females and immature birds. Adult males have black wings with yellow shoulders and a single wing bar. The tail is also dark, with a white tip to the inner webbings of the outer rectrices. Males in breeding plumage are bright yellow with a black cap, wings, and tail. The undertail coverts remain white. Females in breeding plumage are less brilliant yellow and lack the black cap.

SIMILAR SPECIES Winter plumage is similar to the female Lesser Goldfinch (*C. psaltria*), which is yellowish green overall, in contrast to the browner color of the American. The American has a white patch at the base of the tail, rather than the entire inner webbing of the outermost tail feathers of a Lesser Goldfinch. The undertail coverts of the Lesser Goldfinch are yellow. The Pine Siskin (*C. pinus*) can be identified by the heavy streaking on the underparts. It also has patches of yellow, rather than white, in the wings and tail.

HABITAT Along roadsides, in old fields, hedgerows, riparian corridors, open woodlands, and urban areas.

STATUS AND DISTRIBUTION Uncommon to abundant winter resident throughout the state. Occurrence is somewhat irregular, with considerable fluctuation in the number of birds present in a given area from one year to the next. Generally arrives in Texas in late September and departs by mid-May, but may linger into late May and even early June. Very rare summer resident in northeast Texas and in the northeast Panhandle.

American Goldfinch, winter plumage. Photo by Greg W. Lasley.

APPENDIX

The Texas Ornithological Society's List of Birds
Documented in Texas (As of 1 December 2006)

Waterfowl

Black-bellied Whistling-Duck
(*Dendrocygna autumnalis*)
Fulvous Whistling-Duck
(*Dendrocygna bicolor*)
Greater White-fronted Goose
(*Anser albifrons*)
Snow Goose (*Chen caerulescens*)
Ross's Goose (*Chen rossii*)
Brant (*Branta bernicla*)
Cackling Goose (*Branta hutchinsii*)
Canada Goose (*Branta canadensis*)
Trumpeter Swan (*Cygnus buccinator*)
Tundra Swan (*Cygnus columbianus*)
Muscovy Duck (*Cairina moschata*)
Wood Duck (*Aix sponsa*)
Gadwall (*Anas strepera*)
Eurasian Wigeon (*Anas penelope*)
American Wigeon (*Anas americana*)
American Black Duck (*Anas rubripes*)
Mallard (*Anas platyrhynchos*)
Mottled Duck (*Anas fulvigula*)
Blue-winged Teal (*Anas discors*)
Cinnamon Teal

(*Anas cyanoptera*)

Northern Shoveler (*Anas clypeata*)

White-cheeked Pintail (*Anas bahamensis*)

Northern Pintail (*Anas acuta*)

Garganey (*Anas querquedula*)

Green-winged Teal (*Anas crecca*)

Canvasback (*Aythya valisineria*)

Redhead (*Aythya americana*)

Ring-necked Duck (*Aythya collaris*)

Tufted Duck (*Aythya fuligula*)

Greater Scaup (*Aythya marila*)

Lesser Scaup (*Aythya affinis*)

King Eider (*Somateria spectabilis*)

Harlequin Duck (*Histrionicus histrionicus*)

Surf Scoter (*Melanitta perspicillata*)

White-winged Scoter (*Melanitta fusca*)

Black Scoter (*Melanitta nigra*)

Long-tailed Duck (*Clangula hyemalis*)

Bufflehead (*Bucephala albeola*)

Common Goldeneye (*Bucephala clangula*)

Barrow's Goldeneye (*Bucephala islandica*)

Hooded Merganser (*Lophodytes cucullatus*)

Common Merganser (*Mergus merganser*)

Red-breasted Merganser (*Mergus serrator*)

Masked Duck (*Nomonyx dominicus*)

Ruddy Duck (*Oxyura jamaicensis*)

Gamebirds

Plain Chachalaca (*Ortalis vetula*)

Ring-necked Pheasant (*Phasianus colchicus*)

Greater Prairie-Chicken (*Tympanuchus cupido*)

Lesser Prairie-Chicken (*Tympanuchus pallidicinctus*)

Wild Turkey (*Meleagris gallopavo*)

Scaled Quail (*Callipepla squamata*)

Gambel's Quail (*Callipepla gambelii*)

Northern Bobwhite (*Colinus virginianus*)

Montezuma Quail (*Cyrtonyx montezumae*)

Loons and Grebes

Red-throated Loon (*Gavia stellata*)

Pacific Loon (*Gavia pacifica*)

Common Loon (*Gavia immer*)

Yellow-billed Loon (*Gavia adamsii*)

Least Grebe (*Tachybaptus dominicus*)

Pied-billed Grebe (*Podilymbus podiceps*)

Horned Grebe (*Podiceps auritus*)

Red-necked Grebe (*Podiceps grisegena*)

Eared Grebe (*Podiceps nigricollis*)

Western Grebe (*Aechmophorus occidentalis*)

Clark's Grebe (*Aechmophorus clarkii*)

Tubenoses

Yellow-nosed Albatross
(*Thalassarche chlororhynchos*)

Black-capped Petrel (*Pterodroma hasitata*)

Stejneger's Petrel (*Pterodroma longirostris*)

White-chinned Petrel (*Procellaria aequinoctialis*)

Cory's Shearwater (*Calonectris diomedea*)

Greater Shearwater (*Puffinus gravis*)

Sooty Shearwater (*Puffinus griseus*)

Manx Shearwater (*Puffinus puffinus*)

Audubon's Shearwater (*Puffinus lherminieri*)

Wilson's Storm-Petrel (*Oceanites oceanicus*)

Leach's Storm-Petrel
(*Oceanodroma leucorhoa*)

Band-rumped Storm-Petrel
(*Oceanodroma castro*)

Pelicans and Allies

Red-billed Tropicbird (*Phaethon aethereus*)

Masked Booby (*Sula dactylatra*)

Blue-footed Booby (*Sula nebouxii*)

Brown Booby (*Sula leucogaster*)

Red-footed Booby (*Sula sula*)

Northern Gannet (*Morus bassanus*)

American White Pelican (*Pelecanus erythrorhynchos*)

Brown Pelican (*Pelecanus occidentalis*)

Neotropic Cormorant
(*Phalacrocorax brasilianus*)

Double-crested Cormorant
(*Phalacrocorax auritus*)

Anhinga (*Anhinga anhinga*)

Magnificent Frigatebird (*Fregata magnificens*)

Herons and Allies

American Bittern (*Botaurus lentiginosus*)

Least Bittern (*Ixobrychus exilis*)

Great Blue Heron (*Ardea herodias*)

Great Egret (*Ardea alba*)

Snowy Egret (*Egretta thula*)

Little Blue Heron (*Egretta caerulea*)

Tricolored Heron (*Egretta tricolor*)

Reddish Egret (*Egretta rufescens*)

Cattle Egret (*Bubulcus ibis*)

Green Heron (*Butorides virescens*)

Black-crowned Night-Heron
(*Nycticorax nycticorax*)

Yellow-crowned Night-Heron
(*Nyctanassa violacea*)

White Ibis (*Eudocimus albus*)

Glossy Ibis (*Plegadis falcinellus*)

White-faced Ibis (*Plegadis chihi*)

Roseate Spoonbill (*Platalea ajaja*)

Jabiru (*Jabiru mycteria*)

Wood Stork (*Mycteria americana*)

Black Vulture (*Coragyps atratus*)

Turkey Vulture (*Cathartes aura*)

Greater Flamingo
(*Phoenicopterus ruber*)

Birds of Prey

Osprey (*Pandion haliaetus*)

Hook-billed Kite (*Chondrohierax uncinatus*)

Swallow-tailed Kite (*Elanoides forficatus*)

White-tailed Kite (*Elanus leucurus*)

Snail Kite (*Rostrhamus sociabilis*)

Mississippi Kite (*Ictinia mississippiensis*)

Bald Eagle (*Haliaeetus leucocephalus*)

Northern Harrier (*Circus cyaneus*)

Sharp-shinned Hawk (*Accipiter striatus*)

Cooper's Hawk (*Accipiter cooperii*)

Northern Goshawk (*Accipiter gentilis*)

Crane Hawk (*Geranospiza caerulescens*)

Gray Hawk (*Asturina nitida*)

Common Black-Hawk (*Buteogallus anthracinus*)

Harris's Hawk (*Parabuteo unicinctus*)

Roadside Hawk (*Buteo magnirostris*)

Red-shouldered Hawk (*Buteo lineatus*)

Broad-winged Hawk (*Buteo platypterus*)

Gray Hawk (*Buteo nitida*)

Short-tailed Hawk (*Buteo brachyurus*)

Swainson's Hawk (*Buteo swainsoni*)

White-tailed Hawk (*Buteo albicaudatus*)

Zone-tailed Hawk (*Buteo albonotatus*)

Red-tailed Hawk (*Buteo jamaicensis*)

Ferruginous Hawk (*Buteo regalis*)

Rough-legged Hawk (*Buteo lagopus*)

Golden Eagle (*Aquila chrysaetos*)

Collared Forest-Falcon (*Micrastur semitorquatus*)

Crested Caracara (*Caracara cheriway*)

American Kestrel (*Falco sparverius*)

Merlin (*Falco columbarius*)

Aplomado Falcon (*Falco femoralis*)

Gyrfalcon (*Falco rusticolus*)

Peregrine Falcon (*Falco peregrinus*)

Prairie Falcon (*Falco mexicanus*)

Rails and Allies

Yellow Rail (*Coturnicops noveboracensis*)

Black Rail (*Laterallus jamaicensis*)

Clapper Rail (*Rallus longirostris*)

King Rail (*Rallus elegans*)

Virginia Rail (*Rallus limicola*)

Sora (*Porzana carolina*)

Paint-billed Crake (*Neocrex erythrops*)

Spotted Rail (*Pardirallus maculatus*)

Purple Gallinule (*Porphyrio martinica*)

Common Moorhen (*Gallinula chloropus*)

American Coot (*Fulica americana*)

Sandhill Crane (*Grus canadensis*)

Whooping Crane (*Grus americana*)

Shorebirds

Double-striped Thick-knee
(*Burhinus bistriatus*)

Black-bellied Plover (*Pluvialis
squatarola*)

American Golden-Plover
(*Pluvialis dominica*)

Pacific Golden-Plover (*Pluvialis
fulva*)

Collared Plover (*Charadrius
collaris*)

Snowy Plover (*Charadrius
alexandrinus*)

Wilson's Plover (*Charadrius
wilsonia*)

Semipalmated Plover (*Charadrius
semipalmatus*)

Piping Plover (*Charadrius
melodus*)

Killdeer (*Charadrius vociferus*)

Mountain Plover (*Charadrius
montanus*)

American Oystercatcher
(*Haematopus palliatus*)

Black-necked Stilt (*Himantopus
mexicanus*)

American Avocet (*Recurvirostra
americana*)

Northern Jacana (*Jacana spinosa*)

Spotted Sandpiper (*Actitis macu-
larius*)

Solitary Sandpiper (*Tringa
solitaria*)

Wandering Tattler (*Tringa
incana*)

Spotted Redshank (*Tringa
erythropus*)

Greater Yellowlegs (*Tringa
melanoleuca*)

Willet (*Tringa semipalmata*)

Lesser Yellowlegs (*Tringa
flavipes*)

Upland Sandpiper (*Bartramia
longicauda*)

Eskimo Curlew (*Numenius
borealis*)

Whimbrel (*Numenius phaeopus*)

Long-billed Curlew (*Numenius
americanus*)

Hudsonian Godwit (*Limosa
haemastica*)

Marbled Godwit (*Limosa fedoa*)

Ruddy Turnstone (*Arenaria
interpres*)

Surfbird (*Aphriza virgata*)

Red Knot (*Calidris canutus*)

Sanderling (*Calidris alba*)

Semipalmated Sandpiper
(*Calidris pusilla*)

Western Sandpiper (*Calidris
mauri*)

Red-necked Stint (*Calidris
ruficollis*)

Least Sandpiper (*Calidris
minutilla*)

White-rumped Sandpiper
(*Calidris fuscicollis*)

Baird's Sandpiper (*Calidris
bairdii*)

Pectoral Sandpiper (*Calidris
melanotos*)

Sharp-tailed Sandpiper (*Calidris
acuminata*)

Purple Sandpiper (*Calidris
maritima*)

Rock Sandpiper (*Calidris
ptilocnemis*)

Dunlin (*Calidris alpina*)

Curlew Sandpiper (*Calidris
ferruginea*)

Stilt Sandpiper (*Calidris
himantopus*)

Buff-breasted Sandpiper (*Tryngites subruficollis*)
Ruff (*Philomachus pugnax*)
Short-billed Dowitcher (*Limnodromus griseus*)
Long-billed Dowitcher (*Limnodromus scolopaceus*)
Wilson's Snipe (*Gallinago delicata*)
American Woodcock (*Scolopax minor*)
Wilson's Phalarope (*Phalaropus tricolor*)
Red-necked Phalarope (*Phalaropus lobatus*)
Red Phalarope (*Phalaropus fulicarius*)

Gulls and Terns

Laughing Gull (*Larus atricilla*)
Franklin's Gull (*Larus pipixcan*)
Little Gull (*Larus minutus*)
Black-headed Gull (*Larus ridibundus*)
Bonaparte's Gull (*Larus philadelphia*)
Heermann's Gull (*Larus heermanni*)
Black-tailed Gull (*Larus crassirostris*)
Mew Gull (*Larus canus*)
Ring-billed Gull (*Larus delawarensis*)
California Gull (*Larus californicus*)
Herring Gull (*Larus argentatus*)
Thayer's Gull (*Larus thayeri*)
Iceland Gull (*Larus glaucoides*)
Lesser Black-backed Gull (*Larus fuscus*)
Slaty-backed Gull (*Larus schistisagus*)
Western Gull (*Larus occidentalis*)
Glaucous-winged Gull (*Larus glaucescens*)
Glaucous Gull (*Larus hyperboreus*)
Great Black-backed Gull (*Larus marinus*)
Kelp Gull (*Larus dominicanus*)
Sabine's Gull (*Xema sabini*)
Black-legged Kittiwake (*Rissa tridactyla*)
Brown Noddy (*Anous stolidus*)
Black Noddy (*Anous minutus*)
Sooty Tern (*Onychoprion fuscata*)
Bridled Tern (*Onychoprion anaethetus*)
Least Tern (*Sternula antillarum*)
Gull-billed Tern (*Gelochelidon nilotica*)
Caspian Tern (*Hydroprogne caspia*)
Black Tern (*Chlidonias niger*)
Roseate Tern (*Sterna dougallii*)
Common Tern (*Sterna hirundo*)
Arctic Tern (*Sterna paradisaea*)
Forster's Tern (*Sterna forsteri*)
Royal Tern (*Thalasseus maxima*)
Sandwich Tern (*Thalasseus sandvicensis*)
Elegant Tern (*Thalasseus elegans*)
Black Skimmer (*Rynchops niger*)
South Polar Skua (*Stercorarius maccormicki*)
Pomarine Jaeger (*Stercorarius pomarinus*)
Parasitic Jaeger (*Stercorarius parasiticus*)
Long-tailed Jaeger (*Stercorarius longicaudus*)

Pigeons and Doves

Rock Pigeon (*Columba livia*)

Red-billed Pigeon (*Patagioenas flavirostris*)

Band-tailed Pigeon (*Patagioenas fasciata*)

Eurasian Collared-Dove (*Streptopelia decaocto*)

White-winged Dove (*Zenaida asiatica*)

Mourning Dove (*Zenaida macroura*)

Passenger Pigeon (*Ectopistes migratorius*)

Inca Dove (*Columbina inca*)

Common Ground-Dove (*Columbina passerina*)

Ruddy Ground-Dove (*Columbina talpacoti*)

White-tipped Dove (*Leptotila verreauxi*)

Ruddy Quail-Dove (*Geotrygon montana*)

Parrots

Monk Parakeet (*Myiopsitta monachus*)

Carolina Parakeet (*Conuropsis carolinensis*)

Green Parakeet (*Aratinga holochlora*)

Red-crowned Parrot (*Amazona viridigenalis*)

Cuckoos

Dark-billed Cuckoo (*Coccyzus melacoryphus*)

Yellow-billed Cuckoo (*Coccyzus americanus*)

Mangrove Cuckoo (*Coccyzus minor*)

Black-billed Cuckoo (*Coccyzus erythropthalmus*)

Greater Roadrunner (*Geococcyx californianus*)

Groove-billed Ani (*Crotophaga sulcirostris*)

Owls

Barn Owl (*Tyto alba*)

Flammulated Owl (*Otus flammeolus*)

Western Screech-Owl (*Megascops kennicottii*)

Eastern Screech-Owl (*Megascops asio*)

Great Horned Owl (*Bubo v irginianus*)

Snowy Owl (*Bubo scandiacus*)

Northern Pygmy-Owl (*Glaucidium gnoma*)

Ferruginous Pygmy-Owl (*Glaucidium brasilianum*)

Elf Owl (*Micrathene whitneyi*)

Burrowing Owl (*Athene cunicularia*)

Mottled Owl (*Ciccaba virgata*)

Spotted Owl (*Strix occidentalis*)

Barred Owl (*Strix varia*)

Long-eared Owl (*Asio otus*)

Stygian Owl (*Asio stygius*)

Short-eared Owl (*Asio flammeus*)

Northern Saw-whet Owl (*Aegolius acadicus*)

Nightjars

Lesser Nighthawk (*Chordeiles acutipennis*)

Common Nighthawk (*Chordeiles minor*)

Common Pauraque (*Nyctidromus albicollis*)

Common Poorwill
(*Phalaenoptilus nuttallii*)
Chuck-will's-widow
(*Caprimulgus carolinensis*)
Whip-poor-will
(*Caprimulgus vociferus*)

Swifts and Hummingbirds

White-collared Swift
(*Streptoprocne zonaris*)
Chimney Swift (*Chaetura pelagica*)
White-throated Swift
(*Aeronautes saxatalis*)
Green Violet-ear (*Colibri thalassinus*)
Green-breasted Mango
(*Anthracothorax prevostii*)
Broad-billed Hummingbird
(*Cynanthus latirostris*)
White-eared Hummingbird
(*Hylocharis leucotis*)
Berylline Hummingbird
(*Amazilia beryllina*)
Buff-bellied Hummingbird
(*Amazilia yucatanensis*)
Violet-crowned Hummingbird
(*Amazilia violiceps*)
Blue-throated Hummingbird
(*Lampornis clemenciae*)
Magnificent Hummingbird
(*Eugenes fulgens*)
Lucifer Hummingbird
(*Calothorax lucifer*)
Ruby-throated Hummingbird
(*Archilochus colubris*)
Black-chinned Hummingbird
(*Archilochus alexandri*)
Anna's Hummingbird (*Calypte anna*)

Costa's Hummingbird (*Calypte costae*)
Calliope Hummingbird (*Stellula calliope*)
Broad-tailed Hummingbird
(*Selasphorus platycercus*)
Rufous Hummingbird
(*Selasphorus rufus*)
Allen's Hummingbird
(*Selasphorus sasin*)

Trogons

Elegant Trogon (*Trogon elegans*)

Kingfishers

Ringed Kingfisher (*Ceryle torquatus*)
Belted Kingfisher (*Ceryle alcyon*)
Green Kingfisher (*Chloroceryle americana*)

Woodpeckers

Lewis's Woodpecker (*Melanerpes lewis*)
Red-headed Woodpecker
(*Melanerpes erythrocephalus*)
Acorn Woodpecker (*Melanerpes formicivorus*)
Golden-fronted Woodpecker
(*Melanerpes aurifrons*)
Red-bellied Woodpecker (*Melanerpes carolinus*)
Williamson's Sapsucker
(*Sphyrapicus thyroideus*)
Yellow-bellied Sapsucker
(*Sphyrapicus varius*)
Red-naped Sapsucker
(*Sphyrapicus nuchalis*)
Red-breasted Sapsucker
(*Sphyrapicus ruber*)

Ladder-backed Woodpecker (*Picoides scalaris*)

Downy Woodpecker (*Picoides pubescens*)

Hairy Woodpecker (*Picoides villosus*)

Red-cockaded Woodpecker (*Picoides borealis*)

Northern Flicker (*Colaptes auratus*)

Pileated Woodpecker (*Dryocopus pileatus*)

Ivory-billed Woodpecker (*Campephilus principalis*)

Flycatchers

Northern Beardless-Tyrannulet (*Camptostoma imberbe*)

Greenish Elaenia (*Myiopagis viridicata*)

Tufted Flycatcher (*Mitrephanes phaeocercus*)

Olive-sided Flycatcher (*Contopus cooperi*)

Greater Pewee (*Contopus pertinax*)

Western Wood-Pewee (*Contopus sordidulus*)

Eastern Wood-Pewee (*Contopus virens*)

Yellow-bellied Flycatcher (*Empidonax flaviventris*)

Acadian Flycatcher (*Empidonax virescens*)

Alder Flycatcher (*Empidonax alnorum*)

Willow Flycatcher (*Empidonax traillii*)

Least Flycatcher (*Empidonax minimus*)

Hammond's Flycatcher (*Empidonax hammondii*)

Gray Flycatcher (*Empidonax wrightii*)

Dusky Flycatcher (*Empidonax oberholseri*)

Cordilleran Flycatcher (*Empidonax occidentalis*)

Buff-breasted Flycatcher (*Empidonax fulvifrons*)

Black Phoebe (*Sayornis nigricans*)

Eastern Phoebe (*Sayornis phoebe*)

Say's Phoebe (*Sayornis saya*)

Vermilion Flycatcher (*Pyrocephalus rubinus*)

Dusky-capped Flycatcher (*Myiarchus tuberculifer*)

Ash-throated Flycatcher (*Myiarchus cinerascens*)

Great Crested Flycatcher *Myiarchus crinitus*)

Brown-crested Flycatcher (*Myiarchus tyrannulus*)

Great Kiskadee (*Pitangus sulphuratus*)

Social Flycatcher (*Myiozetetes similis*)

Sulphur-bellied Flycatcher (*Myiodynastes luteiventris*)

Piratic Flycatcher (*Legatus leucophaius*)

Tropical Kingbird (*Tyrannus melancholicus*)

Couch's Kingbird (*Tyrannus couchii*)

Cassin's Kingbird (*Tyrannus vociferans*)

Thick-billed Kingbird (*Tyrannus crassirostris*)

Western Kingbird (*Tyrannus verticalis*)
Eastern Kingbird (*Tyrannus tyrannus*)
Gray Kingbird (*Tyrannus dominicensis*)
Scissor-tailed Flycatcher (*Tyrannus forficatus*)
Fork-tailed Flycatcher (*Tyrannus savana*)
Rose-throated Becard (*Pachyramphus aglaiae*)
Masked Tityra (*Tityra s emifasciata*)

Shrikes

Loggerhead Shrike (*Lanius ludovicianus*)
Northern Shrike (*Lanius excubitor*)

Vireos

White-eyed Vireo (*Vireo griseus*)
Bell's Vireo (*Vireo bellii*)
Black-capped Vireo (*Vireo atricapilla*)
Gray Vireo (*Vireo vicinior*)
Yellow-throated Vireo (*Vireo flavifrons*)
Plumbeous Vireo (*Vireo plumbeus*)
Cassin's Vireo (*Vireo cassinii*)
Blue-headed Vireo (*Vireo solitarius*)
Hutton's Vireo (*Vireo huttoni*)
Warbling Vireo (*Vireo gilvus*)
Philadelphia Vireo (*Vireo philadelphicus*)
Red-eyed Vireo (*Vireo olivaceus*)
Yellow-green Vireo (*Vireo flaviviridis*)

Black-whiskered Vireo (*Vireo altiloquus*)
Yucatan Vireo (*Vireo magister*)

Jays and Crows

Steller's Jay (*Cyanocitta stelleri*)
Blue Jay (*Cyanocitta cristata*)
Green Jay (*Cyanocorax yncas*)
Brown Jay (*Cyanocorax morio*)
Western Scrub-Jay (*Aphelocoma californica*)
Mexican Jay (*Aphelocoma ultramarina*)
Pinyon Jay (*Gymnorhinus cyanocephalus*)
Clark's Nutcracker (*Nucifraga columbiana*)
Black-billed Magpie (*Pica hudsonia*)
American Crow (*Corvus brachyrhynchos*)
Tamaulipas Crow (*Corvus imparatus*)
Fish Crow (*Corvus ossifragus*)
Chihuahuan Raven (*Corvus cryptoleucus*)
Common Raven (*Corvus corax*)

Larks

Horned Lark (*Eremophila alpestris*)

Swallows

Purple Martin (*Progne subis*)
Gray-breasted Martin (*Progne chalybea*)
Tree Swallow (*Tachycineta bicolor*)
Violet-green Swallow (*Tachycineta thalassina*)

Northern Rough-winged Swallow
(*Stelgidopteryx serripennis*)
Bank Swallow (*Riparia riparia*)
Cliff Swallow (*Petrochelidon
pyrrhonota*)
Cave Swallow (*Petrochelidon
fulva*)
Barn Swallow (*Hirundo rustica*)

Chickadees and Titmice
Carolina Chickadee (*Poecile
carolinensis*)
Black-capped Chickadee (*Poecile
atricapillus*)
Mountain Chickadee (*Poecile
gambeli*)
Juniper Titmouse (*Baeolophus
ridgwayi*)
Tufted Titmouse (*Baeolophus
bicolor*)
Black-crested Titmouse
(*Baeolophus atricristatus*)
Verdin (*Auriparus flaviceps*)
Bushtit (*Psaltriparus minimus*)

Nuthatches and Creepers
Red-breasted Nuthatch (*Sitta
canadensis*)
White-breasted Nuthatch (*Sitta
carolinensis*)
Pygmy Nuthatch (*Sitta pygmaea*)
Brown-headed Nuthatch (*Sitta
pusilla*)
Brown Creeper (*Certhia
americana*)

Wrens
Cactus Wren (*Campylorhynchus
brunneicapillus*)
Rock Wren (*Salpinctes obsoletus*)
Canyon Wren (*Catherpes
mexicanus*)
Carolina Wren (*Thryothorus
ludovicianus*)
Bewick's Wren (*Thryomanes
bewickii*)
House Wren (*Troglodytes aedon*)
Winter Wren (*Troglodytes
troglodytes*)
Sedge Wren (*Cistothorus
platensis*)
Marsh Wren (*Cistothorus
palustris*)

Dippers
American Dipper (*Cinclus
mexicanus*)

Kinglets and Gnatcatchers
Golden-crowned Kinglet
(*Regulus satrapa*)
Ruby-crowned Kinglet (*Regulus
calendula*)
Blue-gray Gnatcatcher (*Polioptila
caerulea*)
Black-tailed Gnatcatcher
(*Polioptila melanura*)

Thrushes
Northern Wheatear (*Oenanthe
oenanthe*)
Eastern Bluebird (*Sialia sialis*)
Western Bluebird (*Sialia
mexicana*)
Mountain Bluebird (*Sialia
currucoides*)
Townsend's Solitaire (*Myadestes
townsendi*)
Orange-billed Nightingale-
Thrush (*Catharus
aurantiirostris*)
Black-headed Nightingale-Thrush

(*Catharus mexicanus*)

Veery (*Catharus fuscescens*)

Gray-cheeked Thrush (*Catharus minimus*)

Swainson's Thrush (*Catharus ustulatus*)

Hermit Thrush (*Catharus guttatus*)

Wood Thrush (*Hylocichla mustelina*)

Clay-colored Robin (*Turdus grayi*)

White-throated Robin (*Turdus assimilis*)

Rufous-backed Robin (*Turdus rufopalliatus*)

American Robin (*Turdus migratorius*)

Varied Thrush (*Ixoreus naevius*)

Aztec Thrush (*Ridgwayia pinicola*)

Thrashers

Gray Catbird (*Dumetella carolinensis*)

Black Catbird (*Melanoptila glabrirostris*)

Northern Mockingbird (*Mimus polyglottos*)

Sage Thrasher (*Oreoscoptes montanus*)

Brown Thrasher (*Toxostoma rufum*)

Long-billed Thrasher (*Toxostoma longirostre*)

Curve-billed Thrasher (*Toxostoma curvirostre*)

Crissal Thrasher (*Toxostoma crissale*)

Blue Mockingbird (*Melanotis caerulescens*)

Starlings

European Starling (*Sturnus vulgaris*)

Pipits

American Pipit (*Anthus rubescens*)

Sprague's Pipit (*Anthus spragueii*)

Waxwings

Bohemian Waxwing (*Bombycilla garrulus*)

Cedar Waxwing (*Bombycilla cedrorum*)

Silky-Flycatchers

Gray Silky-flycatcher (*Ptilogonys cinereus*)

Phainopepla (*Phainopepla nitens*)

Warblers

Olive Warbler (*Peucedramus taeniatus*)

Blue-winged Warbler (*Vermivora pinus*)

Golden-winged Warbler (*Vermivora chrysoptera*)

Tennessee Warbler (*Vermivora peregrina*)

Orange-crowned Warbler (*Vermivora celata*)

Nashville Warbler (*Vermivora ruficapilla*)

Virginia's Warbler (*Vermivora virginiae*)

Colima Warbler (*Vermivora crissalis*)

Lucy's Warbler (*Vermivora luciae*)

Northern Parula (*Parula americana*)

Tropical Parula (*Parula pitiayumi*)

Yellow Warbler (*Dendroica petechia*)

Chestnut-sided Warbler (*Dendroica pensylvanica*)

Magnolia Warbler (*Dendroica magnolia*)

Cape May Warbler (*Dendroica tigrina*)

Black-throated Blue Warbler (*Dendroica caerulescens*)

Yellow-rumped Warbler (*Dendroica coronata*)

Black-throated Gray Warbler (*Dendroica nigrescens*)

Golden-cheeked Warbler (*Dendroica chrysoparia*)

Black-throated Green Warbler (*Dendroica virens*)

Townsend's Warbler (*Dendroica townsendi*)

Hermit Warbler (*Dendroica occidentalis*)

Blackburnian Warbler (*Dendroica fusca*)

Yellow-throated Warbler (*Dendroica dominica*)

Grace's Warbler (*Dendroica graciae*)

Pine Warbler (*Dendroica pinus*)

Prairie Warbler (*Dendroica discolor*)

Palm Warbler (*Dendroica palmarum*)

Bay-breasted Warbler (*Dendroica castanea*)

Blackpoll Warbler (*Dendroica striata*)

Cerulean Warbler (*Dendroica cerulea*)

Black-and-white Warbler (*Mniotilta varia*)

American Redstart (*Setophaga ruticilla*)

Prothonotary Warbler (*Protonotaria citrea*)

Worm-eating Warbler (*Helmitheros vermivorum*)

Swainson's Warbler (*Limnothlypis swainsonii*)

Ovenbird (*Seiurus aurocapilla*)

Northern Waterthrush (*Seiurus noveboracensis*)

Louisiana Waterthrush (*Seiurus motacilla*)

Kentucky Warbler (*Oporornis formosus*)

Connecticut Warbler (*Oporornis agilis*)

Mourning Warbler (*Oporornis philadelphia*)

MacGillivray's Warbler (*Oporornis tolmiei*)

Common Yellowthroat (*Geothlypis trichas*)

Gray-crowned Yellowthroat (*Geothlypis poliocephala*)

Hooded Warbler (*Wilsonia citrina*)

Wilson's Warbler (*Wilsonia pusilla*)

Canada Warbler (*Wilsonia canadensis*)

Red-faced Warbler (*Cardellina rubrifrons*)

Painted Redstart (*Myioborus pictus*)

Slate-throated Redstart (*Myioborus miniatus*)

Golden-crowned Warbler
(*Basileuterus culicivorus*)
Rufous-capped Warbler
(*Basileuterus rufifrons*)
Yellow-breasted Chat (*Icteria
virens*)

Tanagers

Hepatic Tanager (*Piranga flava*)
Summer Tanager (*Piranga rubra*)
Scarlet Tanager (*Piranga
olivacea*)
Western Tanager (*Piranga
ludoviciana*)
Flame-colored Tanager (*Piranga
bidentata*)

Sparrows

White-collared Seedeater
(*Sporophila torqueola*)
Yellow-faced Grassquit (*Tiaris
olivaceus*)
Olive Sparrow (*Arremonops
rufivirgatus*)
Green-tailed Towhee (*Pipilo
chlorurus*)
Spotted Towhee (*Pipilo
maculatus*)
Eastern Towhee (*Pipilo
erythrophthalmus*)
Canyon Towhee (*Pipilo fuscus*)
Cassin's Sparrow (*Aimophila
cassinii*)
Bachman's Sparrow (*Aimophila
aestivalis*)
Botteri's Sparrow (*Aimophila
botterii*)
Rufous-crowned Sparrow
(*Aimophila ruficeps*)
American Tree Sparrow (*Spizella
arborea*)

Chipping Sparrow (*Spizella
passerina*)
Clay-colored Sparrow (*Spizella
pallida*)
Brewer's Sparrow (*Spizella
breweri*)
Field Sparrow (*Spizella pusilla*)
Black-chinned Sparrow (*Spizella
atrogularis*)
Vesper Sparrow (*Pooecetes
gramineus*)
Lark Sparrow (*Chondestes
grammacus*)
Black-throated Sparrow
(*Amphispiza bilineata*)
Sage Sparrow (*Amphispiza belli*)
Lark Bunting (*Calamospiza
melanocorys*)
Savannah Sparrow (*Passerculus
sandwichensis*)
Grasshopper Sparrow
(*Ammodramus savannarum*)
Baird's Sparrow (*Ammodramus
bairdii*)
Henslow's Sparrow
(*Ammodramus henslowii*)
Le Conte's Sparrow
(*Ammodramus leconteii*)
Nelson's Sharp-tailed Sparrow
(*Ammodramus nelsoni*)
Seaside Sparrow (*Ammodramus
maritimus*)
Fox Sparrow (*Passerella iliaca*)
Song Sparrow (*Melospiza
melodia*)
Lincoln's Sparrow (*Melospiza
lincolnii*)
Swamp Sparrow (*Melospiza
georgiana*)
White-throated Sparrow
(*Zonotrichia albicollis*)

Harris's Sparrow (*Zonotrichia querula*)

White-crowned Sparrow (*Zonotrichia leucophrys*)

Golden-crowned Sparrow (*Zonotrichia atricapilla*)

Dark-eyed Junco (*Junco hyemalis*)

Yellow-eyed Junco (*Junco phaeonotus*)

McCown's Longspur (*Calcarius mccownii*)

Lapland Longspur (*Calcarius lapponicus*)

Smith's Longspur (*Calcarius pictus*)

Chestnut-collared Longspur (*Calcarius ornatus*)

Snow Bunting (*Plectrophenax nivalis*)

Grosbeaks and Buntings

Crimson-collared Grosbeak (*Rhodothraupis celaeno*)

Northern Cardinal (*Cardinalis cardinalis*)

Pyrrhuloxia (*Cardinalis sinuatus*)

Rose-breasted Grosbeak (*Pheucticus ludovicianus*)

Black-headed Grosbeak (*Pheucticus melanocephalus*)

Blue Bunting (*Cyanocompsa parellina*)

Blue Grosbeak (*Passerina caerulea*)

Lazuli Bunting (*Passerina amoena*)

Indigo Bunting (*Passerina cyanea*)

Varied Bunting (*Passerina versicolor*)

Painted Bunting (*Passerina ciris*)

Dickcissel (*Spiza americana*)

Blackbirds and Orioles

Bobolink (*Dolichonyx oryzivorus*)

Red-winged Blackbird (*Agelaius phoeniceus*)

Eastern Meadowlark (*Sturnella magna*)

Western Meadowlark (*Sturnella neglecta*)

Yellow-headed Blackbird (*Xanthocephalus xanthocephalus*)

Rusty Blackbird (*Euphagus carolinus*)

Brewer's Blackbird (*Euphagus cyanocephalus*)

Common Grackle (*Quiscalus quiscula*)

Boat-tailed Grackle (*Quiscalus major*)

Great-tailed Grackle (*Quiscalus mexicanus*)

Shiny Cowbird (*Molothrus bonariensis*)

Bronzed Cowbird (*Molothrus aeneus*)

Brown-headed Cowbird (*Molothrus ater*)

Black-vented Oriole (*Icterus wagleri*)

Orchard Oriole (*Icterus spurius*)

Hooded Oriole (*Icterus cucullatus*)

Streak-backed Oriole (*Icterus pustulatus*)

Bullock's Oriole (*Icterus bullockii*)

Altamira Oriole (*Icterus gularis*)

Audubon's Oriole (*Icterus graduacauda*)
Baltimore Oriole (*Icterus galbula*)
Scott's Oriole (*Icterus parisorum*)

Finches
Pine Grosbeak (*Pinicola enucleator*)
Purple Finch (*Carpodacus purpureus*)
Cassin's Finch (*Carpodacus cassinii*)
House Finch (*Carpodacus mexicanus*)
Red Crossbill (*Loxia curvirostra*)
White-winged Crossbill (*Loxia leucoptera*)

Common Redpoll (*Carduelis flammea*)
Pine Siskin (*Carduelis pinus*)
Lesser Goldfinch (*Carduelis psaltria*)
Lawrence's Goldfinch (*Carduelis lawrencei*)
American Goldfinch (*Carduelis tristis*)
Evening Grosbeak (*Coccothraustes vespertinus*)

Old World Sparrows
House Sparrow (*Passer domesticus*)

GLOSSARY

AURICULAR area below eye that covers the ear opening.

AXILLARY area on the underside of the wing where it attaches to the body.

BREAST equivalent to the chest.

BREAST BAND stripe across the breast.

BREAST SPOT small, usually dark, area of feathers in the center of the breast.

CAP top of the head.

CULMEN ridge of upper mandible.

DIHEDRAL angle of the wings of a flying bird, forming a shallow V.

EAR PATCH area around ear opening; synonymous with "auricular."

EYE LINE contrasting line of feathers that begins in front of the eye and continues behind it.

EYE-RING pale or contrasting feathers encircling the eye.

EYEBROW contrasting line of feathers above the eye; synonymous with "supercilium."

FACIAL DISKS rounded disks of feathers that encompass eyes and ears; characteristic of owls.

FLANK area along the side of the body, between the belly and the wing.

FLIGHT FEATHERS primaries and secondaries of the wing and the tail.

FRONTAL SHIELD extension of the bill onto the forehead.

GORGET iridescent throat feathers on a hummingbird.

LORE area between the eye and the bill.

MALAR STRIPE stripe along the sides of the chin; synonymous with "whisker" or "mustache."

MANTLE area including the back and the top of the wings.

CENTRAL CROWN STRIPE stripe down the center of the top of the head.

MUSTACHE stripe along the sides of the chin; synonymous with "malar stripe."

NAPE back of the neck.

PRIMARIES outermost flight feathers on the wing.

PRIMARY COVERTS feathers covering the base of the primaries.

RECTRICES long feathers forming the tail.

RUMP area between the uppertail coverts and the back.

SCAPULARS area between the back and the wings.

SECONDARIES flight feathers between the primaries and the body.

SECONDARY COVERTS feathers covering the bases of the secondaries.

SHOULDER feathers covering the bases of the secondary coverts.

SPECTACLE eye-ring attached to pale lores.

SPECULUM brightly colored upper surface of secondaries, usually associated with ducks.

SUPERCILIUM line of contrasting feathers above the eye; synonymous with "eyebrow."

TERMINAL BAND stripe across the tip of tail.

UNDERPARTS chest, belly, flanks, and undertail coverts.

UNDERTAIL COVERTS feathers covering underside of the base of the tail.

UPPERPARTS back, rump, and wings.

UPPERTAIL COVERTS feathers covering upperside of the base of the tail.

WHISKER stripe along the sides of the chin; synonymous with "mustache" or "malar stripe."

WING BAR pale tips of coverts forming a distinct line on the folded wing.

WING LINING area of feathers on underside of wing at base of flight feathers.

SUGGESTED REFERENCES

American Ornithologists' Union. 1998. *Check-list of North American Birds.* 7th edition. Washington, D.C.: American Ornithologists' Union.

Attwater, H. P. 1892. List of birds observed in the vicinity of San Antonio, Bexar County, Texas. *Auk* 9:229–238, 337–345.

Bailey, V. 1905. *Biological Survey of Texas.* Washington D.C.: U.S. Department of Agriculture.

Blankenship, T. L., and J. T. Anderson. 1993. A large concentration of Masked Duck (*Oxyura dominica*) on the Welder Wildlife Refuge, San Patricio County, Texas. *Bull. Texas Ornith. Soc.* 26:19–21.

Brush, T. 2000. First nesting record of Blue Jay (*Cyanocitta cristata*) in Hidalgo County. *Bull. Texas Ornith. Soc.* 33:35–36.

———. 2005. *Nesting Birds of a Tropical Frontier: The Lower Rio Grande Valley of Texas.* College Station: Texas A&M University Press.

Bryan, K., T. Gallucci, G. Lasley, M. Lockwood, and D. H. Riskind. 2006. A Checklist of Texas Birds. Austin: Natural Resources Program, Texas Parks and Wildlife Dept.

Bryan, K. B., and J. Karges. 2001.

Recent changes to the Davis Mountains avifauna. *Texas Birds* 3(1):41–53.

Diamond, D. D., D. H. Riskind, and S. L. Orzell. 1987. A framework for plant classification and conservation in Texas. *Texas Journal of Science* 39:203–221.

Dittmann, D. L., and G. W. Lasley. 1992. How to document rare birds. *Birding* 24:145–159.

Dixon, K. L. 1990. Constancy of margins of the hybrid zone in titmice of the *Parus bicolor* complex in coastal Texas. *Auk* 107:184–188.

Dunn, J. L., and K. L. Garrett. 1997. *A Field Guide to Warblers of North America.* Boston: Houghton Mifflin Co.

Heindel, M. 1996. Solitary Vireos. *Birding* 28:458–471.

Howell, S. N. G., and S. Webb. 1995. *A Guide to the Birds of Mexico and Northern Central America.* Oxford: Oxford University Press.

Kutac, E. A., and S. C. Caran. 1993. *Birds and Other Wildlife of South Central Texas.* Austin: University of Texas Press.

Lehmann, V. W. 1941. Attwater's Prairie Chicken: Its life history and management. *North American Fauna* 57. U.S. Dept. of the Interior.

Lockwood, M. W. 1995. A closer look: Varied Bunting. *Birding* 27(2):110–113.

———. 1996. Courtship behavior in Golden-cheeked Warblers. *Wilson Bulletin* 108(3):591–592.

———. 1997. A closer look: Masked Duck. *Birding* 29(5):386–390.

———. 2001. *Birds of the Texas Hill Country.* Austin: University of Texas Press.

Lockwood, M. W., and B. Freeman. 2004. *The TOS Handbook of Texas Birds.* College Station: Texas A&M University Press.

Lockwood. M. W., and A. Werchan. 2003. Odd "nesting" behavior in Greater Roadrunner. *Bull. Texas Ornith. Soc.* 36:11–12.

Lyndon B. Johnson School of Public Affairs of the University of Texas at Austin. 1978. Preserving Texas' natural heritage. *Policy Research Project Report* 31:1–34.

Moldenhauer, R. R. 1974. First Clay-colored Robin collected in the United States. *Auk* 91:839–840.

National Geographic Society. 2002. Field Guide to the Birds of North America. Washington, D.C.: National Geographic Society.

Neck, R. W. 1986. Expansion of Red-crowned Parrot, *Amazona viridigenalis,* into southern Texas and changes in agricultural practices in northern Mexico. *Bull. Texas Ornith. Soc.* 19:6–12.

Oberholser, H. C. 1974. *The Bird Life of Texas.* Austin: University of Texas Press.

Peterson, J. J., G. W. Lasley, K. B. Bryan, and M. Lockwood. 1991. Additions to the breeding avifauna of the Davis Mountains. *Bull. Texas Ornith. Soc.* 24:39–48.

Peterson, J. J., and B. R. Zimmer. 1998. *Birds of the Trans Pecos.* Austin: University of Texas Press.

Peterson, R. T. 1960. *A Field Guide to the Birds of Texas.* Boston: Houghton Mifflin Co.

Pulich, W. M. 1976. *The Golden-cheeked Warbler: A Bioecological Study.* Austin: Texas Parks and Wildlife Dept.

———. 1988. *The Birds of North Central Texas.* College Station: Texas A&M University Press.

Rappole, J. H., and G. W. Blacklock. 1985. *Birds of the Texas Coastal Bend: Abundance and Distribution.* College Station: Texas A&M University Press.

Rylander, K. 2002. *The Behavior of Texas Birds.* Austin: University of Texas Press.

Seyffert, K. D. 2001. *Birds of the Texas Panhandle.* College Station: Texas A&M University Press.

Sibley, D. A. 2000. *The Sibley Guide to Birds.* New York: Alfred A. Knopf.

———. 2003a. *The Sibley Field Guide to Birds of Eastern North America.* New York: Alfred A. Knopf.

———. 2003b. *The Sibley Field Guide to Birds of Western North America.* New York: Alfred A. Knopf.

Simmons, G. F. 1925. *Birds of the Austin Region.* Austin: University of Texas Press.

Wauer, R. H. 1996. *A Field Guide to Birds of the Big Bend.* Houston, Tex.: Gulf Publishing.

White, M. 2001. *Birds of Northeast Texas.* College Station: Texas A&M University Press.

INDEX

Species with full accounts are listed in **bold**.